COLLECTOR'S GUIDE TO
ASHTRAYS

IDENTIFICATION
& VALUES

Nancy Wanvig

COLLECTOR BOOKS

A Division of Schroeder Publishing Co., Inc.

The current values in this book should be used only as a guide. They are not intended to set prices, which vary from one section of the country to another. Auction prices as well as dealer prices vary greatly and are affected by condition and demand. Neither the Author nor the Publisher assumes responsibility for any losses which might be incurred as a result of consulting this guide.

Searching For A Publisher?

We are always looking for knowledgeable people considered experts within their fields. If you feel that there is a real need for a book on your collectible subject and have a large comprehensive collection, contact Collector Books.

Photography: Scott Archer
Cover design: Beth Summers
Book layout: Karen Geary

Additional copies of this book may be ordered from:

Collector Books
P.O. Box 3009
Paducah, KY 42002-3009

@ $19.95. Add $2.00 for postage and handling.

Copyright © 1997 by Nancy Wanvig

This book or any part thereof may not be reproduced without the written consent of the Author and Publisher.

Printed in the U.S.A. by Image Graphics, Paducah, KY

DEDICATION

This book is dedicated to my husband, Tom,
whose help and encouragement were invaluable.

ACKNOWLEDGMENTS

As I started my ashtray collection, many dealers at shows and malls shared their information with me. However, the general theme was that they did not know much about the subject and there was really no comprehensive information available. But helpful and nice they were.

Gary John Gresl, a dealer and owner of Milwaukee Antique Center, got me started when he mentioned the probable future of ashtrays. He was always there to answer questions and advise. He even tested some metal when I did not know what they were.

While collecting ashtrays, I had to find out more about them. I spent most of my days for two years doing research at the Milwaukee Public Library. I will always be grateful for their kind help so freely given. Special thanks to Ruth Ruege, in charge of the Art, Music, and Recreation department.

Special thanks to Carolyn Washburne of Washburne Literary Services. Her encouragement, editing, and proofreading were a great help.

The photographs on the cover and in the book were made by Scott Archer, Mukwonago, Wisconsin. In addition to his beautiful work, he helped to make twelve tedious all-day picture sessions a lot easier. I cannot say enough about his qualifications.

Finally, I want to thank my family, including my children, Linda and John, for their continuing support and encouragement. Their patience still amazes me. My husband, Tom, drove me all over the country, packed and unpacked ashtrays, collected prices for the database, and paid all my bills!

With all this help, I hope I have put together a book that you will enjoy.

ABOUT THE AUTHOR

Nancy Wanvig, born in Pennsylvania in 1933, studied retailing and graduated from Cornell University with a master's degree. Besides New York State, she has lived in New Jersey, Germany, California, and Wisconsin.

Always interested in art and design principles, she started to collect different types of art during her travels. This was particularly true when the author fulfilled a lifelong goal and spent three weeks in China.

Although Mrs. Wanvig gained experience in the collectibles market by selling some family antiques, she eventually became interested in buying unusual ashtrays, ones that she had never seen before. Realizing that smoking was declining in the United States, she checked with the ashtray manufacturers and found that production of these ashtrays had stopped many years ago.

Her fascination with these old and unique ashtrays grew and led to an extensive collection, gathered from all over the United States. Subsequently, she decided to write this book for collectors and dealers about the ashtrays available on the antique collectible market.

CONTENTS

CONTENTS

INTRODUCTION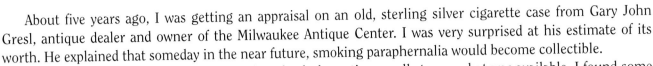

About five years ago, I was getting an appraisal on an old, sterling silver cigarette case from Gary John Gresl, antique dealer and owner of the Milwaukee Antique Center. I was very surprised at his estimate of its worth. He explained that someday in the near future, smoking paraphernalia would become collectible.

This sounded interesting, and I decided to check the antique malls to see what was available. I found some dusty ashtrays for $1.00 or $2.00, as well as some advertising ashtrays that were cleaner and cost a few dollars more. The workers in the malls told me that the advertising ashtrays, in particular, were beginning to sell.

This was all I needed to hear. I decided this was my new collectible, and I soon learned about "the thrill of the hunt." I thought ashtrays were a perfect collectible because they were cheap and plentiful. Also, they would increase in value over time.

As I began to look for and study about ashtrays, I realized that I was just seeing the very tip of the iceberg. I soon began to uncover amazing pieces with unique histories. My research became more and more interesting. You could not keep me away from antique shows, flea markets, and antique malls. When I found older ashtrays, it was if I had uncovered a bit of Americana, something right out of old businesses, old-fashioned drugstores, old saloons, and people's homes. What fun I had.

I did have one problem though, the pricing. There seemed to be no consistency to the pricing of ashtrays within malls or shows. I could find the same ashtray in the same mall marked anywhere from $4.00 to $25.00. Also, if there was information about the ashtray on the tag, it was often incorrect. There were no books about different types of ashtrays to help either dealers and collectors with these subjects. It seemed to me that some helpful information was needed.

From this point on, I started to collect prices in a database so that I would know what I should pay. Eventually I had many prices that were representative of the market at that time. I also expanded my search to collect old and unusual ashtrays in various parts of the country. It was not long before I decided to write a book, sharing this information with you. With more information available about ashtrays, more people will begin to collect. Then the prices will begin to stabilize. Also, hopefully, more interesting ashtrays, now stored away in closets, attics, and basements, will come on the market, and soon there will be many new excited ashtray collectors. One thing is certain about ashtrays, they don't make them like they used to! Hope you enjoy the book.

PRICING ASHTRAYS

One of the main reasons I wrote this book is to help establish a price guide for ashtrays. It is not unusual to find the same ashtray in the same antique mall or shows with prices as divergent as $25.00, $17.00, $12.00, $8.00. Eventually dealers will need information to use when determining ashtray prices, and collectors need to know what is a fair price. I hope this book will help.

The prices listed in this book are to be used only as a guide. They have been influenced by rarity as well as by demand. I have been pricing in different parts of the country for four years, but have more prices from the Midwest and East. I have found that some ashtrays are more numerous, and less expensive, near where they were made, particularly in the glass and china categories.

Unless otherwise stated, the price refers to excellent condition, that is—almost like new. However, since ashtrays were made to be used and to have cigarettes extinguished in them, most bear some marks, such as discoloration, dents, or cracked glaze. I feel that signs of wear directly related to smoking are more acceptable than cracks or injury do to careless handling.

Some of the prices may seem too high or too low now, but this is not unexpected. Ashtrays are such a new collectible, and as time passes, more collectors, supply and demand, and even better reference books will all play a role in helping to stabilize prices. Remember, this book with its pricing information is to be used as a guide only.

BRIEF HISTORY OF
SMOKING AND ASHTRAYS

Americans in the 1950s smoked over 542 trillion cigarettes each year. How did this come about? What is the future of cigarette smoking now? And how does all this affect ashtrays?

Smoking in some form was discovered in Europe at least by the 1500s. In 1603, King James of England declared smoking a filthy habit saying it was harmful "to the brains." In 1638, China issued a decree threatening decapitation to all tobacco smokers. The Russians in power also deplored the habit. Offenders were to be deported to Siberia.

After the Crimean War of 1853, cigarette smoking became popular among British and French soldiers who adopted the habit from the Turkish officers. About that time, hand-rolled cigarettes, using Turkish tobacco, were introduced in America. By the 1900s the tobacco industry had grown, and soon became one of the major growth areas of the twentieth century economy.

In the 1880s it became socially acceptable for men to smoke cigarettes, but it was not until the late 1920s that smoking gained acceptance for women. Also, about this same time the cigarette became the most popular form of smoking tobacco.

Early brands of cigarettes came in colorful packages with magnificent designs. As smoking increased, the ashtray made its appearance on the scene. In 1857, according to an English dictionary, the "ash pan" appeared as a new word. This was usually shaped like a cup, with no rests for cigars or cigarettes. However, in 1887 the same dictionary referred to the ash pan as "ash-tray," and thus the name became known.

Soon ashtrays were designed for different uses. There were small individual ones for the dining table, larger ones for the parlor, fancy ones for the ladies' boudoir, and practical ones for the kitchen. Artistic styles in vogue at the time also influenced the style of ashtrays. The Victorian style, with its ornate decoration, was very popular in the late nineteenth century. This soon gave way to Art Nouveau, with its flowing lines and graceful decorative themes. Art Deco appeared during the 1920s and 1930s. The very chic lady walking a sleek dog is a good example of this style. Angles, bold colors, and new materials, such as chrome and plastics, became popular, and played an important role in the Art Deco movement. Later, more inexpensive metals, such as tin, appeared on the market.

During the Great Depression years in the United States, when people could not afford to entertain outside the house, the game of bridge became very popular. Soon special ashtrays were designed for this and other card games. Promoters also used ashtrays with advertising on them as free premiums. Doctors, hospitals, schools, and insurance firms all placed ads on them. Even artists designed them. Soon all kinds of styles and materials were used. And many of these ashtrays were beautiful and expensive.

Other needs also led to new types of ashtrays. New models were designed for smoking while driving a car, and some were for smoking in bed. There were magnetic ashtrays for cars, beanbag ones for uneven surfaces, ones with candles for bedside, and as money became more plentiful in the 1940s, ones for Christmas and other holidays. People put ashtrays in every room and on almost every table. Companies specialized in the manufacture of them, and unique ashtrays were patented.

Now health experts have said that about 420,000 people die each year from diseases associated with smoking. If people could be persuaded to stop smoking, life expectancy would increase more than if cancer could be eliminated. President Bill Clinton has called for a smoke-free America by the year 2000.

Many companies have passed no-smoking rules at work, and many states have no-smoking laws in public places. Now there are even laws to help protect the public from second-hand smoke. Anti-smoking campaigns, and medical support to help people stop, have definitely reduced the number of cigarette smokers, and obviously, this influences the manufacture of ashtrays. Plain glass ones are still available, and many of the better department stores carry crystal ashtrays, especially at Christmas. But the interesting advertising and lovely ashtrays from the first half of the twentieth century are no longer being made. This part of Americana belongs to the past.

ABBREVIATIONS

The following abbreviations have be used in this book in order to provide you with detailed descriptions in the limited space available. No periods were used after initials or abbreviations.

/	with	l	long
alum	aluminum	lg	large
amet	amethyst	lt	light
appl	applied	mk	mark
bbl	barrel	OJ	Occupied Japan
bsk	bisque	o/l	overlay
C	century	orig	original
c	copyright	Pat	Patented
ca	circa	pcs	pieces
cen	center	ped	pedestal
cvd	carved	pic	picture
d	diameter	porc	porcelain
dbl	double	rd	round
decor	decoration	rect	rectangle
dk	dark	sgn	signed
dtd	dated	sm	small
emb	embossed, embossing	SP	silver plated
eng	engraved, engraving	sq	square
ext	extended	std	standard
fig	figural	TM	Trademark
h	high	tri	triangle
int	interior	w	wide
irid	iridescent	w/o	without

FUNCTIONAL ASHTRAYS

This group of ashtrays I collected because they were made by known manufacturers. Most of them are lovely, and many of the designs were a surprise to me. I never knew some of these existed, and am very happy to have them among my collection. I have divided this group into three areas, depending on where they were manufactured: the United States, Europe, or Japan.

Besides our own American manufacturers, there are many well-known foreign ones. Among these are Staffordshire, Wedgwood, Hummel, Royal Doulton, Royal Bayreuth, and Noritake. More pottery and porcelain ashtrays can also be seen in other areas of the book.

Following are some helpful terms for this section:

Arita: Japanese port that shipped blue and white porcelain, exported to Europe, where the porcelain inspired production of Delft and other blue and white wares.

Backstamp: Mark on the bottom that tells the manufacturer, and sometimes the date.

Ceramic: Products such as earthenware, porcelain, brick, glass, and vitreous enamels made by firing at high temperatures.

China: As used in this section, earthenware or porcelain tablewares.

Delft: Blue and white pottery decorated in Dutch scenes; made in Holland.

Imari: Japanese porcelain patterns, usually with orange and blue stylized flowers; widely copied by Europeans as well as Americans in the eighteenth and nineteenth centuries; refers to area where shipped; those marked Fukaguwa are very good quality.

Kutani: Japanese porcelain from 1650–1750, with decorations of warriors, animals, birds; most found today are nineteenth century.

Luster decoration: Type of colored decoration giving an iridescent effect; popular import in 1920s for novelty tableware items, often in blue, tan, and mother of pearl.

Majolica: Earthenware covered with opaque tin glaze before firing, usually nineteenth century.

Matte finish: A dull finish, opposite of shiny.

Moriage: Refers to applied clay put on like cake decoration, often done with dots or slip trailing; can also be hand-shaped clay added to an item.

Onion Pattern: Derived from Chinese pomegranate pattern, copied by Europeans and Americans.

Polychrome: Many colors used; often refers to Delft.

Porcelain: A hard, fine grained, nonporous, translucent ceramic ware; fired at high temperatures.

Pottery: Manufacture of clay ware, especially earthenware, as distinguished from porcelain and stoneware.

POTTERY & PORCELAIN ASHTRAYS FROM AMERICA

Rookwood Pottery was established in 1879, in Cincinnati, Ohio, and produced superior lines of art pottery. Fortunately, most of their work was marked; the reverse "RP" monogram is the most familiar. Rookwood also made advertising ashtrays as well as those in their regular art line. Several examples of their ashtrays are shown in Plate 1. The company experienced trouble during the Depression, and finally closed in 1967.

Roseville produced art pottery from 1892 to 1954. They used hundreds of glazes, from matte to gloss. Their animals and portraits usually bring higher prices than their floral pieces. The Pine Cone ashtray, in Plate 1, is from a well-known line.

Red Wing was founded in 1878, and for the most part produced utilitarian wares. By 1930, they added dinnerware and art pottery to their stoneware lines. Production stopped in 1967. Note the red wing-shaped ashtray in Plate 2. This one is the anniversary model, celebrating their seventy-fifth. There is another ashtray just like this but without the anniversary inscription on the back. The celebration model is worth $10.00 to $15.00 more.

The Frankoma Pottery opened in 1933, and continued until sold in 1991. Their body ware was changed in 1954 from honey tan to red brick clay. The pottery items made before 1942 had no mold number on the back. This, along with the glaze, helps to determine the age. Their covered wagon ashtray is a favorite of mine. It fits in nicely with an American history collection of ashtrays, and is shown there.

PLATE 1 (left to right):

Row 1:

Rookwood, fish fig on back rim, blue, 6" d, 1945 . . . . $125.00

Roseville, Pine Cone, comes in brown also, 4¾" l, 1935 . . . . $ 85.00

Rookwood, raven fig at back of ashtray, 4", 7¼" l, 1952 . . . . $195.00

Rookwood, fish shape, blue, 5⅝" w, 1949. . . . . $ 70.00

Rookwood, devil's head, black with green inside, lion mark on bottom, 5¼" w, 1930 . . . . $235.00

Row 2:

Rookwood, advertising ashtray for an insurance company, 5¾" d, 1938 . . . . $ 60.00

Roseville, Wincraft, square, green, raised flower & branch at one corner, 4½" side, 1948 . . . . $ 40.00

Roseville, Snowberry, round, shades of dk rose, raised branch, 5¼" d, 1946. $ 45.00

PLATE 2 (left to right)

Row 1:

Frankoma, fish shape, shown in black, cigarette rests in center, 7½" l . . . . $ 16.00

Frankoma, large four-leaf clover, marked, color is woodland moss, about 6" d, 1958–1964. . . . . $ 12.00

Frankoma, fish shape, brown, cigarette rests in center, 7½" l . . . . $ 16.00

Row 2:

Red Wing, slashed ball shape, pink outside, off-white inside, matte finish, 4½" d. . . . . $ 11.00

McCoy, stylized fish shape, marked McCoy, 4¼" l . . . . $ 10.00

Red Wing, burgundy color, red wing shape, anniversary model, 7¼" l . . . . $ 75.00

Red Wing, open book with rests in center, 6½" l, 4⅞" w. . . . . $ 14.00

Cowan, blue duck, marked, cigarette rest on head, match holder in tail, 4" l, 1928 . . . . $ 60.00

Red Wing, orange duck, like Cowan duck above, 4" l . . . . $ 32.00

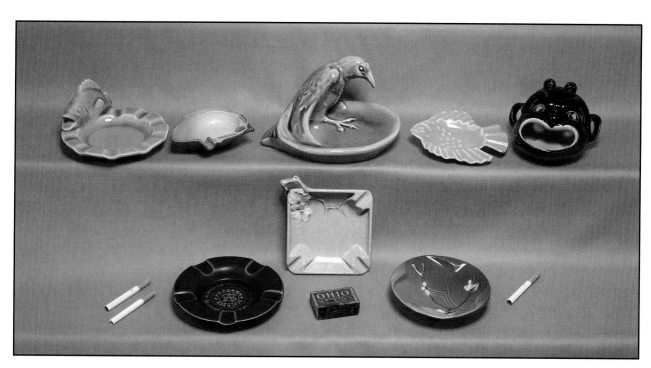

PLATE 1

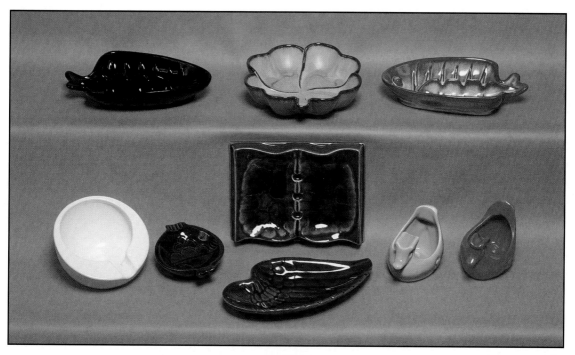

PLATE 2

POTTERY & PORCELAIN ASHTRAYS FROM AMERICA

Haeger Pottery was founded in 1914 and is still in business. The mark, Royal Haeger, was used after 1938, and was considered their premium line. Known for their commercial artware, they made advertising ashtrays as well as other types. Sometimes paper labels were used for their early products.

The Hall China Company was established in 1903 and continued production until 1985. They made many types of wares, and are well known for their collectible teapots. They are the largest manufacturer of them in the world. They also made many advertising ashtrays, especially for hotels and restaurants.

Fiesta dinnerware was manufactured by the Homer Laughlin Pottery, starting in 1936. It was a casual style, made in bright, solid colors. In the 1950s, some new colors were added, and they are currently bringing higher prices. All marketing was originally through the Woolworth stores. Ashtray production stopped in 1973.

In 1938, Homer Laughlin also introduced his Harlequin dinnerware. It is similar to Fiesta which has rings on the rim, while Harlequin has rings just before the rim.

The Currier and Ives ashtray, in Plate 4, is very hard to find. It has no connection to the Currier and Ives pattern by Royal, shown in Plate 5. Instead, it relates to Currier and Ives prints.

PLATE 3 (left to right)
Row 1:
Hall, red ceramic with cream inside, match pack holder & rest at cen back, 5⅝" l $35.00
Haeger, manufacturer's sample, usually worth more, 3¾" d, possibly the 1940s $20.00
Hall, example of advertising ashtray, cigarette holder and 2 snufferettes, marked, 5½" l $35.00
Shenango, decorative pattern around rise, match holder at back, 3¾" d $25.00
Hall, color is warm yellow, match holder near back, 4¾" l $25.00

Row 2:
Hall, wine, scalloped wide rim with small flowers in relief, 5" d $15.00
Shawnee, coaster-ashtray, part of bridge set, outline of club in relief in coaster part, 5⅛" l $10.00
Brush-McCoy, double frog, mark-042, 6½" l $55.00
Haeger, marked, but not Royal Haeger, 4" square $10.00
Shawnee, pale green with concentric rings, marked, 5" d $12.00

PLATE 4 (left to right)
Row 1:
Fiesta, by Homer Laughlin, 1950s color gray, 5½" d $72.00
Winfield, leaf shape, blue & cream background, bamboo pattern from 1937, 3¾" l . . . . $ 5.00
Currier & Ives, not by Royal, "The Skating Pond," rare in ashtray, 6" w $35.00
Harlequin, by Homer Laughlin, saucer-ashtray, hard to find, 6¼" d, 1938 . . . . $76.00
Winfield, leaf shape, cream color with yellow & blue design cen, 3¾" l . . . . $ 5.00
Amberstone, by Homer Laughlin, produced for supermarket promotion, also in amber, 5½" d, 1967 . . . . . $18.00

Row 2:
Harlequin, by Homer Laughlin, Basketweave pattern, rose, 4½" d $45.00
Hyalyn, purple, not so well known pottery, hard to find, 5" l . . . . $ 8.00
Camark Pottery, older style, gold inside, strong deco lines, 4" w, probably 1920s $15.00
Vernon Kilns, Modern California, lavender, 4½" d $11.00
Harker Ware, from a dinnerware pattern, gray, 4⅝" d . . . . $ 8.00

PLATE 3

PLATE 4

POTTERY & PORCELAIN ASHTRAYS FROM AMERICA

The Royal China Company manufactured Currier & Ives dinnerware in the 1950s. This china was transfer printed with scenes taken from prints by Currier & Ives, and was given as premiums through the A&P food stores. The blue, round ashtray in Plate 5 is the easiest to find. The green ashtray of the Old Curiosity Shop series is also fairly easy to find; the pink one, more difficult.

The grouping of ashtrays seen in Plate 6 is from many different manufacturers. The Indian face, by McMaster in Canada, is a different and interesting treatment. The Pennsbury Pottery ashtrays, round with beige background, were produced to sell in gift shops along the Pennsylvania Turnpike in the 1950s and 1960s. The ashtray from Mayer China Company is a salesman's sample. They are always worth more than the regular ashtray on the antique market.

Russel Wright dinnerware is highly collectible and still easy to find. Many of their patterns have a more modern style. The one pictured in Plate 6 is from the Sterling pattern.

PLATE 5 (left to right)

Row 1:

Old Curiosity Shop, by Royal, green background, 5½" d, 1950s $10.00

Franciscan, Desert Rose pattern, individual, 3½" d. $20.00

Sascha Brastoff, painted flowers with some enamel, about 6½" sq $23.00

Lara Aileen, Calif., set with larger shoe cigarette box, smaller shoes are ashtrays, add-on flowers & leaves . . $13.00

Franciscan, soft rose color, 4½" l $12.00

Old Curiosity Shop, by Royal, pink background, 5½" d, 1950s $10.00

Row 2:

Van Briggle, black & gray ceramic, bridge set, spade & club, about 3¼" l, four-piece set. $70.00

Franciscan, Apple pattern, individual, 4½" l $18.00

Currier & Ives, by Royal, popular blue & white pattern in park scene, 5½" d, 1950s $12.00

Van Briggle, Persian Rose color, matte finish, 6⅛" l, early back mark, probably 1921–1922 . . . . $40.00

Van Briggle, black & gray ceramic, rest of bridge set, diamond & heart, about 3¼" l, priced above

PLATE 6 (left to right)

Row 1:

Russel Wright, Sterling pattern, color-gray suede, almost round,
    match pack holder center back, 6" d. $75.00

No mark, match holder in center with tray at base, nicely done, but nothing on bottom, 5½" d $25.00

McMaster, Canada, Indian face in relief, 6¾" d $30.00

Carlin Comforts, interesting shape, white interior, 4⅜" l $12.00

No mark, similar to Hall China, 6 snufferettes & 2 rests, 6¼" d. $25.00

Row 2:

Pennsbury Pottery, *Its making down,* 5" d, 1950–1970 . . . . $20.00

Mayer China, salesman's sample, hotel ware, 3½" d $10.00

No mark, aqua ashtray with pen holder, shape popular in 1940s, 1950s, 1960s, 8" l $12.00

Wisconsin Porcelain Company, pic of old fashioned car, plentiful, 4" d. . . . . $ 7.00

Pennsbury Pottery, with black rooster, 5" d, 1950–1970. . . . . $18.00

PLATE 5

PLATE 6

POTTERY & PORCELAIN ASHTRAYS FROM ENGLAND

Wedgwood is easily recognized in its various forms of porcelain: Queen's Ware, creamware, bone china, basalt, and jasper, the last being the best known. It was founded in 1759 and is still in business. Jasperware is an unglazed, fine stoneware decorated with classic figures, usually in white relief. It comes in black, several shades of blue, white, green, lilac, terra-cotta, and some yellow. Both terra-cotta and yellow are hard to find.

Wedgwood had great success with his creamware because it was lighter in weight which many people preferred. He made a set for the Queen, now called Queen's Ware. He also made bone china, somewhat thinner.

The single word "Wedgwood" must be stamped on the back with the correct spelling. Later wares are stamped with the date; earlier wares are stamped with a date code. After 1891, "England" was added to the stamp; after 1905, "Made in England" was added.

PLATE 7 (left to right)   **All ashtrays Jasper, by Wedgwood.**
Row 1:
Yellow round, Primrose introduced 1977, white Prumus Blossom pattern, 4⅜" d $40.00
John Wedgwood's signature, Oct. 14th, 1961, backstamped 1961, 3⅝" d $50.00
Dark blue/white round, laurel leaf border, 4½" d $30.00
Black round, grape leaf border, center plain, 5¼" d $32.00
Moon shot, lg lt blue round, white moon & rocket in white raised decor, 7" d $70.00
White/yellow diamond, Wedgwood Collectors Society, oak leaf border, 5¾" l, 1978 . . . . $60.00
Black round, grape leaf border, center plain, 3½" d $25.00
Pink/white round, grape leaf border, 4½" d $27.00
Blue/white ridged rim, round, 4½" d $18.00
White/blue round, grape leaf border, 4½" d $22.00

Row 2:
Rare – very dark navy blue/white round, laurel leaf border, 3⅝" d, prior to 1950 . . . . $55.00
Olive/white round, grape leaf border, 4½" d $18.00
Terra-cotta heart, bridge set, oak leaf border, color only made 2 years, 4¾" l, 1959 . . . . $28.00
Lilac club, bridge set, oak leaf border, 4½" w $30.00
Eagle & stars round, lg black round, 13 stars & eagle in white raised decor, 6⅞" d, 1971 . . . . $36.00
Blue spade, bridge set, oak leaf border, 4⅜" l, 1966 . . . . $27.00
Olive diamond, bridge set, oak leaf border, 5¾" l, 1962 . . . . $22.00
Navy/white round, grape leaf border, 3⅝" d, old $25.00
Aqua round, grape leaf border, 4½" d $25.00

PLATE 8 (left to right)   **All ashtrays by Wedgwood.**
Row 1:
Blue/beige Dragon pattern, bone china, black edging, 4⅜" d $12.00
Blue/white square Queen's Ware, embossed, 3¼" sq, ... $14.00
White/pink round Queen's Ware, embossed 3⅞" d, 1949 . . . . $12.00
Kutani Crane pattern, bone china, 4½" d $12.00
Set blue Queen's Ware, 2 pcs, lt blue lg rd ashtray, cigarette cup with grape leaf border in white, 1957 . . . $20.00
White/sage green diamond, embossed Queen's Ware, 4½" l, 1950 . . . . $25.00
White round Queen's Ware, embossed, grape leaf border, 4⅜" d, 1938 . . . . $13.00
Gray/white square Queen's Ware, embossed, 3¼" sq, 1957 . . . . $14.00
Napoleon Ivy, bone china, green edge/ivy in center, as used by Emperor at St. Helena, 4¼" d, 1955. . . . . . $15.00

Row 2:
Black Dragon pattern, off-white bone china, black pattern/gold edging, 4½" d, prior to 1950 . . . . $15.00
Governor's Palace, Williamsburg, Virginia, creamware, 4¼" d $11.00
White oval Queen's Ware, off-white, grape leaf border on rim, 4⅝" l, 1950 . . . . $12.00
Gunston Hall, home in Va., creamware, 4¼" d $10.00
U.S. Frigate Constitution, blue pic of ship with blue border, creamware, 4⅜" d, 1951 . . . . $11.00

PLATE 7

PLATE 8

POTTERY & PORCELAIN ASHTRAYS FROM ENGLAND

In England, there are many pottery-making districts, and Staffordshire is one of the best known. Early in the eighteenth century, separate potteries sprang up, many of which are still in operation today. Some of these factories are famous, such as Wedgwood, Royal Doulton, Spode, and Royal Worcester. Others include Maling, Mason's, Crown Devon, Royal Winton, and Moorcroft.

Royal Winton and Lancaster & Sandland Ltd. are both Staffordshire potteries, and often make use of English scenes for their themes. Crown Devon does the same. See Oliver Twist, The Jolly Drover, Old London, and Coaching Days, all in Plate 9.

Mason's ashtrays, shown in Plate 10, are both from the same mold but are different patterns. Although Mason's started in 1813, they sold to Morley in 1848, and then later to Ashworth. Their older work is much better.

Blue Willow was originally copied from the Japanese by the English potters in the 1700s, and both the Japanese and the Americans are still making it. The ashtray pictured is not marked, and its maker is unknown.

The two Moorcroft ashtrays, in Plate 10, are good examples of tube lining, a raised clay outline around the flowers. Moorcroft is also noted for his lovely glazes.

PLATE 9 (left to right)
Row 1:
Lancaster & Sandland Ltd., Sandland Ware, *Oliver Twist Asks For More,* 4⅛" sq. $17.00
Crown Devon, *The Swan Inn* from Coaching Days pattern, 5½" l $25.00
Matchbox cover, horse scene $20.00
Lancaster & Sandland, shell shape, purple, pic of Gabard Inn, 4" l $15.00
Crown Devon, set cigarette cup & ashtray, Jonroth, pic of *Ausable Chasm,* N.Y.,
    cream china, ashtray 4½" sq $28.00
Royal Winton, cream porcelain, *Bridge at Norwood, Bermuda,* 4" sq $25.00

Row 2:
Lancaster & Sandland Ltd., Sandland Ware, *The Jolly Drover Pub,* 4" sq $14.00
Royal Winton, Grimwades, Oriental scene, black background, set cigarette box & four ashtray, box 5⅛" l. . $50.00
Royal Winton, Grimwades, Old London pattern, 4½" l $25.00

Plate 10 (left to right)
Row 1:
Moorcroft, wine flower, aqua ceramic, great glazes, triangle, 5½" side $65.00
Moorcroft, Hibiscus, flowers a favorite theme, beige ceramic, 6¼" l $55.00
Lancaster & Sandland Ltd., green earthenware, Trojan scene in gold, 9" l, after 1935. . . . . $10.00
Lancaster Ltd., period dressed lady, ashtray unusual shape, 5½" l $12.00
Coalport, Revelry pattern, 5½" d, prior to 1976. . . . . $20.00

Row 2:
Mason's, Plantation Colonial pattern, for Carl Forslund, 3½" sq $19.00
Blue Willow, Oriental influence, manufacturer unknown, 5½" d. $15.00
Royal Falcon Ironstone, J.H. Weatherby & Sons, London Pride, *Piccadilly Circus,* 4⅜" d. $14.00
Mason's, Manchu pattern, Oriental influence, 3½" sq, prior to 1960s $10.00

PLATE 9

PLATE 10

POTTERY & PORCELAIN ASHTRAYS FROM ENGLAND

Royal Doulton, founded in 1815, originally made sewage pipes, but in the twentieth century began making figurines and jugs, as well as fine artware. In 1968, they combined with other firms, still making some tablewares. The Spode Company is very old, making pottery as early as 1770. In 1843, Copeland purchased it, and continued its production. Now the company's name is Worcester Spode, Ltd.

Clarice Cliff designed for the Wilkinson and Newport Pottery in Burslem, England. She created Bizarre Ware pottery between 1925 and 1935, which had a tremendous influence on the Art Deco style ceramics.

The dog picture, in Plate 12, was painted by Cassilus Coolidge, Rochester, New York, from 1872 to 1934. It is his most famous. His prints sell today for about $75.00.

PLATE 11 (left to right)

Row 1:
Spode, cream pottery, Homeward scene, green edge, 4½" sq . . . . $ 20.00
Royal Doulton–Dick Turpin, match holder & ash dump, no rests, 3" h $130.00
Royal Staffordshire, designed from old platter made from hand-engraved copper from 1824, 5¼" sq . . . . $ 12.00
Royal Doulton–Old Charley, ashtray, 3⅛" h $115.00
Maling, Newcastle-on-Tyne, no luster, 4" sq, prior to 1963 . . . . $ 10.00

Row 2:
Maling, Newcastle-on-Tyne, luster, part of same scene as above, 4⅞" d, early 1950s . . . . $ 15.00
Royal Winton, Summertime pattern, like chintz, 4" sq. . . . . $ 50.00
Royal Doulton–Farmer John, ashtray, 3" h . . . . $ 90.00
Royal Winton, Empire pattern, like chintz, 3¾" l . . . . $ 20.00
Maling, flower pattern, Newcastle-on-Tyne on back, slip lining like Moorcroft used, 4¾" d . . . . $ 60.00
Clarice Cliff, Charlotte pattern, bird shape, Royal Staffordshire, Burslem, England, 5" l . . . . $ 25.00
Royal Doulton–Parson Brown, ashtray, 3¼" h . . . . $ 98.00
Tuscan China, bone china, flowers in relief, unusual pattern, 4⅜" sq . . . . $ 12.00
Royal Doulton, Old English scenes, *The Gleaners,* 4¾" w . . . . $ 65.00

FROM ENGLAND, IRELAND, POLAND

Ireland has produced lovely porcelain and pottery over the years. Belleck is a very thin porcelain, manufactured in a town of that name in Ireland. Started in 1859, the company continues to this day. The glaze is a creamy ivory color with a pearl-like luster. See Plate 12 for two of its more popular patterns.

Wade Potteries started in England in 1810, making mostly industrial products. In 1947, a new pottery was opened in Northern Ireland that made figurines, giftware, dinnerware, and advertising products.

The Cmielow factory started in Poland in 1789, a very old pottery. Still in operation in 1930, it is hard to date from its backstamp, because the mark stays the same for long periods of time.

The large ashtray on the bottom shelf in Plate 12 was made by Homer Laughlin of the United States. I put it here because the picture related to the chess ashtray.

PLATE 12 (left to right)

Row 1:
Carringaline Pottery, pic man fishing, 5⅜" d . . . . $ 9.00
Carlton Ware, set ashtray & cigarette box, ashtray is 6¾" l, prior to 1958 . . . . $90.00
Cmielow, Made in Poland, 3¾" sq . . . . $ 8.00
Arklow Pottery, *Blarney Castle in Cork,* 5½" d . . . . $ 8.00

Row 2:
Wade, rounded parallelogram with horse & rider, 6½" l, recent. $24.00
Belleck, Thorn pattern, base 4" sq $35.00
Wade, triangle with scene, 3½" side, 1953 on $15.00
Homer Laughlin, great pic of dogs playing poker & 1 cheating, *A Friend In Need,* 7¼" sq. $40.00
Wade, shamrock shape with shamrocks in center, 3½" l, 1953 on $14.00
Belleck, Shamrock pattern, 4⅜" d, 1946–1955 . . . . $30.00
Wade, ripple rim with *Irish Jaunting-Car* in center, 4⅝" d $17.00

PLATE 11

PLATE 12

POTTERY & PORCELAIN ASHTRAYS FROM FRANCE

The city of Limoges, France, became the center of the French porcelain industry in the mid-eighteenth century. The porcelain had vivid colors and lavish gold decoration. After 1891, the word "France" was added to the backstamp. Limoges factories are known for their excellent porcelain tableware.

Quimper is a tin enamel-glazed earthenware pottery with hand-painted decoration. It started in Quimper, France, in 1600. The marks are HB Quimper, HR Quimper, or Henriot Quimper. The factory was sold in 1983 to a couple from the U.S., ending the family control. See Plate 13.

PLATE 13 (left to right)
Row 1:
Haviland, cup, saucer/ashtray, mark incised, 6" d . . . . $ 48.00
Limoges, lady in ball gown, back-Marque Deposee, 5¼" l . . . . $ 40.00
Limoges, hand painted, mark in black, Giraud, 3½" d . . . . $ 12.00
Quimper, cat is cigarette holder, match holder, and ashtray, HB Quimper, no country mark, 6½" l, old . . . $140.00

Row 2:
Limoges, over picture in cen, *Paris 1961,* mark Limoges, France, 4⅜" sq, 1961 . . . . $ 18.00
Limoges, Limoges, France stamped in green, EM Limoges in gold, 4" d, after 1935 . . . . $ 20.00
Quimper, heavy, Hen Riot Quimper France mark, 5½" d, 1977 . . . . $ 45.00
Limoges, Napoleon Bonaparte, recent mark, 6" l . . . . $ 25.00
Quimper like, Luc-Sur-Mer mark, 3⅞" d . . . . $ 25.00
Quimper, cigarette & match holder & striker, ashtray with 1 rest, HB Quimper mark,
    no country, 2¾" h, old . . . . $ 80.00

POTTERY & PORCELAIN ASHTRAYS FROM HOLLAND

Delft is earthenware coated with a thin opaque tin glaze with blue or polychrome designs painted on it. This type of pottery has been made since the 1600s, in other countries as well as Holland, where the patterns had a Dutch theme. The word Delft was taken from the Dutch village where most of it is still being made today. The demand for Delft items peaked in the mid 1700s. Be sure the ashtray has the country mark of Holland stamped on the reverse side, because some Delft is also made in Holland, Michigan.

The pieces of Delft that are my favorite are polychrome, which means many colors. Most common are green, reddish-brown, and gold. See the polychrome ashtray with the sterling rim. This work is lovely, with beautiful colors and an intricately embossed rim.

PLATE 14 (left to right)   **All hand painted from Holland.**
Row 1:
Delft, hand-painted windmill scene, pattern numbers, 3 rests, 6½" d $15.00
Delft polychrome, De Porcelyne mark, Holland, 3¼" sq $25.00
Delft, mug shape, 3 rests, 2 handles, 3¾" h $25.00
Delft, with fig 2 shoes, scalloped rim, factory mark & number, 4" d $24.00
Delft polychrome, Royal Delft mark, Holland, brownish-pink & gold, 4" l $30.00
Delft, hand-painted flowers, Blau Delft mark, Holland, 5⅞" d $13.00

Row 2:
Gouda, Holland mark, matte finish, 4½" d $30.00
Gouda, Art Deco design, matte finish, signed Sydney, 3½" sq, 1926 . . . . $45.00
Gouda, mark Holland, glaze finish, 4⅛" d $28.00
Delft, horseshoe shape, some glaze cracks, very old, 4¾" l, prior to 1921 . . . . $25.00
Delft polychrome, De Porcelyne mark, 4⅝" l, prior to 1921 . . . . $50.00
Gouda, Holland, glaze finish, 4⅜" d $35.00
Delft polychrome, sterling rim with flowers in relief, signed Eiesva, 3½" d $80.00
Gouda, Holland, matte finish, 5½" l $25.00

PLATE 13

PLATE 14

POTTERY & PORCELAIN ASHTRAYS FROM GERMANY

Majolica is a pottery glazed with an opaque tin enamel. Made since the 1300s, it regained popularity in the mid-1800s. Pieces found today are not usually signed. They are also expensive. See Plate 15.

Royal Bayreuth was founded in Bavaria in 1794, and is much sought after. From 1870 to 1919 the back stamp contains a crest, and the mark Royal Bayreuth, and the word "Bavaria." Those pictured in Plate 15 and 16 are from this time.

Bavaria, now a state in Germany, was originally the center of that country's pottery industry. Bavaria was used alone in the backstamp until 1871, after which Germany was added. Many of the ashtrays that have only the Bavarian stamp are old, around the turn of the century.

Johann Haviland was a German porcelain manufacturer from 1907 to 1924. Among other items, he was known for his pictorial souvenirs, produced from engraved plates. See Plate 16.

Hummel figurines were first made in 1934, and are based on the drawings of Sister Berta Hummel, manu-factured by Goebel. Their backstamps are helpful in dating the ashtrays. Of course, the earlier ones are worth more. Some ashtrays can be found that were made by Goebel but are not Hummels, such as Friar Tuck. This particular ashtray is worth more because not very many were made.

PLATE 15 (left to right)
Row 1:
Majolica, accordion player cigar holder, match holder, ashtray, match striker, 6½" h, no mark, very old . . . $350.00
Royal Bayreuth, Corinthian pattern, marked, 4¼" sq, prior to 1919 . . . . $ 30.00
Majolica, Chinaman with cigarette holder, match striker, no mark, 5½" h, old $180.00
Royal Bayreuth, lobster claw ashtray, marked, 6" l, prior to 1919 . . . . $ 65.00
Royal Bayreuth, picture of boy with donkey, 3⅞" sq, marked, prior to 1919 . . . . $ 50.00
Majolica, string instrument player cigarette holder, match holder, ashtray, 4¼" h $150.00

Row 2:
Bavaria-Selb, pic of American Indian/pipe, match holder at back, hexagon, 6¾" l, early 1900s $110.00
No mark, very similar to Royal Bayreuth, pic of two women & goats, 3⅛" sq, old . . . . $ 35.00
Royal Bayreuth, pic of three goats, marked, 5½" l, prior to 1919. . . . . $ 75.00
Majolica, horn cigar holder, match holder, ashtray, match striker, 6½" h, no mark, very old $275.00
No mark, pic of Rotterdam Maasbruggen, flowers, possibly made in Germany, 4¾" sq, very old . . . . $ 15.00
Royal Bayreuth, enamel & paint on three storks in center, one wide rest, nice, marked, 5½" w. $130.00

PLATE 16 (left to right)
Row 1:
Johann Haviland, Bavaria, *Frankfurt,* pictorial engraved souvenirs, 4¾" l, early 1900s . . . . $ 15.00
Villeroy & Boch, design from an old print, manufacturer still in business, 7⅜" l . . . . $ 20.00
CICO, Bavaria, Germany, 7½" d, early 20th century . . . . $ 40.00
Goebel, Friar Tuck, #ZF 43/II, 4" h, 1956 . . . .$165.00
Johann Haviland, Bavaria, *Aschaffenburg,* pictorial souvenirs, 5" d, early 1900s . . . . $ 15.00

Row 2:
Hummel, Let's Sing, #114, 3½" h $175.00
No mark, pipe fig, cobalt edge with gold dusting, German, 5" w . . . . $ 28.00
Plunger type, embossed scenes like a beer stein, 6" h. . . . . $ 70.00
Villeroy & Boch, designed by Paloma Picasso, Heinrich-Castellon, 4" d . . . . $ 20.00
Hummel, Happy Pastimes, #62, 3⅜" h $135.00

PLATE 15

PLATE 16

POTTERY & PORCELAIN ASHTRAYS FROM GERMANY

Meissen, a town in Germany, was where the first true porcelain body was produced. Pottery has been made in Meissen since 1710. The crossed swords are their trademark. Dresden, also a town in Germany, produces fine porcelain. Dresden often refers to wares made there or in Meissen; however, this name does not include wares made at the famous Meissen factory. They, and they alone, are marked with the crossed swords.

In Plate 17, there is a lovely old ashtray made by the Kalk Manufacturing Company, whose factory was located in the same area of Germany. Their trademark is crossed arrows, not to be confused with Meissen's crossed swords.

PLATE 17 (left to right)
Row 1:
Dresden, hand painted, add-on roses, crown over N, no country, artist initials, 4¼" w, end 19th C. . . . . $ 65.00
No mark, ashtray with attached cigarette holder and two match strikers, heavy, 3⅝" h, old . . . . $ 60.00
Bavaria, Tirschenreuth, match holder & ashtray, place card holder, no Germany in mark,
  2" h, very old . . . . $ 50.00
Kalk, crossed arrows, Victorian style, very old, lovely, 7½" w, around turn of century . . . . $ 95.00
Dresden, very fine work, mark #071 with Germany, 2½" sq . . . . $ 25.00
Cupid ashtray set, set of cigarette holder/cupid & ashtray, #6430, ashtray 5" sq, old. $115.00

Row 2:
Raised flowers, one of my favorites, slightly raised flowers on rim, 5" d, prior to 1950 . . . . $ 20.00
Rosenthal, set of cigarette holder & ashtray, fine decoration, paper labels over stamp,
  ashtray is 3½" sq . . . . $ 35.00
Rosenthal, fine white porcelain with raised decoration on outside, 4¼" d, 1950s . . . . $ 20.00
Horse & rider, figural, #19493, fine detail work, 3⅜" h . . . . $ 35.00
Dresden, crown over N, decoration all around rise, 5" d. . . . . $ 35.00

FROM ITALY, PORTUGAL & SPAIN

The Capo-Di-Monte factory was established near Naples in 1743, and later moved to Spain. They made a fine porcelain with a lot of relief decoration. In 1834 another factory acquired the molds and continued to produce, using the same marks. Over the years other factories have made porcelain in the same way, which is now referred to as the Capo-Di-Monte style. As is so often the case, the older wares were better.

PLATE 18 (left to right)
Row 1:
Vestal Aucobaca, Portugal, heart shape, 2 rests, 5¾" l $14.00
Pintado-A-Mtao, Berardos, Portugal, 8¾" d, 1942. . . . . $18.00
Italy, typical of much of their pottery, 4⅛" d, probably around 1950s $10.00

Row 2:
Capo-Di-Monte style, R. Capodimonte, one of the newer marks, 6" sq $28.00
Egro, Wien mark, School for Lipizzan Horses, nice work, porcelain, 3½" d $12.00
Italy, Siena, extended rests, 3⅞" l, old $14.00
Italy, Florentine, old scene of horses & men in Florentine-style dress, nice, heavy, 2⅞" h $20.00

PLATE 17

PLATE 18

POTTERY & PORCELAIN NIPPON ASHTRAYS

Western trade opened with Japan in 1865. In 1890, the McKinley Tariff Act required all items of foreign manufacture to be marked with the country of origin. This was satisfactory until 1921, when Congress added that the country name must be marked in English. Until then Japan had used "Nippon," their name for Japan. When both Nippon and Japan occur in the back stamp, it refers to the years after 1921.

Quality varied with the Nippon ashtrays, and the more desirable pieces had fine art work. Those marked Nippon-Noritake were always of the highest quality. Moriage decoration was commonly used. Nippon porcelain marked "hand painted Nippon" was only manufactured from 1891 to 1921. These were usually fine, quality pieces. The most expensive pieces had their decorative scenes all around the piece, not just in the front. Less expensive ashtrays might have had only one scene. There are reproductions of Nippon, so be sure you know what Nippon looks like, and its marks, before you invest.

PLATE 19 (left to right) **All Nippon unless noted.**
Row 1:
High rise extended rests, Noritake, roosters and flowers, all around, some moriage, 5" d $140.00
Nippon Noritake Toke Kaisha Japan, flowers on wide rim, not true Nippon age, 5" d . . . . $ 20.00
Plate type, pink flowers, 3 rests, 5" l . . . . $ 45.00
Match holder, Noritake, part of set of next ashtray, beautiful work, some moriage, 5½" l
Bowl on flat pedestal, Noritake, part of set, scenes all around, 3⅛" h, price is for set $375.00

Row 2:
Plate type, flowers & vines, gold edge, 5" l . . . . $ 45.00
Dish with extended rests, Noritake, house & meadow scene, rim plain, 3⅞" d . . . . $ 65.00
Large square, Noritake, house & meadow scene, brown moriage, 5½" sq . . . . $ 80.00
Separate matchbox holder, makes nice set with other ashtrays, 4½" l . . . . $ 50.00
Cup with two extended rests, Noritake, nicely done, lots of moriage, trees & houses, 4⅝" l . . . . $ 95.00
Plate type, Noritake, green dragon cen, designs all around rim, nice moriage, roughly 5" d . . . . $ 90.00

POTTERY & PORCELAIN NORITAKE ASHTRAYS

Many lovely pieces were made in Japan by Noritake, both in the Nippon area and later. The earliest pieces, from 1904 to 1921, had both Noritake and Nippon marks. But by the early 1920s, the pieces were marked with a green "M" in a wreath, standing for Morimura, the name of the company's founder. The country's name was marked as Japan. Sometime during the mid-1920s a red mark came to be used. The green mark was used until 1953, when the "M" was changed to an "N," standing for Noritake. For more detailed information consult books on Noritake.

PLATE 20 (left to right)
Row 1:
Round with match holder on back rim, cards & sticks cen, green mark, 4¾" d . . . . $ 85.00
Cup type, orange, black, lg gold rests, green mark, 5¼" d . . . . $ 80.00
Figural frog, luster on boat & green frog, 4¼" l . . . . $ 95.00
Figural pelican, opalized tray, wine rim, luster on pelican, green mark, 5" d $130.00

Row 2:
Square, four rests, tree in meadow pattern, red mark, 3¾" w . . . . $ 50.00
Horses' heads in relief in center, orange rise, 5½" d $175.00
Cup type with rests making handles, stylized flowers inside, green mark, 5½" l . . . . $ 72.00
Orange rectangle, horse scene in cen, green mark, 4¾" l . . . . $ 80.00

PLATE 19

PLATE 20

POTTERY & PORCELAIN NORITAKE ASHTRAYS

The first ashtray on Plate 21, very collectible now, was at one time sold for $1.00 with a premium. Early Noritake was always well made, and the designs were good as well. This high quality helps to keep the prices high. But do look carefully to make sure that it has not been mended if you are paying top dollar. Also, be sure the back stamp is really Noritake.

PLATE 21 (left to right)

Row 1:

Lady holding out skirt, luster, red mark, 4¼" sq, early to mid 1920s $125.00

Hexagon, swans in center, black moriage on rise, green mark, 6¾" d . . . . $ 90.00

Tray, cigarette box, four small ashtrays, set, blue with Wedgwood appearance, red mark,
   very nice, white moriage $400.00

Victorian picture, more recent Noritake, 3⅞" square, 1940 . . . . $ 18.00

Row 2:

Small, flat hexagon, luster, couple dancing in center, green mark, 3½" d, mid to late 1920s . . . . $ 50.00

Small cup, one rest, tree in meadow scene all around, luster, 2¼" d, probably early 1920s . . . . $ 25.00

Cup type, stylized flowers around rim, brown moriage on cigarette rests, green mark, 5½" d . . . . $ 95.00

Cigarette cup holder with ashtray, red mark, 3¾" d, 1920s . . . . $ 85.00

Small spade, opalized with butterfly center, red mark, 3¼" l . . . . $ 40.00

POTTERY & PORCELAIN ASHTRAYS WITH JAPAN MARK ONLY

All the ashtrays in Plate 22 have just a Japan mark, unless noted. They are from different times, mostly from the 1920s on. Some ashtrays have the mark written in Japanese characters. These were probably made for use within Japan. Ashtrays marked Occupied Japan will be discussed in Section V.

The ashtrays with the Japan mark are made for export. They vary greatly in quality and probably should be judged on the workmanship. Many of them have luster, which was very popular during the 1920s, but it can also be found on more recent ashtrays.

The Hummel-like ashtray is one of the better ones that I have seen of that type. Be careful not to be fooled if you want to buy Hummel. Japan makes many Hummel-type ashtrays and figurines, but the real Hummels will always have the Hummel mark.

PLATE 22 (left to right)

Row 1:

Hummel-style, *Music Maker,* Nepco-Japan mark, about 5½" w $25.00

Oriental boy, signed Will George, matte finish on tray , great work, 3¼" h $75.00

Bowl with three extended rests, moriage decoration, bowl is 4⅛" d $50.00

Dragonware, moriage used for gray dragon, often found in gift shops, no mark, 3⅝" l $10.00

Panda, animal & bamboo figural, China mark, 4½" h $15.00

Row 2:

Clown, figural, opalized tray, the rest is luster finish, 3" h $30.00

Luster triangle, pink flowers on sides, 5" sides $14.00

Bowl, ashtray top is removable, holes for cigarettes, Ardalt-Japan mark, 4½" d $30.00

Oriental man, no mark, nice work, robe decorated all around, 2½" w $28.00

Green dish, basketweave pattern, Marutomoware-Japan mark, 4½" d . . . . $ 8.00

Blue enamel, matchbox holder, copper cut out work, 2½" h, China, old $35.00

Dog, figural with nine cigarette holders, luster, double T in diamond mark, 3" h $25.00

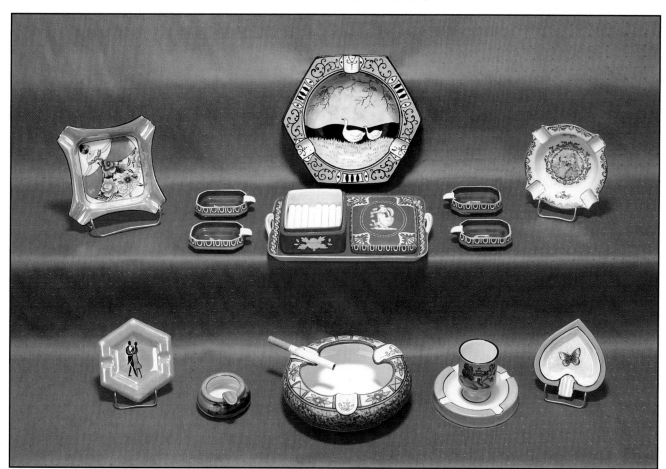

PLATE 21

PLATE 22

POTTERY & PORCELAIN ASHTRAYS WITH JAPAN MARK ONLY

These ashtrays, all from Japan, are a mixture of exports and ashtrays made for their own use in Japan. The two large ashtrays on the bottom shelf in Plate 23 were made for Japanese use and are made in the Kutani and Imari style. The clown figural cigarette holder has no ashtray, but I liked it because of its Deco style.

PLATE 23 (left to right)

Row 1:
Elephants, figurals, Deco style, elephants finished on both sides, 3" h $25.00
Small square, luster sides, tree in meadow scene, double T in circle (Takito) mark, 3⅛" sq $20.00
Bowl, large, rust & blues, 3 rests on center top edge, not made for export, mark in Japanese, 8" d........ $25.00
Hexagonal, red background, moriage, 2" sides $15.00
Small square, tree, house, hills, water, moriage, 3⅛" sq... $18.00
Clown, figural next to cigarette holder & match pack holder, both Japanese script & made in Japan, 4" h.... $30.00

Row 2:
Kutani-type bowl, three rests on center top edge, mark in Japanese, not made for export, 6⅜" d $12.00
Lefton-type squares, two, white with violets, Japan mark, 3" l.................................... $ 6.00
Dish, two men sitting, moriage, geometric design on rim, 5" d.................................... $35.00
Box shape, early deco style, black sides with designs, Trico mark, 2½" sq........................ $15.00
Imari-type bowl, medium, three rests on center top edge, mark in Japanese, 6½" d $12.00

POTTERY & PORCELAIN ASHTRAYS MADE BY LEFTON

Lefton is a name of an importer, operating in the United States and selling porcelains made in Japan to America. The company was founded in 1940 and is still active. All wares are clearly marked, fired on or with a paper label. Numbers below the mark are for identification only. Ashtrays imported by Lefton are very easy to find, and usually not very expensive. The older they are, the more desired and thus more expensive. There are good books in the library about Lefton that will give you some help in identifying the ashtrays and show you the different backstamps. There are more styles than these delicate, add-on types pictured in Plate 24.

Note: Be very careful when washing this type of Lefton china. Put towels or rubber liner in sink or use a plastic dishpan.

PLATE 24 (left to right)

Row 1:
Oval dish shape, pink, add-on roses & two violets, leaves, pink bird fig, 5" l, after 1955................. $24.00
Swan, small, white with gold and add-on violets, 3" w, 1950–1955 .... $15.00
Tub shape, oblong, white, add-on roses, violets, leaves, some gold dusting, 5¼" l, 1948–1953 .... $20.00
Swan, small greenish-gray, three small pink flowers, some gold dusting, 3⅛" l, 1948–1953............. $18.00
Swan, small, white, flowers & leaves, cigarette rests in tail, 3½" l.................................. $15.00
Oval dish shape, pink, add-on roses & leaves, pink bird figurals, 5" l, after 1955 .... $20.00

Row 2:
Oval dish shape, white, add-on roses & leaves, 4¾" l, 1950–1955 .... $15.00
Dish shape, part of set, rd, pink, add-on flowers, gold dusting, 3½" d, 1950–1955, see below for tall cup .. $20.00
Dish shape, rd, white, add-on flowers in pink & blue, scalloped sides, 3⅜" d, 1950–1955 .... $15.00
Sleigh, small pink & yellow roses/green leaves, gold dusting, cigarette rests at top of back, 3½" l, 1950–1955.. $25.00
Tall cigarette cup set & ashtray (above), pink, add-on flowers, gold dusting, ruffled edges, set price above
Swan, large, white, bisque, colored flowers, leaves, 2 rests near tail, 4" l, 1950–1955................. $35.00
Bisque tray, some pink, ornate cupids in relief, 4⅝" l... $20.00
Dish shape, rd, pink roses at top, 3⅜" d, 1949–1955 .... $18.00
Dish shape, rd, pink, add-on flowers in pink & blue, some gold dusting, 3½" d, 1950–1955............. $18.00

PLATE 23

PLATE 24

GLASS ASHTRAYS

We are all aware of the appearance and many qualities of glass. It can be clear and seen through, translucent, or opaque. It can be molded, cut, painted, and layered. The old Venetian techniques have produced beautiful glass, and the newer glass art techniques have produced glass equally breathtaking. In this section I will discuss Depression glass, elegant Depression glass, glassware of the '40s, '50s, and '60s, and art glass.

Depression glass is the term given inexpensive glassware made in the late 1920s and through the 1930s. Much of this glass was colored — pink and green being among the favorites — but amber, blue, black, crystal, red, yellow, and white were also used. People had little money to buy new glass, and these tableware items were often used as premiums when other products were purchased. For instance, the advertisers would include a free glass plate in a large bag of flour. Perhaps the smaller bag of flour would include a cup. Women thought this was great! It gave them a chance to buy their staples and obtain a new set of dishes, which they would not have been able to afford.

Another way that this glassware was promoted was through Woolworth's and other large chain stores. Remember, it was cheap and could be sold profitably for very little money. Colored glass was new and was also cheerful on the table during these difficult times.

Elegant Depression glass is the term given to glassware, mostly handmade, that was sold in jewelry and other better stores as gifts. These items were made by the best glass manufacturing companies of the time, and the products were usually lovely. The quality of elegant Depression glass is completely different from regular Depression glass, although the time of manufacture was the same. I have included some of the ashtrays manufactured by Cambridge, Duncan and Miller, Fostoria, Heisey, and Imperial. There are other companies that are just as good that I do not have room to include.

Glassware of the '40s, '50s, and '60s describes glass made in those years by inexpensive and expensive manufacturing processes. It was often made by the same manufacturers active in the Depression glass era.

The term *art glass* in this book refers to glass made from the late nineteenth century on, but not typical of general production lines. It is expensive and of limited production. This glass comes from many different countries. Some examples are also shown here.

When caring for glass ashtrays, be very careful not to knock them in the sink. If possible, use a plastic pan, and line the sink with thick towels. Most glass can be safely soaked, but iridescent glass can be harmed by very hot water and strong soap. If the ashtray is just plain glass, you can use dish detergent and soak it for 15 minutes. This will help to loosen dirt, tar, and paper labels. Dishwasher detergent is much stronger and should not be used unless you know it will not harm the glass.

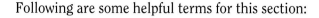 

Following are some helpful terms for this section:

Akro Agate: Items made from solid, marbleized, opaque glass.

Amberina: Clear and translucent, shading from light amber to ruby red.

Aventurine: Translucent glass with sparkling inclusions of gold, copper, and chromic oxide.

Black glass: The look of solid black, but when held to sun or strong light, color can be seen through it, most often amethyst.

Bohemian: Term often used to refer to glass that is cut or etched from color to clear; made in a province of Czechoslovakia.

Burmese: Type of art glass with pink shading to yellow; popular between 1885 and 1895.

Cameo: Made from multiple layers of glass in which the outer opaque layer is cut away to leave the design in relief.

Carnival: Usually patterned glass that is pressed with an iridescence to look expensive, but was often given away at carnivals early in this century; made 1905–1925, reissued in 1950s when popularity revived.

Cranberry: Refers to color of glass; made by adding traces of gold to molten glass.

Crystal: Colorless lead glass; also a term referring to colorless glass.

Custard: Creamy or yellowish milk glass often found in early twentieth century.

Engraved: Design cut into glass by small wheels coated with abrasive.

Etched: Inexpensive method of design by which patterns are scratched in acid-resistant wax and acid is applied; results in the appearance of being engraved.

Flashed: Application of very thin layer of colored glass over another color.

Frosted: A frost-like appearance to surface of glass.

Gilding: Process of decoration by application of gold leaf, paint, or dust.

Hobnail: Refers to pattern of small raised knobs known as prunts; popular from Civil War to present.

Intaglio cut: Design depressed below surface, giving an image in relief.

Iridescent glass: Has a shimmering quality.

Luster: Surface painted with metallic oxide, resulting in shiny metallic surface.

Milk: Opaque glass of white color.

Mold: Form used for shaping molten glass, or decorating the item.

Opalescent: Glass reflecting light, like an opal, milky-white translucent.

Opaque: Glass that cannot be seen through; appears solid.

Overlay: To finish with a layer of glass or another kind of decoration.

Peach blow: Partially opaque glass where surface is shaded from cream to pink or red, sometimes over opaque white.

Pressed: Inexpensive substitute for free-blown glass; formed in mold by mechanical pressure.

Sandwich: Type of glass resulting from a method of pressing glass so that it looks like lace.

Satin: Dipped in acid or sand blasted to give a dull, matte finish.

Vaseline: Sometimes referred to as uranium glass; use of uranium oxide in making glass to produce an effect of brilliant, yellow-green glass.

Whimsy: Object made for fun or to show skill of glassmaker, such as Venetian glass sailboats.

DEPRESSION GLASS ASHTRAYS

All the ashtrays discussed on the next few pages belong in the Depression glass category. These ashtrays were inexpensively made and often given away as an advertising premium. They were also sold at five-and-dime stores, a way for the families to obtain new tablewares for little or no money.

When color was introduced to these items, it was an immediate hit. It helped to bring a bit of gaiety into the house while the country was going through the Great Depression. The pressed patterns were also very popular because they somewhat resembled the expensive cut glass.

Tablewares were much more complicated during these years. If possible, people used a specific dish for every type of food. And in many cases there was an ashtray to match the pattern of dishes. Sometimes these ashtrays were given away as an advertising premium in the same way as the other dishes. Smoking was becoming very popular, and there were many ashtrays.

Some of the better known Depression manufacturers are mentioned here, and some of their works are shown on the following plates.

ANCHOR HOCKING, BARTLETT COLLINS, FEDERAL

Manhattan is one of the most easily spotted patterns in Depression glassware. The pink Manhattan, shown in Plate 25, is possibly a reproduction. However, in 1929, Westmoreland did make some larger pieces in a similar design in both pink and crystal, and this piece could be theirs. Snufferettes were more common during the 1920s than the 1930s. Remember that new ashtrays in established patterns do occasionally show up. To protect your purchases, it is best to buy from a reputable dealer. Also, know about your subject before you buy.

The green Bartlett Collins in Plate 26 was made with the match striker in long strips on the rim. This was great for use before safety matches came into common use.

PLATE 25 (left to right)

Row 1:

Manhattan round, Anchor Hocking, can also come with gold rim, 4" d, 1938–1943 . . . . $11.00
Block optic, Anchor Hocking, crystal, 4" d, 1929–1933 . . . . $30.00
Manhattan pink, probably by Westmoreland, one snufferette, 3¾" d $18.00

Row 2:

Manhattan with ad, *Anchor Hocking, 38 years of progress, 1905–1943,* 4" d $15.00
Serva snack set, Anchor Hocking, one rest in the corner next to cup, 10" l $15.00
Manhattan square, Anchor Hocking, with gold on rim, 4½", 1938–1943 . . . . $20.00
Manhattan round with ad, Anchor Hocking, *Post Cereals,* 4" d $13.00

PLATE 26 (left to right)

Row 1:

Federal, lt amber round, 5⅛" l, 1930s . . . . $ 5.00
Federal, crystal round, hobs on bottom, *Glassware by Federal,* 4" d $11.00
Federal, green cup on legs, Deco lines, 2⅜" h, probably late 1920s, early 1930s $12.00
Federal, Williamsburg, pressed pattern, crystal, 4" d . . . . $ 7.00
Federal, lt blue round, 5⅛" l, possibly late 1930s or 1940s . . . . $ 5.00

Row 2:

Federal with ad, *Glassware By Federal,* blue letters, 4" d $12.00
Federal, Williamsburg, pressed pattern, amber, 4" d . . . . $ 8.00
Bartlett Collins, green round, match holder center, match strikers on rim, 5⅝" d, late 1920s $18.00
Federal, Diana, irid amber, 4⅛" sq, 1937–1941 . . . . $ 8.00
Bartlett Collins, black amethyst with ad, *Sapulpa, Oklahoma,* 4" sq $15.00

PLATE 25

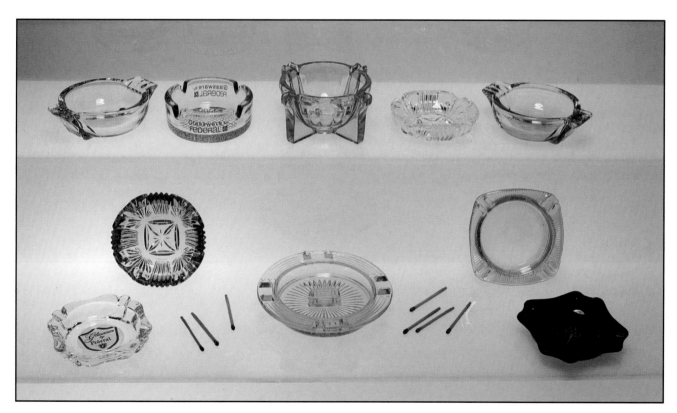

PLATE 26

GREENSBURG GLASS WORKS AND KNOX GLASS

Animals have always fascinated glass designers, and not just during the Depression years. The elephant has probably been reproduced in glass, pottery, and metal more than any other animal.

Early in the 1930s Greensburg Glass Works made a series of animals that were raised in the center or on the rim of an ashtray. Plate 27 shows some of their ashtrays and one cigarette box. These are the only four colors that I have seen: pink, green, amber, and black amethyst. About this time, the Greensburg Company was sold to L.E. Smith, and in some cases, you will see credit given to L.E. Smith for their manufacture.

Probably in the 1930s, the Knox Glass Company made the Pacemaker ashtray. It shows a horse standing in the center of the tray and both the horse and ashtray were made in different colors. Later, the Pacemaker ashtray was produced by American Glass.

In the early 1940s, this Pacemaker ashtray was selected by William Randolph Hearst to give to tourists when they visited the Hearst Castle. Later, in 1974, they were sold at the Roosevelt Raceway in New York. The mold has not been reproduced.

PLATE 27 (left to right)
Row 1:
Elephant, black amethyst, Greensburg Glass Works, 6" d, early 1930s $30.00
Scotty, amber, same as above $25.00
Scotty, black amethyst, on back rim with match holder, manufacturer unknown, 4⅝" sq $27.00
Pacemaker, crystal horse, 5¼" d, 3½" h, late 1930s $15.00
Pacemaker, black horse, blue fired on ashtray, same as above $35.00
Scotty, black amethyst, 6" d $26.00

Row 2:
Elephant, green, 6" d $25.00
Scotty cigarette box, pink, Greensburg Glass Works, 3¾" l, 3¾" h, early 1930s $30.00
Bulldog, green, Greensburg Glass Works, 5" l, 3" h, early 1930s $35.00
Scotty, small; pink, 4" d $20.00
Scotty, green, Greensburg Glass Works, 6" d, early 1930s $25.00

HAZEL ATLAS

Hazel Atlas made many, many household items, and their variety of ashtrays continues to be easy to find in antique malls. Some were just for everyday, while others were for very good. See the Ships ashtray in Plate 28 for one of my favorites. It is hard to find with the sails in good condition. The jar shown in Plate 28 is not very easy to find. Too bad I cannot turn the top of the jar inside out, as it is in much better condition inside.

I have seen the cobalt blue, oval ashtray labeled from the Moderntone pattern by Hazel Atlas, but this is incorrect. It was made by Hazel Atlas but is not Moderntone. It is a lovely cobalt blue and has Deco lines.

PLATE 28 (left to right)
Row 1:
Crystal oval, swirl pattern in bottom, 6¼" l . . . . $ 9.00
Ovide, fired-on gray, 3½" sq, 1930s . . . . $ 7.00
Jar, marked, top in poor condition but hard to find, 2⅝" h, 1930s . . . . $ 15.00
Dutch boy & girl, match holder center, 5¾" d, late 1920s . . . . $ 28.00

Row 2:
Ships, Hazel Atlas, cobalt ashtray, 5" d, late 1930s $100.00
#9785, series of ribs at right angles on bottom, 4¼" sq, 1936–1939 . . . . $ 8.00
Hazel Atlas ad, for *Jars, Packers Vessels,* pattern under rim, 5¾" d, old . . . . $ 27.00
Six-pointed star, blue, pattern on bottom, 6 rests, 4¾" w, 1936–1939 . . . . $ 15.00
Six-pointed star, crystal, same as blue one . . . . $ 12.00
Cobalt blue oval, 5½" l, early 1930s–1940 . . . . $ 15.00

PLATE 27

PLATE 28

HAZEL ATLAS

In Plate 29, there are some ashtrays from the Windmill and Checkerboard series. The four small ashtrays with the checkerboard rims and the larger ashtrays with the Dutch boy and girl, and the carnival windmill are all from the same series. Ashtrays with checkerboard rims are quite easy to find.

PLATE 29 (left to right)

Row 1:

Florentine #1, (Poppy #1), uneven rim edge, has coaster ring in bottom, 5½" d, 1932–1935............ $25.00

Florentine #2, (Poppy #2), green even rim edge, coaster ring in bottom, crystal, 3¾" d, 1932–1935 ..... $18.00

Windmill & Checkerboard, crystal, marked, match holder center, 4" d, late 1920s..................... $12.00

Double ashtray, probably Hazel Atlas, green, two rests, good for card games, 4¾" l, 1930s............. $13.00

Florentine #2, (Poppy #2), yellow, same as above $28.00

#757½, miscellaneous items, crystal, marked, 4" d, 1936–1939 .... $10.00

Green oval, 5½" l, early 1930s–1940 .... $13.00

Row 2:

Moderntone, pink with metal rests in cen, 4" d, 1934–1942, & also late 1940s–early 1950s $40.00

Windmill & Checkerboard, green marked, match holder center, 4" d, late 1920s.................. $12.00

Windmill & Checkerboard, green, marked, 4" d, late 1920s $11.00

Carnival, windmill in relief, match holder on rim, 5¾" d, late 1920s..................... $30.00

#757½, miscellaneous items, green, 4" d, 1936–1939 .... $15.00

Windmill & Checkerboard, pink marked, match holder center, 4" d, late 1920s................. $12.00

#757½, miscellaneous items, green, match holder center, 4" d, 1936–1939........................ $15.00

HOCKING GLASS, INDIANA, AND NATIONAL

I recently found a green Miss America ashtray, at least I thought so, until I looked at the pictures of the Miss America pattern very closely. Unfortunately, the rays in the center of the ashtray meet and extend almost to the rise, but in Miss America they do not. I haven't found one yet, so be careful before you buy.

The colors of the bridge set by Indiana represent very different time periods. The crystal and amber pieces were both made during the late 1920s to the 1980s. But the blue and dark green are only from recent years. The pattern remains the same, regardless of when they were made. Other colors were also made.

The Royal Ruby and Forest Green Queen Mary ashtrays, in Plate 30, were made by Hocking Glass and were entitled to use that patented color name. For more about this, see ashtrays of the 1940s, 1950s, and 1960s.

PLATE 30 (left to right)

Row 1:

Waterford, Hocking Glass, "waffle," crystal, 4" d, 1938–1944 .... $ 8.00

Sandwich, Indiana, bridge set, 2 clubs & 1 heart, early colors, 3½" w, late 1920s–today $14.00

Waterford, Hocking Glass, "waffle," white with green inside, 4" d, 1938–1944 .... $ 7.00

Queen Mary, Hocking Glass, oval cigarette holder, 2" h.............................. $ 6.00

Sandwich, Indiana, bridge set, olive diamond, later color, 3¼" w, late 1920s–today................... $14.00

Princess, Hocking Glass, green, 4½" sq, 1931–1935 .... $72.00

Row 2:

Queen Mary, Hocking Glass, Royal Ruby, 3½" d, 1950s .... $ 4.00

Pineapple & Floral, #618, Indiana, 4½" l, 1932–1937.......................... $18.00

Sandwich, Indiana, bridge set, two spades, early colors, 3⅛" w, late 1920s–today $14.00

Queen Mary, Hocking Glass, crystal, 4¼" sq, 1936–1949 .... $ 5.00

National, set of three, hobs in center, definite rests on rim, cobalt, crystal, olive, largest 5¼" d, set price .. $20.00

Queen Mary, Hocking Glass, "Vertical Ribbed," crystal, 3½" d, 1936–1949 .... $ 4.00

Queen Mary, Hocking Glass, Forest Green, 3½" d, 1950s........................... $ 6.00

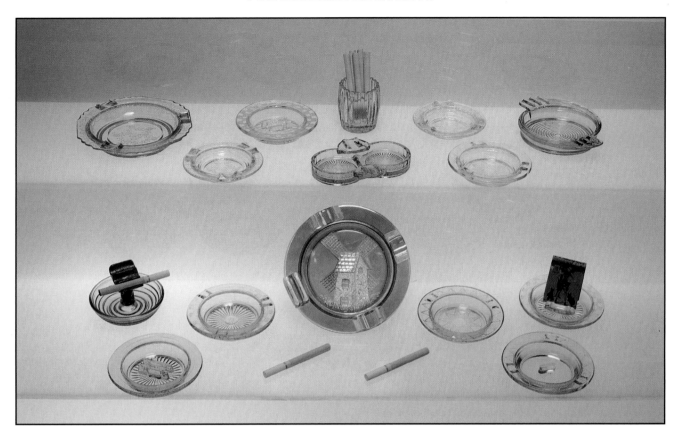

PLATE 29

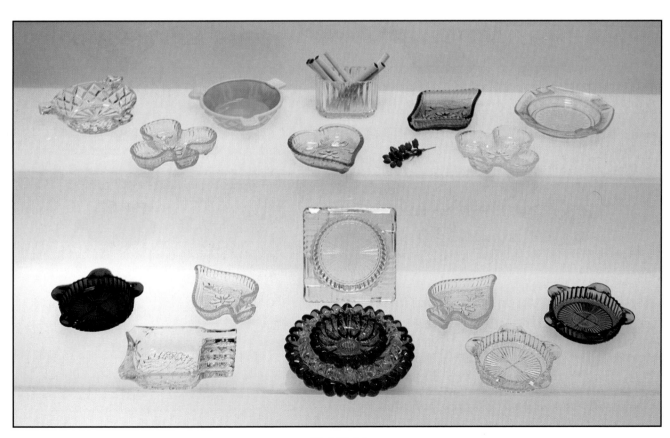

PLATE 30

JEANNETTE, MACBETH-EVANS

Jeannette made many very nice patterns throughout the Depression years. Adam, Sunflower, and Windsor Diamond were three of these patterns that included ashtrays. Their colors were strong, and I heard one person refer to them as "happy" colors. Happy colors were certainly needed during the Great Depression.

In Plate 31, there is a MacBeth-Evans ashtray that is very easy to find in antique malls, but seldom listed with the correct manufacturer. It also varies greatly in price from $2.00 to $45.00. Pink is the easiest color to find.

PLATE 31 (left to right)   **All Jeannette unless noted.**
   Row 1:
   Adam, pink, 4½" sq, 1932–1934 . . . . $30.00
   MacBeth-Evans, #7541-A, green, 3¼" sq, 1932 . . . . $ 8.00
   Homespun (Fine Rib), coaster ashtray, cross-hatch on bottom, 3¾" sq, 1939–1949 . . . . $ 7.00
   Kitchenware, Jad-ite, hexagon, match holder center, 4½" w, mid-1930s $10.00
   Adam, lt yellow, no pattern on rib due to small size, 3⅞" sq, 1932–1934 . . . . $20.00
   MacBeth-Evans, #7541-A, pink, 3¼" sq, 1932 . . . . $10.00
   Sunflower, one snufferette in center, 3¾" d, 1930s $12.00

   Row 2:
   Windsor Diamond, green, match holder center, two snufferettes on rims, 5¾" d, 1936–1946 . . . . $47.00
   Green oval, kitchen ware & miscellaneous item, 4¼" l, 1934 . . . . $15.00
   Windsor Diamond, blue delphite, note pattern is on reverse side only, match holder center, 5¾" d $47.00
   Large round, match holder center, 4 rests, 5¾" d, 1934 . . . . $15.00
   Homespun (Fine Rib), cross-hatch bottom, rectangle, 4⅜ x 3", 1939–1949 . . . . $ 9.00
   Windsor Diamond, pink, same as above Windsor Diamonds $36.00

McKEE, NEW MARTINSVILLE, AND OWENS ILLINOIS GLASS CO.

The McKee glass and ashtray, often called "Bottoms Up" was a fun piece but somewhat impractical, because you could not put the glass down until it was empty. The ashtray part of this set has two snufferettes, popular in those times for putting out the cigarette. The color shown in Plate 32 was called jade.

PLATE 32 (left to right)
   Row 1:
   New Martinsville, green, match strikers on outside rise in three places, 4½" d, about 1915 . . . . $ 25.00
   New Martinsville, crystal, matchbox holder with slit in front of it for match pack, two snuff,
      4⅛" d, Pat. #, 1923 . . . . $ 13.00
   McKee "Bottoms Up," jade, two pieces, can find pieces separately, ashtray is 4" d, 1932 . . . . $140.00
   New Martinsville, crystal, matchbox holder only in center, 4½" d, 1920s . . . . $ 10.00
   New Martinsville, #728, green, opening for match pack holder, Pat # app., 4⅜" d, for Diamond Match Co.. . $ 15.00

   Row 2:
   New Martinsville, ruby dish on three small legs, 4" d $10.00
   New Martinsville swan, crystal with colored decoration, 1 rest in tail, 2¾" h $25.00
   Round with match holder center, pressed pattern on bottom, 4⅞" d, early 1930s $10.00
   New Martinsville, triangle/match striker on rims, three wide rests, 4½" sides, old glass $25.00
   Owen Illinois, Sager Safetray, patent applied for, five rests in center, matchbox holder &
      match pack holder, 6¼" d $25.00
   McKee Glass, shell shape, ad for company in Jeannette, PA, 5⅝" l. $13.00
   New Martinsville, crystal, matchbox holder & slit recessed for match pack, 4⅝" l, 1920s–1930s $13.00
   New Martinsville, Moondrops, amethyst, 6" d, 1932–1940 . . . . $19.00

PLATE 31

PLATE 32

L.E.SMITH, U.S.GLASS, WESTMORELAND

The L.E. Smith Glass Company made some wonderful black amethyst ashtrays in the late twenties and thirties. Because of their Art Deco influence, they were very popular. I've pictured two of them in Plate 33.

The large, green ashtray was made by U.S. Glass and has a cigarette pack holder, a match pack or matchbox holder, and two snufferettes. It is from their pattern, Flower Garden with Butterflies. Match holders of this shape and size were made to hold a match pack by using the center slot, or a matchbox by using the whole outside. This shape helps in dating, because it was not made until after match packs were frequently used.

The Primo coaster-ashtray, in Plate 33, is also by U.S. Glass. It does not have the Primo pattern on it, but was probably made to go with it. I've been told that the Primo glass fits exactly into the ring made for the glass.

PLATE 33 (left to right)

Row 1:

L.E. Smith, #503 black amethyst, match holder, 6½" d . . . . $ 18.00
L.E. Smith, crystal duck, one rest in tail, 4½" l . . . . $ 8.00
Westmoreland, ruby English hobnail, smooth hobs, hard to find, 4½" sq, 1920s–1940s . . . . $ 40.00
Westmoreland, English hobnail low-hat, milk glass, 4½" l . . . . $ 15.00
U.S. Glass, Flower Garden With Butterflies cigarette pack holder, matchbox holder & match pack holder,
    two snuff, 6" d, late 1920s $185.00
L.E. Smith, #90/4, black amethyst, three legs which become rests at top, 3" h, 5" d . . . . $ 20.00

Row 2:

Pipe holder & ashtray, amethyst, 6⅝" l, patented June 1923 . . . . $ 15.00
Glasses and ashtray, pink, possibly designed for card table, mfgr not identified, 7⅜" w . . . . $ 60.00
U.S. Glass, Primo coaster ashtray, "paneled Aster," two snufferettes, two rests, 5¼" l, early 1930s . . . . . . $ 10.00
Westmoreland, listed as candle holder & ashtray in book, matchbox holder, 6½" l, 1924 . . . . $ 20.00
Pipe holder & ashtray, amber, 6⅝" l, patented June, 1923 . . . . $ 12.00

PRESSED PATTERNS OF THE DEPRESSION ERA

Since the Depression years, pressed patterns have been an inexpensive way of decorating glass. Pictured in Plate 35 are some attractive ashtrays featuring the ever-popular Buttons and Bows and Moon and Stars patterns. There are many good pattern books that show various patterns and their names.

The Daisy Button pattern was thought to be created by cut glass designers who were probably looking for a less expensive way to decorate glass. At first, the manufacturers marketed it under many different names or altered the pattern. Most tableware manufacturers produced this pattern during the 1930s and 1940s.

PLATE 34 (left to right)

Row 1:

Daisy Button pattern, cup on three legs, blue, 2¼" h . . . . $ 8.00
Moon & Stars pattern, olive oval dish shape, four rests, 4⅜" l $12.00
Daisy Button pattern, five snufferettes, crystal, 4" d . . . . $ 9.00
Bubbles and Lines, ripple rim, crystal, 4" d . . . . $ 7.00
Daisy Button pattern on bottom, ridges on outside, small square, light blue, 2⅝" sq . . . . $ 5.00
Type of cross-hatch bottom, green square, 3¼" sq . . . . $ 8.00
Hobnails on bottom, deep square, lt blue, nicely made, 3¼" sq . . . . $ 9.00
Daisy Button pattern, cup on three legs, amberina, 2¼" h $10.00

Row 2:

Daisy Button, large green square, 5½" sides $14.00
Daisy Button pattern, green fan, 5¼" w $10.00
Moon & Stars pattern, amberina oval dish, 4⅜" l $14.00
Pattern includes stars, crystal rectangle, 3¾" l . . . . $ 8.00
Daisy Button pattern, blue fan, 5¼" w $10.00
Daisy Button pattern, clover shape, lovely cobalt, 6¾" l $15.00

PLATE 33

PLATE 34

GLASS ASHTRAYS WITH VARIATIONS ON AN EARLY THEME

As smoking became more prevalent in the early part of the twentieth century, tobacco jars were often kept near the man's favorite chair. Sometimes the tops of the jars were a combination jar top and ashtray. There are three shown in Plate 35.

About the same time, from early in the twentieth century to the 1930s, many of the ashtrays looked very much the same. They were large, often with a matchbox holder, and had large rests, suitable for cigars or cigarettes. Most seemed to be quite plain. Occasionally they were in green, carnival, or amber, but most often these ashtrays were made in crystal.

The ashtrays in Plate 36 are a different type, but again all similar. This group is all flat. They were probably made from 1910 to the 1930s. Again, colors are somewhat limited. The large crystal ashtray that looks like the Manhattan pattern is probably not Manhattan. Interestingly, Westmoreland made some in a similar, but larger, pattern in the 1920s. This might belong to that group. It would probably fetch about the same price, though.

PLATE 35 (left to right)

Row 1:

Jar top, three rests, matchbox holder back rim, 4¾" d . . . . $ 9.00

Jar top, no rests, matchbox holder, deep depression for ashes, 4¾" d, 1915 . . . . $12.00

Green, two rests, matchbox holder & match pack holder, rays in center not out to rise, 4⅜" d $10.00

Protecto, reg U.S. Pat. Off., two rests, matchbox & match pack holder, 5½" l $23.00

Extended rests, three rests & one in matchbox holder, even rays not all way out, 5¾" l $15.00

Jar top, four rests, matchbox holder, 5¾" d . . . . $ 9.00

Row 2:

Plain green, no rests, matchbox holder, depressed center for ashes, 5¼" d . . . . $ 9.00

Different shape, three regular rests & one rest in matchbox holder, pressed pattern on bottom, 4¾" l $12.00

Diamond Match Co., two rests, two match pack holder, made for Diamond Match Co., 4" l $13.00

Blue milk glass, three rests, matchbox holder & match pack holder, 4" d $16.00

Round, no rests, match pack holder, 4" d . . . . $ 9.00

Green, two rests, six snufferettes, 4¼" d $17.00

PLATE 36 (left to right)

Row 1:

Carnival polo player, three rests, matchbox holder & match pack holder, 5½" d $40.00

Ridges on rim, three rests, matchbox holder & match pack holder, rays to rise, 5½" d $13.00

Pink agatized glass, four rests, four snuff, bump in center for pipes, 6" d, 1910 . . . . $25.00

Manhattan type, four rests, four snuff, matchbox holder, maybe by Westmoreland, 7" d, 1920s $20.00

Carnival, three rests, plain rim, matchbox holder, 5¾" d, 1910 . . . . $25.00

Row 2:

Ripple rim, dk amber, matchbox holder & match pack holder, rays to rise, 5¾" d $14.00

Green checkerboard rim, three rests, matchbox holder & match pack holder, rays to rise, 5¾" d $15.00

Large carnival, six rests, matchbox holder & match pack holder, rays to rise, 7½" d $20.00

Green checkerboard rim, four rests, matchbox holder & match pack holder, rays not all way to rise, 5¾" d . . $15.00

Carnival checkerboard rim, three rests, matchbox holder & match pack holder, rays to rise, 5¾" d $15.00

PLATE 35

PLATE 36

AKRO AGATE

The Akro Agate company was founded in Clarksburg, Virginia, in 1914. In the beginning, they made mostly marbles — hence, the term "Aggies." In later years, they made children's dishes and many novelty items, including ashtrays.

In 1936, Akro Agate obtained the molds of Westite, a similar manufacturer. Westite's colors were drab in comparison to Akro Agate, and Westite products were usually not marked. Akro Agate's mark is a crow flying through the letter "A" with an Aggie in each claw and one in his mouth. Despite the differences, Westite's products are considered collectible along with Akro Agate.

After World War II, the popularity declined. This and competition from foreign markets influenced the closure of Akro Agate in 1951.

PLATE 37 (left to right)   **All Akro Agate unless noted.**
Row 1:
Cigarette holder & ashtray, maybe Westite, lemonade & oxblood, base 5" d . . . . $ 50.00
Leaf, some yellow in bottom, 4" l . . . . $ 10.00
Blue rectangle, 4" l . . . . $ 9.00
Rare, ruby clear/match holder, ruby ashtray, matches on a roll fastened at top, 5¾" h $180.00
Red & cream rectangle, 4" l . . . . $ 9.00
Lemonade & oxblood, popular color demands higher price, 3" sq . . . . $ 15.00
Cigar lighter & ashtray, Vidrio Products Corp., patented, 6" l . . . . $ 65.00

Row 2:
Blue hexagon, nice blue marbling, two wide rests, two narrow rests, 4¼" w . . . . $ 30.00
Yellow, very little marbleizing, 3" sq. . . . . $ 8.00
Gray & red, Westite, 3" sq. . . . . $ 8.00
Pen holder, two rests, 4¾" l . . . . $ 25.00

DEPRESSION ERA GLASS ASHTRAYS – UNIDENTIFIED

I have not been able to identify many of the ashtrays that I have in my collection. However, they are typical of the Depression era ashtrays. The glass is old, the patterns were pressed, the styles are from that time. The next three plates, 38, 39, and 40, will show some of these Depression ashtrays.

PLATE 38 (left to right)
Row 1:
Matchbox holder, pressed pattern on bottom, space in center for ashes, 4" l $10.00
Ruby flash, pressed pattern, flash on rim, four rests, 3¼" sq . . . . $ 8.00
Coaster & ashtray, two snuff but no rests, 4" d . . . . $ 9.00
Frosted glass/cobalt ball, holds cigarette tip to water-filled ball & water extinguishes cig, 5½" d, pat. 1935. . . $35.00
Italy, pressed pattern, only in crystal, 4⅜" d . . . . $ 4.00
Cup top, lt pink, heavy, fits on top of cup, two rests, two snuff, hole for ashes, 3¼" d $15.00
Square pattern center, pressed pattern, four rests, 3⅜" sq . . . . $ 8.00
Star, rests at points, sits on five tiny feet, 4¾" w . . . . $ 9.00

Row 2:
Round with bubbles, three rests, 5½" d $13.00
Art Deco, two rests, elongated lines, 4" l . . . . $ 8.00
Crisscross with dots, pressed pattern on bottom, 3¼" l $13.00
Fan, amethyst, Daisy Button pattern, 4" l $10.00
Oval, lt pink, matchbox holder & match pack holder, three rests, 5⅜" l $16.00
Good Luck, two rests, four snuff, matchbox holder, slit recessed in front for match pack, 4¼" l $16.00
Scotty, pressed pattern, 2 rests opposite corners, 3" l . . . . $ 7.00
Nest of three, very easy to find, shows different treatments — ruby flash, pink, crystal, largest is 5⅝" d . . . $15.00

PLATE 37

PLATE 38

DEPRESSION ERA GLASS ASHTRAYS – UNIDENTIFIED

If you choose to collect glass ashtrays, you will have chosen one of the most difficult materials to work with. Most glasswares are not marked, and the ones that are will only tell you the manufacturer. You must be very careful to validate what might be written on the price ticket. Some of the time that information is incorrect. Also, you can spend hours looking through books for a picture like your ashtray. But if you can finally identify it, you will feel great.

You can get much information just from the feel of the object and how it was made. Because of the difference between Depression glass and elegant Depression glass, you can probably tell how the ashtray was purchased or acquired originally. A good reason for collecting glass ashtrays now is that the current prices are not as high as it is with many china patterns.

Some of the ashtrays in the next two plates may have been made in the twenties. Note the windmill scene, and the large amber round with match striker, both found in Plate 40.

PLATE 39 (left to right)

Row 1:

Round milk glass with two rests, matchbox holder & match pack holder, pattern on bottom, 5" d $15.00
Round milk glass with pattern bottom, nine rests, 4" d . . . . $ 8.00
Blue milk glass, pattern on bottom only, four rests becoming legs, 6" d $15.00
Unusual edge, milk glass, flower in relief in center, pattern on bottom, 3¾" d . . . . $ 8.00
Milk glass with matchbox holder, oval, three rests, 5" l $14.00
Milk glass cup with three legs, Daisy Button, three rests, 2¼" h . . . . $ 9.00

Row 2:

Blue, pressed pattern on bottom, six rests, 4¾" d $11.00
Two extended rests, pressed pattern with tree on each side, rays on bottom, 4¾" l $10.00
Blue fired-on, popular mold, 4" sq $11.00
Leaf, one rest, rib pattern on bottom, 5⅜" l . . . . $ 5.00
Cobalt blue, pat. number applied for, two raised rests in center, match pack holder, 4¾" d, possibly 1940s . . $ 9.00

PLATE 40 (left to right)

Row 1:

Carnival, each three rests, smallest 3⅜" d, largest 5½" d, set $10.00
Yellow, knobs under rim, 4¾" d . . . . $ 8.00
Match pack holder center, green, two rests in center next to match holder, pattern on bottom, 4⅛" l $18.00
Cup with three legs, amberina, Daisy Button pattern, 2⅛" h $12.00
Crinkle Ware, pale amber, four rests, 4¼" d . . . . $ 8.00
Green with two rests, matchbox holder & match pack holder at back rim, rays all way out, 5½" w $16.00

Row 2:

Deep rise, green, 4 rests, 3¾" d . . . . $ 5.00
Pattern under rim, dk amber, two large rests, even length rays in center, 4" d $10.00
Small green, pressed pattern on sides & bottom, 4 rests, 2¾" d . . . . $ 7.00
Fan, amber, Daisy Button pattern, 4" l $10.00
Large round, dk amber, match striker on rim, pipe knob cen, four snuff, four rests, 6" d, old $20.00
Carnival, same as larger above, 3⅜" d, price above
Scotty dogs, impressed in bottom, 4¾" l $15.00
Windmill scene, fired-on orange, three wide rests, different, 5¼" d, old $25.00

PLATE 39

PLATE 40

ELEGANT DEPRESSION GLASS ASHTRAYS

During the Depression years, there was also a need for handcrafted glassware. Beautiful items were made, and the manufacturers' names became well known for their lovely work. These items could be found for sale in jewelry and better department stores. Of course, the prices matched the quality of their work.

Because this work was so fine, collectors have given it the name of elegant Depression glass, as opposed to just Depression glass, even though they were both made during the same period, mainly the 1930s.

Elegant Depression ashtrays can be found as part of a named pattern, just as with Depression glass. Sometimes the patterns were etched; other times the patterns were beautiful because of the shape acquired by handcrafting. Colors were still important, probably for the same reasons, but crystal also became increasingly important. Below is some information about better-known manufacturers and their handmade ashtrays.

CAMBRIDGE

Cambridge Glass was founded in 1901, in the town of Cambridge, Ohio, and continued production there until 1958. Not only did they always make fine dinnerware, but they also introduced color to their lines that became popular with the American public. Glassworkers, who later worked for Cambridge, discovered amberina by accident in the early 1880s. A gold ring slipped from a worker's hand and fell on a lump of glass at the end of a blow pipe. The unusual color of amberina was created when the the glass and ring were heated together several times. The process was patented in 1883. Today, the manufacturers add gold powder to the molten glass.

Cambridge's early dinnerware lines were of heavy glass with pressed patterns, called Near Cut. Later, the manufacturer eliminated this style and continued with clear and engraved patterns. The most commonly used mark on this is the "C" in a triangle. However, I have only seen one ashtray with this mark.

Cambridge used romantic names for their colors, such as moonlight blue, emerald green, willow blue, Crown Tuscan, and ebony. They also made a black with a matte finish, which they called "Ebon."

PLATE 41 (left to right)
Row 1:
Mt. Vernon, #1624, one snufferette in center, two rests on rim, 3½" d, late 1920s–1940s $10.00
Yellow, small square from holder set below, 2½" sq
Moonlight blue for two people, two rests in center of rim, pie crust rim mold, 6⅛" l $22.00
Caprice footed shell, crystal, 2 rests near center back, 2¾" l, 1940s–1957 . . . . $11.00
Holder, set of four, two moonlight blue, two yellow, holder is 5¼" l $35.00
Moonlight blue engraved, small flower, 2½" sq $16.00
Cambridge square, crystal, 3½" d, 1952–mid 1950s . . . . $ 9.00

Row 2:
Caprice, moonlight blue triangle, small rest at each point, 2⅞" side, 1940s–1957 . . . . $17.00
Yellow stacking, #1715 miscellaneous, one rest in center, 1½" high, prior to 1949 . . . . $ 7.00
Caprice, set of 3, yellow is 3" d, crystal is 4" d, moonlight blue is 5" d, 1940s–1957 . . . . $46.00
Slashed ball shape, note that the rest does not go all the way out to edge, 3⅜" l $15.00
Caprice footed shell, moonlight blue, two rests near center back, 2¾" l, 1940s–1957 . . . . $14.00

PLATE 42 (left to right)
Row 1:
Amethyst round, four rests, heavy, 4⅜" d . . . . $ 20.00
Cambridge square, ebony, 6½" d, 1952–mid 1950s . . . . $ 15.00
Nude stem, crystal stem & ashtray, also comes with colored ashtrays, 6½" h $155.00
Black square, Cambridge calls black gloss "Ebony," 3½" sq . . . . $ 11.00

Row 2:
Golf ball stem, pale amber, card holder & cigarette holder, ashes in ashtray base, 3½" h. . . . . $ 70.00
Amberina-like hat, color called "Carmen," two rests on top rim, 3¼" l . . . . $ 17.00
Footed ruby ashtray, beautiful color, 3" h . . . . $ 50.00
Ebon oval, non-glossy black is called "Ebon," rests at ends, 7" l . . . . $ 15.00
Green stacking, #1715 miscellaneous, one rest in center, 1½" h, prior to 1949 . . . . $ 9.00
Golf ball stem with amethyst ashtray, lovely color, 3½" h . . . . $ 60.00

PLATE 41

PLATE 42

DUNCAN AND MILLER

George Duncan and Sons started a glass factory in 1874, and John Miller was a designer for the company in the beginning. By 1891, Duncan and Sons merged with seventeen other companies in Pittsburgh. But after a disastrous fire took place in 1892, the association dissolved. Duncan opened a new plant in Washington, Pennsylvania, in 1900, calling it Duncan and Miller, and continued to prosper until 1955, when they sold to U.S. Glass in Tiffin, Ohio.

Duncan and Miller made many pressed patterns in their early days. But they are known for their beautiful clean lines in lovely colors. Note the intensity of the ruby in the duck in Plate 43. Their sandwich glass, opalescent glass, and colored glass will usually fetch at least 25 percent more than their crystal glass. I suspect that Duncan and Miller ashtrays will continue to increase in price as more people begin collecting ashtrays. Duncan and Miller ashtrays were never marked, regardless of when they were made.

Note: Be very careful when washing good crystal. Do not let slippery soapsuds cause an accident. Line the sink with terry cloth towels if you do not use a plastic pan.

PLATE 43 (left to right)
> **Row 1:**
> **Duck,** large, 7" l x 5" w $40.00
> **Cloverleaf,** also in colors, 3" d.. $15.00
> **Cantebury,** 3" club, 1937 .... $ 9.00
> **Sandwich,** crystal, 3" sq, 1924–1955 .... $ 9.00
> **Duck,** small, 4½" l x 3" w $20.00
> **Tear drops,** individual size, 3" d, 1936–1955 .... $ 7.00
> **Sylvan,** leaf shape, 3½" l, 1940 .... $11.00
> **Duck cigarette box,** decorated/flowers, 6¼" l $75.00
>
> **Row 2:**
> **Caribbean,** also comes in blue, 4½", 1936–1955 .... $16.00
> **First Love,** engraved pattern, one the their most popular, 3½" l x 2½" w, started 1937 .... $17.00
> **Masters,** mold name, also colors, pattern name not identified, 2¾" d $13.00
> **Lilly of the Valley,** embossed and frosted flower stem, 7" l $35.00
> **Sandwich,** pressed pattern, 2 rests at opposite corners, 3¾" x 2½", 1924–1955 .... $10.00
> **Tear drops,** 5" d, 1936–1955 .... $11.00
> **Patio,** 3½" sq $15.00

PLATE 44 (left to right)
> **Row 1:**
> **Cantebury,** amber is 4½" l, chartreuse is 3½" l, 1937, set............................ $25.00
> **Masters,** small cobalt blue cup, 1⅝" h $16.00
> **Sanibel,** fish, pink opalescent, Duncan called cranberry pink, other colors too, 3¾" l, 1930s $50.00
> **Cloverleaf,** amber, 1 rest, Duncan's cloverleaf has a depression on back in center, 3" d, 1930s–1940s...... $15.00
> **Patio,** sapphire blue, 4½" sq $17.00
>
> **Row 2:**
> **Terrace,** cobalt blue, 3½" sq, 1930s $38.00
> **Duck,** small, ruby color, 4½" l x 3" w.. $50.00
> **Caribbean,** blue, part of cigarette holder with ashtray as top, 3" d, 1936–1955....... $28.00
> **Club,** amber, 3 rests, 3" h $20.00
> **Cloverleaf,** sapphire blue, one rest, depression on back in center, 3" d, 1930s–1940s..... $19.00
> **Terrace,** ruby, ridges on outside of rise, 3½" sq, 1930s $38.00

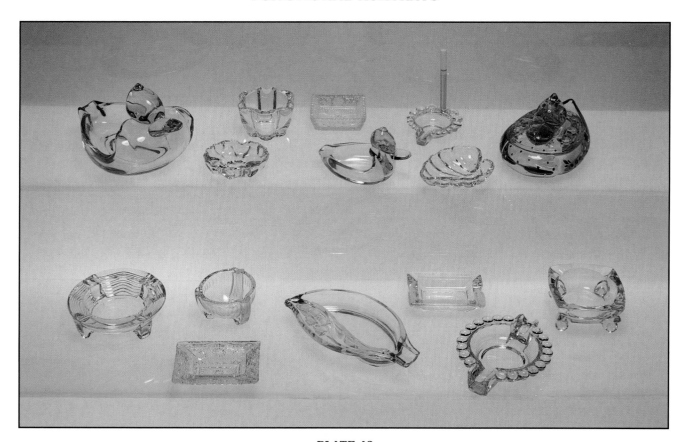

PLATE 43

PLATE 44

FENTON

The Fenton brothers, Frank and John, founded the Fenton Art Glass Company in Martin's Ferry, Ohio, in 1906. The next year Frank built his own factory in Williamstown, West Virginia.

The company made over 130 patterns of good carnival glass, mostly between 1907 and 1920. They also made custard, chocolate, opalescent, and stretch glass. They have been very successful over the years, continuing to stay in touch with current tastes.

In the 1920s, Fenton made a line of handmade items incorporating mosaic and threading techniques. Many of their products have been said to rival the finest antique glassware. The company made items during the Depression years, as well as later. More Fenton ashtrays are pictured in the 1940s, 1950s, and 1960s section.

PLATE 45 (left to right)
Row 1:
Footed ashtray, three feet, ruby, 1½" h, 1934–1936 . . . . $25.00
Rose oval, pressed mold, 4½" l . . . . $ 9.00
Milk glass, flower raised up in center to support pipe, also cigarette rests, 6½" d $40.00
Footed ashtray, cobalt blue, 1½" h, 1934–1936 . . . . $28.00

Row 2:
Footed ashtray, three feet, crystal, 1½" h, 1934–1936 . . . . $20.00
Small green square, probably Fenton, 2" sq $10.00
Cobalt stretch glass, Depression type, three rests, four snufferettes, 4⅞" d, 1927 . . . . $28.00
Footed ashtray, jade, 1½" h, 1934–1936 . . . . $25.00

FOSTORIA

The first factory opened in Fostoria, Ohio, in 1887, and continued until 1891. They later moved to Moundsville, West Virginia, and continued a long line of production until they sold in 1983. Although they started in pressed tablewares and lamps, they expanded to complete lines of dinnerware in crystal and colors. In the late 1930s, Fostoria was the largest manufacturer of handmade dinnerware in the world. They closed in 1986, unable to meet foreign competition.

Fostoria is perhaps best known for their popular American pattern in their elegant Depression line. This was introduced in 1915, and was made continuously until they closed. When looking at Fostoria pieces, remember that they were handmade, and the edges should be smooth. Fostoria's Spool pattern has no circle in the center, see Plate 46. Be careful, Fostoria imitations do have a circle in the center. More Fostoria ashtrays are in the 1940s, 1950s, and 1960s section.

PLATE 46 (left to right)
Row 1:
Mayfair, frosted, 3⅞" sq . . . . $ 9.00
Sun ray, one rest each end, 4" l, 1935–1944 . . . . $ 8.00
Trojan, topaz yellow, small, 3⅞" d, 1929–1944 . . . . $27.00
Mayfair, ruby, 3⅞" sq $15.00
American, oval with matchbox holder, 5" l, 1915–1986 . . . . $28.00
Fairfax, rose, 4" d, 1927–1944 . . . . $18.00
Mayfair, topaz yellow, 3⅞" sq . . . . $ 8.00

Row 2:
Round/matchbox holder, probably Fostoria, 4½" d, maybe 1920s because holder will take only a box $15.00
American, two rests at opposite corners, 2⅞" sq, 1915–1986 . . . . $ 8.00
Milk glass, 3½" sq, #2675 . . . . $11.00
American, oval, 3¾" l, 1915–1986 . . . . $ 9.00
Spool, set of 3 (3" topaz, 4"crystal, 5⅜" blue), 1938–1944 . . . . $21.00
Versailles, blue, etching around rim only, one rest, 4" d, 1928–1944 . . . . $30.00
Mayfair, crystal, rose embossed in center, 3⅞" sq $11.00
Colony, set of 3 (3" sq, 3¾" sq, 4¾" sq), 1920s–1970s $35.00

PLATE 45

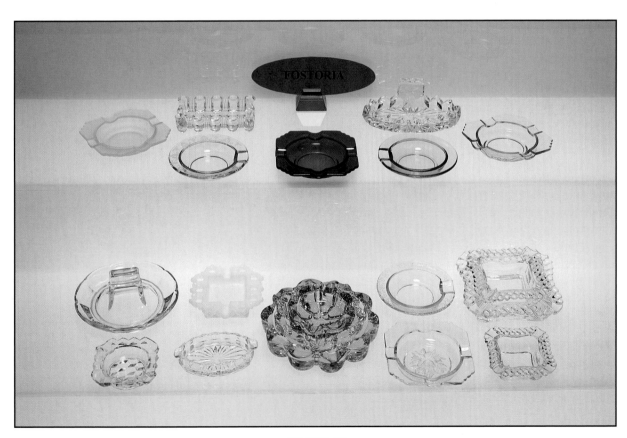

PLATE 46

HEISEY

Heisey and Company was founded in Newark, Ohio, in 1895. They continued producing fine, handcrafted dinnerware with graceful lines until they closed in 1957. Heisey also used romantic names for their colors, such as Sahara yellow, Flamingo pink, Moongleam green, Limelight green, and Dawn. Some of these colors varied in intensity, however. In the Empress pattern, the ashtrays were in colors. Only later were they made in crystal. Heisey called the crystal in Empress pattern Queen Ann.

The Heisey trademark is an "H" inside a diamond. It was not used on very early wares, but after 1902, all pieces were marked, usually with their logo. If they could not mark it because of the pattern, a paper label was used. Note the small rectangular ashtray in Plate 48. It does not have a mark but does have a label.

When they closed, Heisey sold some of their molds to Imperial, who used these molds with the Heisey trademark. However, Imperial removed the Heisey trademark in 1968. If you see the Heisey trademark, be sure that it really was made by Heisey.

Collectors consider Heisey glass to be a sound investment. I believe that as more Heisey ashtrays come on the market, and more collectors buy them, their prices will continue to increase.

Since Heisey continued in production until 1957, they made glasswares during the 1940s, 1950s, and 1960s period. They also made many of their patterns for long periods of time.

PLATE 47 (left to right)
Row 1:
Set of two, Victorian pattern, cigarette holder & ashtray with two rests, 5" l, 1933–1953 . . . . $75.00
Provincial, 3" sq $13.00
Crystolite, 3¼" sq, late 1930s–late 1950s $10.00
Crystolite, ashtray-coaster, 3" d, late 1930s–late 1950s $10.00
Orchid, etching in bottom only, 3" sq, 1940–1957 . . . . $28.00
Ridgeleigh, 2⅝" sq . . . . $ 6.00
Coalport, 2 rests, 2⅝" d, 1937–1946 . . . . $10.00
Ridgeleigh, 4¼" d $20.00

Row 2:
Crystal round, heavy, pattern not identified, 3½" d $15.00
Diamond, club, spade, heart, bridge set, all Ridgeleigh pattern, 3¼" w, set price $40.00
Lariat, 4" d $15.00

PLATE 48 (left to right)
Row 1:
Duck, Verly's mold, possibly made by Heisey, but not verified, 6½" l . . . . $ 80.00
Empress, Moongleam green, elongated diamond, 7" l, prior to 1938 . . . . $200.00
Match holder at back, heavy, 5½" w, probably in 1930s or earlier . . . . $ 38.00
Queen Ann, elongated diamond, 7" l, 1938 . . . . $ 30.00
Ashtray with metal holder, ashtray etched, cigarette or match holder at back, metal duck in front, 5" l . . $ 45.00

Row 2:
Amber small cup type, probably Heisey, 3⅜" w . . . . $ 16.00
Waverly, small beading, 3" l . . . . $ 21.00
Lodestar, color called Dawn, bottom is a star, 5¼" d . . . . $ 80.00
Military hat, one rest at top in front, 4" l . . . . $ 30.00
Small tray, called ashtray in Heisey book, decor in blue and gold, 4⅜" d . . . . $ 25.00

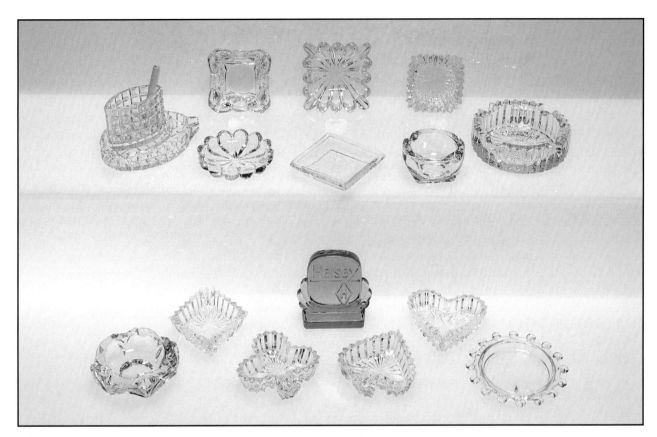

PLATE 47

PLATE 48

IMPERIAL

The Imperial Glass Company was founded in Bellaire, Ohio, in 1901. Early in this century, they began making pressed carnival glass. They also made some art glass during the first part of this century. In 1914, their Nu Cut line was introduced to imitate cut glass. It became very popular and was soon introduced in color.

From 1916 to 1920, they used a luster process and made a line called Imperial Jewels, now referred to as stretch glass. During the 1930s, they started to produce milk glass and by 1950, were one of the leading milk glass manufacturers. Today their art, carnival, and stretch glass is all highly collectible.

In 1936, Imperial started to make the Candlewick pattern, one of the most popular and easily recognized glass patterns of all times. Most pieces are crystal, but there are enough colors to make nice groupings. All light blue, ruby red, and cobalt colors were made before the 1940s; the others were added after 1940. Some of the Candlewick has etched patterns. See some examples in Plate 50.

The Candlewick pattern does not have a coaster ashtray, as far as I know. There is one that looks as though it could be one, but it really is a coaster with spoon rest. There is a small depression in the extended spoon rest for the handle of the spoon. See Plate 49.

In Plate 50, there are two ashtrays that many people claim are Candlewick. They are in Row 2, second and fifth from the left. Despite all my research, I have not found any verification of this.

PLATE 49 (left to right)   **All ashtrays are Candlewick by Imperial.**
   Row 1:
   Square, 3¼" and 4½", each. $34.00
   Heart, crystal, 4½", prior to 1940. . . . . $10.00
   Round, sometimes referred to as "individual," 2¾" d . . . . $ 9.00
   Rectangle, 4⅜" l . . . . $ 6.00
   Round with extended rests, two long rests, also match pack holder, 4¼" d $25.00

   Row 2:
   Round with extended rests, two long rests, 4¼" d $14.00
   Crystal set, 4" d, 5" d, 6" d. $25.00
   Coaster/spoon rest, *not* an ashtray, despite sometimes being marked as such, 3¾" d $13.00

PLATE 50 (left to right)   **All ashtrays are Candlewick by Imperial.**
   Row 1:
   Round with etching, flower in center, 6", prior to 1940 . . . . $ 22.00
   Eagle ashtray, some frosting, 6½" l . . . . $ 60.00
   Eagle ashtray, 6½" l . . . . $ 60.00
   Rare pink, with eagle and stars, old, 6" d $100.00

   Row 2:
   Large pink, 6" d. . . . . $ 12.00
   Round, probably not Candlewick, with row of small rounds in bottom, three rests, 3¾" d . . . . $ 8.00
   Small Viennese blue, 4" d. . . . . $ 8.00
   Round, large, match pack holder, and two rests in center, 6" d. $150.00
   Round, probably not Candlewick, with row of small rounds on top and on bottom, 3½" d . . . . $ 9.00
   Round with etching, Viennese blue, etching in center, 4" d, prior to 1940 . . . . $ 16.00
   Medium yellow, 5" d . . . . $ 10.00

PLATE 49

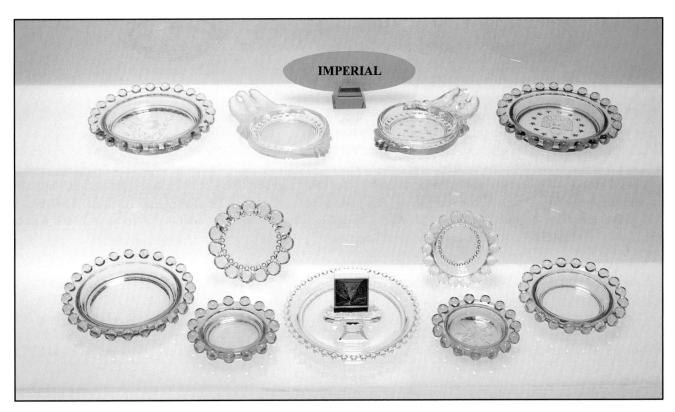

PLATE 50

IMPERIAL

In 1958, Imperial Glass acquired some of the Heisey molds, and in 1960, Imperial also acquired the molds from Cambridge. Note the Amberglo long oval in Plate 51. It was made from one of the Cambridge's molds and even has Cambridge's color name.

After 1951, they used an "I" over a "G" for their Imperial Glass trademark. In 1973, Imperial Glass was acquired by Lenox and an "l" was added to the Imperial trademark. After several more times of changing hands, it went bankrupt in 1982, selling assets and, yes, molds to other companies.

The Candlewick pattern was also made by Boyd after they acquired some molds from Imperial. The Candlewick ashtrays are clearly marked, and no confusion should occur. See Boyd's vaseline Candlewick cigarette box under the black light in Plate 68B. Even though of recent manufacture, it is lovely, and the price will probably increase.

PLATE 51 (left to right) **All ashtrays are Imperial unless noted.**
  Row 1:
  Boyd Candlewick heart, vaseline, marked, 4½" w $12.00
  Special molds, Imperial Glass, Bellaire, Ohio, in bottom, 2¼" h $15.00
  Purple slag, 4¾" sq $20.00
  Boyd slag Candlewick, marked, 2¾" d . . . . $ 5.00
  Special molds, similar to above but smaller, 1½" h. $12.00
  Boyd Candlewick eagle, vaseline, marked, 6½" l $18.00

  Row 2:
  Brown Candlewick, by Imperial, later color, 5" d . . . . $ 8.00
  Cape Cod, comes in colors also, 4" l, 1932–1984 . . . . $15.00
  Boyd Candlewick cigarette box, vaseline, 5⅜" l. $22.00
  Amberglo oval, 7" l, after 1960 . . . . $13.00
  Oval, 4" l, after 1958 . . . . $ 9.00
  Boyd Candlewick heart, cobalt blue, marked, 4½" w. $15.00
  Square with scene, appears to be the God of Thunder, 3½" sq . . . . $ 8.00

TIFFIN

The Tiffin Glass Company, part of the United States Glass Company, was founded in Tiffin, Ohio, in 1887. In 1959, U.S. Glass was sold, but the Tiffin plant was reopened in 1963 as the Tiffin Art Glass Company. Work continued, but Tiffin was sold again in 1966 to Continental Can and again in 1969 to Interpace. Tiffin finally closed in 1980. Their ashtrays were made from Depression years through 1940s, 1950s, and 1960s.

Tiffin made many lovely handmade lines of tablewares and decorative items over the years, but they are perhaps best known for their black, satin glass, produced in the twenties. Tiffin's cloverleaf is similar to Duncan and Miller's, but the bottom is almost flat while Duncan's has a definite depression. Neither is marked. Tiffin items sometimes have paper labels, or it may be missing.

PLATE 52 (left to right)
  Row 1:
  Cobalt cloverleaf, 4¾" l $28.00
  Twilight blue cloverleaf, 4¾" l $40.00
  Amber rectangle, 3⅝" l $14.00
  Amethyst cloverleaf, 4¾" l $24.00

  Row 2:
  Nest of two, oval, 4" l $16.00
  Vaseline color, oval, 7" l. $30.00
  Cascade, two extended rests, 1935, 5" l $15.00

PLATE 51

PLATE 52

GLASS ASHTRAYS FROM THE 1940s, 1950s, and 1960s

The Depression glass and elegant Depression glass manufacturers continued to design and produce long after the 1930s. The time frame following the Depression era is commonly called the 1940s, 1950s, and 1960s. The glass ashtrays in this time span have changed somewhat from earlier years. The glass itself is better and the edges are usually more rounded, even if they are machine made. The designs were usually bigger, as were many items in the 1950s.

1940s, 1950s, and 1960s ANCHOR HOCKING

Royal Ruby and Forest Green were two color names which Anchor Hocking patented for their use. The name had nothing to do with the pattern. In fact, it was used for many items that they made in red or green. Some of this color glass was made during the Depression, but most falls into this category. If you buy ashtrays of these colors, look for the Anchor Hocking trademark on the back. The market is flooded with look-alikes in all colors.

PLATE 53 (left to right)

Row 1:

Forest Green, hexagonal, 5¾" w. . . . . $ 8.00
Anchor Hocking ad, *75 years,* shows different trademarks, 5½" d, 1980 . . . . $15.00
Amber, large square, marked, 5¾" . . . . $ 5.00
Amber, mid square, marked, 4⅝" . . . . $ 4.00
Crystal, mid square, marked 4⅝" . . . . $ 4.00
Forest Green, mid square, marked, 4⅝" . . . . $ 5.00

Row 2:

Royal Ruby, mid square, marked, 4⅝" . . . . $ 6.00
Forest Green, small square, marked, 3⅜" . . . . $ 4.00
Fire-King Oven Ware, turquoise blue, not marked, 4¾" sq, 1957–1958 . . . . $ 9.00
Fire-King Dinnerware, peach luster, coaster-ashtray, not marked, 3¼" d, 1952–1963 . . . . $ 4.00
Forest Green, large square, marked, 5¾" . . . . $ 7.00
Royal Ruby, small square, marked, 3⅜" . . . . $ 5.00
Fire-King dinnerware, Jade-ite Restaurant Ware, not marked, 4¼", 1950–1953 . . . . $ 8.00
Royal Ruby, leaf, marked, 4½" l, 1940–1960 . . . . $ 4.00
Crystal, small square, marked, 3⅜" . . . . $ 3.00

1940s, 1950s, and 1960s FENTON

Do not ignore Fenton ashtrays with their name on the bottom. Even though Fenton has only been marking this way since 1970, they are still considered collectible. Paper labels were used from 1920 until 1970, but they were missing usually, and it was difficult to know the glassware's manufacturer. At least this way, we know that the newer ashtrays we find are Fenton's.

PLATE 54 (left to right)

Row 1:

Slashed ball shape, ruby, hobnails, 4" h, 1970+ $20.00
Amber with hobnails, four rows of hobnails, 3½" d, prior to 1970 . . . . $18.00
Moondrops, cigarette box & lid, 4⅞" l $36.00
Slashed ball shape, milk glass, 4" h $25.00

Row 2:

Amberina round, five rests across center, 6⅜" d, prior 1970 . . . . $13.00
Fan, opalescent topaz, hobnail, 5½" l, 1940–1948 . . . . $37.00
Bridge set, milk glass, diamond, spade, heart, club, 3¼" d, set price . . . . $30.00·
Amber with hobnails, four rows of hobnails, 6¼" d, prior 1970 . . . . $11.00

PLATE 53

PLATE 54

1940s, 1950s, and 1960s FENTON

Fenton's designs and workmanship have always been top quality. They made many ashtrays during this time period as well as during the Depression era. Note the ribbed, blue opalescent square in Plate 55. This is very similar to Beatty Rib, which is rare. This costs much less, and is just as attractive.

PLATE 55 (left to right)

Row 1:

Cobalt blue, four rows of hobnails, mark on bottom, 6¼" d, 1970 +.................................. $13.00

Milk Glass large octagon, three rows hobs on rise, more on bottom, 6½" w.......................... $10.00

Blue round, opalescent, four rests in center, mark on bottom, 6⅜" d, 1970 +........................ $14.00

Row 2:

Milk glass octagon, three rows of hobs on rise, more on bottom, 4" d................................ $ 9.00

Milk glass rectangle, three rows on rise, bottom plain, 4¼" l, 1950s................................ $ 8.00

Square opalescent, blue, like rare Beatty Rib, 4¼" sq, 1951...................................... $45.00

Fan, opalescent blue, hobnail, 5½" l, 1940–1954 .... $33.00

Oval, lt blue, pressed pattern on rim not identified, marked on bottom, 6" l, after 1970 .... $12.00

White round, four rows of hobnails, rim provides rests, marked on bottom, 3¾" d, after 1970 .... $ 9.00

1940s, 1950s, and 1960s FOSTORIA

Fostoria eventually became the largest manufacturer of handmade dinnerware in the world, carrying their excellent techniques into the 1940s, 1950s, and 1960s. One of their most popular patterns was the Coin pattern, which is considered a hot collectible today. There are many coin reproductions on the market, so if you are considering a purchase, be sure that the coins in the ashtrays are frosted. Note the blue, one coin ashtray in Plate 56: the coin is not frosted. Although it was well made, it is probably a reproduction.

Fostoria's biggest problem occurred in the 1980s, when 40 to 60 percent of all handmade wares purchased by Americans were inexpensive imports. This was up from 20 percent in 1960. Unfortunately, Fostoria was not able to compete. They closed in 1986.

PLATE 56 (left to right)

Row 1:

Four coin, emerald green, 7¾" d $45.00

Myriad, one rest each end, 2⅞" l, 1941–1945.. $12.00

Century, long cigarette supports on both sides of ashtray, 2¾" sq $11.00

Coin cigarette cup, amber, 3⅜" h... $25.00

Small round, light blue, 2¼" d... $12.00

Place card holder, ashtray with two rests, blue, 2½" h, after 1949 .... $11.00

Four coin, olive green, 7¾" d $30.00

Row 2:

Four coin, red, 7¾" d $20.00

Two coin, amber, 3¾" l $15.00

One coin, blue, probably a reproduction, coin not frosted, 5" d .... $ 8.00

Myriad, one rest each corner, 3¾" l, 1941–1945 .... $13.00

Large center coin, can be used for pipes also, 7⅞" d $28.00

PLATE 55

PLATE 56

1940s, 1950s, and 1960s
HAZEL WARE, JEANNETTE & VIKING

Hazel Ware was formerly Hazel Atlas during the Depression years. See Plate 57 for their Capri blue and Moroccan Amethyst ashtrays. Both of these names probably referred to color more than pattern. They made many patterns in the 1940s, 1950s, 1960s time frame. Viking was also very active during this era. They acquired many of their molds from other companies, and it is sometimes hard to tell who made what.

PLATE 57 (left to right)

Row 1:

Viking, amber, large slashed ball, round bottom, 4" w... $13.00
Viking, blue, slashed ball shape, 3⅜" w .... $ 9.00
Moroccan Amethyst, by Hazel Ware, Executive Set/box, 2 ashtrays, silver rimmed, 3¾" d, 1960s........ $17.00
Floragold, Louisa by Jeannette, coaster-ashtray, iridescent amber, 4" sq, 1950s...................... $ 8.00
Viking, amber, slashed ball shape, 3⅜" w... $ 9.00
Viking, gray, slashed ball shape, 3⅜" w .... $ 9.00
Viking, amber, large slashed ball, triangle bottom, 4" w $15.00

Row 2:

Moroccan Amethyst, by Hazel Ware, rests at points, 6⅞", 1960s $10.00
Viking Convention, A.F.G.W.U.–1953, six rests, 5⅛" d $14.00
Moroccan Amethyst, probably Hazel Ware, rests in mid-side, 5⅝" side, 1960s......................... $ 8.00
Capri, by Hazel Ware, azure blue, two rests, 3¼" d, 1960s .... $ 6.00
Harp, by Jeannette, coaster-ashtray, 4¾" l, 1954–1957... $ 6.00
Capri, by Hazel Ware, azure blue, 6⅞", 1960s $12.00

1940S, 1950S, AND 1960S WESTMORELAND

Westmoreland made English Hobnail, another well-known pattern, from the 1920s to the 1940s. Most of the colors belong to the Depression era, but amber and crystal belong here. When I bought the ashtray in Plate 58, I was amazed how more rounded the hobs felt than those in many other hobnail patterns.

Panel Grape in milk glass was one of Westmoreland's more popular patterns. See Plate 58 and notice that one has decorated rims and one has plain rims. Of course, the decorated one costs more, about half again as much.

PLATE 58 (left to right)

Row 1:

Old Quilt, 4" sq $10.00
Slashed ball shape, 3¼" w, carnival-type colors $24.00
Pedestal, not soap dish, four rests at corners, called "mist," 3⅞" h, 1954–1984.................... $ 8.00
Blue square, called Brandywine Blue, about 3¼" sq $14.00
Panel Grape, milk glass, 4" sq, 1950–1970s $15.00

Row 2:

Panel Grape, iridescent, 4" sq $25.00
Panel Grape, flower decorated, 4" sq, 1950–1970s... $25.00
Old Quilt, 6½" sq $14.00
Round milk glass, hobnails on rise & bottom, 3 rests, nice, 4½" d $12.00
English hobnail, amber, two cigar rests, two cigarette rests, 4½" sq $25.00

PLATE 57

PLATE 58

UNIDENTIFIED ASHTRAYS FROM THE 1940S, 1950S, and 1960S

As I mentioned before, glasswares from this time span can often be detected just by looking at them. The glass was better quality, the manufacturing process was better, and the item was often bigger, as were most household items in the 1940s and 1950s. The ashtrays pictured in Plates 59 and 60 show a group that fits all these criteria. However, when you are really only guessing, you do make mistakes.

In Plate 60, there are two ashtrays that have large balls around their outer edge. Easy to find on the market, they come in several colors, and two sizes, with 12 balls or with 18 balls. I have tried and tried to identify them, but with no success. They definitely do not belong to the Imperial's Candlewick pattern, even though some of Candlewick's serving pieces do have large balls.

PLATE 59 (left to right)

Row 1:

Heavy square, club type, 4½" sides. $13.00

Milk & clear square, nice result, 4" sq $10.00

Goat, impressed in bottom, three rests, 4¼" d. $15.00

Unusual rests, basketweave-type pattern pressed on bottom, 4¾" d . . . . $ 8.00

Milk & clear cup-shape, three rests, 2¾" h $10.00

Row 2:

Club, card games popular in this time period, 5¼" l $15.00

Large round, pressed pattern on bottom, twelve rests, 6¼" d $14.00

Small square, pressed crackle-like pattern on bottom, 3" sq . . . . $ 7.00

Triangle, like Capri, but not, blue, 5½" sides . . . . $ 6.00

PLATE 60 (left to right)

Row 1:

Amberina, unusual shape, three rests, 2⅝" h $11.00

Small green square, four small feet, 3½" sq . . . . $ 9.00

Cobalt, two rests in center, great design & color, Deco lines, 5" l $20.00

Large black, three rests at angles to rim, thick glass, 5¾" d. $12.00

Pale Pink, four extended rests, 4¼" w . . . . $ 9.00

Amber square, four rests on inside, 4" sq. . . . . $ 8.00

Green square, four small feet, have seen it in crystal, 4½" sq $11.00

Row 2:

Green round, pressed pattern on bottom, four rests extended inward, 5½" d $10.00

Ruby with rose, flowers in center and under rise, ripple rim, 4½" d $18.00

Cranberry balls, iridescent, twelve balls, 5⅛" d $14.00

Amethyst round, bottom telescopes inward, 4½" d. $10.00

Yellow balls, pale yellow, twelve balls, 5⅛" d . . . . $ 8.00

Deep green, small, two rests, 3⅛" d . . . . $ 9.00

Azure blue, pressed pattern on bottom, 4 rests, 6⅛" d $10.00

PLATE 59

PLATE 60

ART GLASS ASHTRAYS

In this category I have put many different kinds of glass ashtrays, most of them made in this century. They are decorative, artistic, expensive, and limited in production. The different kinds of ashtrays pictured here include aventurine, black Bohemian, cut, hand blown, intaglio, opalescent, overlay, satin, vaseline, and Venetian. There are many other kinds, but I do not have ashtrays representing them.

In Plate 61, there are two cut ashtrays that are very nice. Their cut is deep, and they have elaborate geometric designs. One is probably American cut and from the brilliant cut glass period, from 1880 to 1905.

There are also two ashtrays in Plate 61 that are very lovely in their basic shape lines. One is by Lalique and the other by Steuben.

The paperweight-type ashtrays are particularly interesting. The multicolored one is marked "St C" standing for St. Clair, the manufacturer. Since others imitate him, make sure the ashtray is marked, if you are paying for St. Clair.

A picture of all red and cobalt glass is always very striking. But the ashtrays in Plate 62, can all stand on their own merits. The cigarette cup and ashtray set is an example of ribbon work, originating on the island of Murano, in Venice, Italy. But the quality in this set suggests that it came from a lower grade of manufacturer.

Unfortunately, the silver in the center has come off the red ashtray with the Venetian scene, although you can see the canal scene when you look closely. However, the cobalt and silver ashtray with the Venetian canal scene is in much better condition.

The very dark red ashtray is a color I have not very often seen in cut overlay. The name given to this color is "port."

PLATE 61 (left to right)   **All handmade.**

Row 1:
Cut glass, Austrian, center appearance like jewel, 5¼" d .... $ 90.00
Lalique, lion face, some frosting, signed, 5¾" d, after 1945 .... $255.00
Val St. Lambert, one of pair, three rests each, signed, Belgium, 3¾" sides, price for pair .... $ 15.00
Steuben, signed, 5½" l .... $ 75.00
Cut glass, probably from American brilliant period, 5" d, around turn of century $110.00

Row 2:
St. Clair, five multicolored flowers, marked, 4" d $65.00
Lalique, fish in center, signed, 3¾" h $95.00
St. Clair, three yellow flowers, marked, 3" d $50.00
Val St. Lambert, one of pair, three rests each, signed, Belgium, 3¾" sides, price for pair, see above
Oval paperweight type, five blue flowers, ground bottom, 6" l $38.00

PLATE 62 (left to right) **All handmade.**

Row 1:
Red over white, white lining, also comes in blue & white, yellow & white, 4½" d $13.00
Venetian set, cigarette holder and ashtray, a typical Venetian design, ashtray is 4⅝" d. $45.00
Rare cloisonné dish, made with glass and brass, lavender glass, blue flowers, 3" d. $90.00
Czechoslovakia, cobalt with lots of gold, enameled flowers, 3¼" d. $80.00
Ruby bowl, three rests, enameled flowers, 4" d $16.00
Cobalt & crystal cut, 4½" d $20.00

Row 2:
Murano, Italy, artist signed, shades of blue, heavy, 4¼" d $150.00
Venetian, sterling rim, gondola scene, cobalt, old glass, 3¾" l .... $ 55.00
Dark red cut to crystal, unusual color called "port," nice pattern, probably Czechoslovakia, 4½" d ...... $ 80.00
Cobalt, heavy, 6⅞" d .... $ 22.00
Venetian, ruby with sterling design, center silver worn off, hexagon, 5" w .... $ 35.00
Small cobalt cut to crystal, deep cut, lovely pattern, two wide rests, probably quite old, 3⅛" d .... $ 55.00
Red cut to crystal, 3½" d .... $ 40.00

PLATE 61

PLATE 62

ART GLASS ASHTRAYS

In Plate 63, there are four examples of cut glass. I have grouped these together because they show a different type of cutting than that found in American brilliant period. They have a more shallow cut and are definitely not as sharply cut. However, they are fine examples of their own style.

There is a small crystal ashtray in Plate 63 that is signed Daum France. Although it does not say Daum Nancy, France, it was made in one of the Daum factories, perhaps not located in Nancy. It is heavy for its size, and nicely made.

The multicolored swirled glass, shaped something like a cup, is the only Japanese glass ashtray in my collection. See Plate 64.

The green cased glass ashtray with white decor and colored flowers on the outside, and then a layer of clear glass, is Turkish. It is always fun to find something different. I will have to read about Turkish glass to find out more about it. This piece is certainly colorful.

Art glass is very difficult to price. I have been collecting prices from many areas in the United States for over four years. However, because of the limited production, there are many ashtrays that I have not seen more than once or twice. I have talked to other dealers and studied about this type of art glass before deciding on the prices listed here. Even with these precautions, I may not have established a fair price. As more ashtray books come on the market, there will be more knowledge to help price in this art glass category.

PLATE 63 (left to right)   **All hand made.**
Row 1:
Waterford, heavy, signed, ashtray raised up on pillow-like glass, 4¾" d $60.00
Horse's head, nice work, 4" h $30.00
Cut-slashed ball type, one rest, flower pattern, W. Germany, 4" w, 1945–1990 . . . . $22.00
Engraved square, pineapples and flying birds with twigs in mouth, 3½" sq $15.00
Cut, interesting pattern, part of which is frosted, W. Germany, 5½" d, 1945–1990 . . . . $38.00

Row 2:
Cut crystal, heavy, nice pattern, four rests, 5½" d $18.00
Daum, France, signed this way, heavy, two rests, somewhat square, 2¼" sides $15.00
Intaglio, cupids, octagon, two rests, 3" l, 1920s $25.00
Paperweight type, five sides, white flower at bottom, 3" h $23.00
Cut rectangle, geometric patterns, large rests, 4" x 2¾" $12.00
Name card holder & ashtray, ashtray intaglio, 3¾" l, holder is 4" h, 1920s $50.00
Waterford, heavy, signed, 5" d $45.00

PLATE 64 (left to right)   **All hand made.**
Row 1:
Bubble body, popular style in 1940s & 1950s, 5¼" sides $25.00
Bohemian, two layers glass, white cut to amber, gold decor, 4" d, around turn of century $60.00
Turkish glass, heavy, green, triangular, 4½" sides $22.00
Small green triangle, three rests, 3½" sides . . . . $ 9.00
Green satin glass, Greek key pattern on top of glass bowl, brass insert of rests & dump, etched on rim,
   three feet, 3¾" h, old $30.00
Gold bowl, three rests, enameled flowers, heavy, hand blown, 5" d $15.00

Row 2:
Gold & white bowl on pedestal, heavy, hand blown, 3" h . . . . $ 17.00
Pewter fret work, green glass set into ornate pewter pattern of birds & flowers, 4" d, old . . . . $ 20.00
Steuben Hawks, gold decor over yellow glass, brass rest center, 3⅜" d . . . . $ 80.00
Murano, multicolor swirled, heavy, black bottom, 7¼" w $100.00
Intaglio, amber octagon, cupid fishing, 3" l . . . . $ 25.00
Swirl glass, Lenwile Glass of Ardalt, Japan, heavy with three rests, 4" l . . . . $ 22.00
Sterling overlay, slashed ball shape, sterling pattern of flowers & leaves, possibly Tiffin, 4" w . . . . $ 75.00

PLATE 63

PLATE 64

ART GLASS ASHTRAYS

It is very easy to make mistakes when identifying art glass. I was sold the glass and brass rim with raised decor as Phoenix glass. See Plate 65. When I studied Phoenix glass, I found I had made a mistake. The birds in the ashtray are not similar to any Phoenix design, and the quality of the glass is not as good.

In Plate 65, the satin glass dish with Cupid feet is probably not very old. It could be considered Victorian-like in style. However, the cut glass oval with the brass rim and lovely pattern in relief is probably quite old and might very well be from Victorian times. The cutting is deep and sharp.

The glass box with two ashtrays is probably from the 1940s or 1950s. It is banded in chrome with a chrome handle. During this time span, chrome was very popular. This really is not art glass and not handmade.

Some of the ashtrays in Plate 66 are very old, possibly from Victorian times or the turn of the century. The blue one with the gold color rim with raised decor is thought to be from the turn of the century. It is French and the glass is opaline. While the blue rectangle with the brass edge is lovely, it is not as old.

In Plate 66, the black ashtray on a brass stand is from Czechoslovakia during the 1920s. The leaves across the top which make a rest is a style similar to one often used by Royal Bayreuth in their china ashtrays. The small blue round is also imported, this time from China. This opaline ashtray has a simple pattern pressed into it. The brass is also etched. "China" is scratched on the bottom, and the ashtray is very old.

The large, smoky gray ashtray with the bubbles was made by Erickson. See Plate 66. This is typical of his work, and if you look carefully, you will see that the bubbles all line up and graduate in size. He does excellent work, well worth the price you have to pay for one of his ashtrays.

Frances and Michael Higgins are also designers of special glassware, and their work often resembles several layers of glass slumped together. The ashtray shown here is typical of their style.

The black ashtrays, also in Plate 66, are good examples of Italian art glass with metallic and color swirls. Copper metallic was often used with opaque black glass for a striking effect.

PLATE 65 (left to right)

Row 1:

Cut crystal oval, rim & rests with pattern in relief, 6" l, perhaps turn of century . . . . $ 48.00
Wave Crest, called ash receiver, 4¼" w $125.00
Satin glass, brass rim & Cupid legs, 5¼" d . . . . $ 35.00
White opaline set, lighter, cigarette holder, & ashtray, etched metal rims, ashtray is 3⅜" d . . . . $ 28.00
Duck, marked, "France" on bottom, one rest, 7" l . . . . $ 25.00

Row 2:

Phoenix-like glass, pressed mold, brass rim is nice, 4" d, probably quite old . . . . $ 27.00
Cigarette box & two ashtrays, chrome band around items, hobs on bottoms of ashtrays, 3⅛" sq . . . . $ 14.00
Ashtray with Rose, part of set, 3½" l, see price below
Cigarette cup & ashtray, pressed pattern, part of set, ashtray above, 4" h, from 1940s–1950s . . . . $ 25.00
Ornate stand, ashtray made for stand, brass colored metal, stand is 3¾" d, not very old . . . . $ 10.00

PLATE 66 (left to right)

Row 1:

French opaline, no mark, 5" d, very old $70.00
Italian black square, copper metallic & blue, two rests, 4½" l $25.00
Multicolor, pale green with gold, blue & white, texture blown in, 5¾" d $10.00
Blue rectangle, very heavy, brass trim claw feet, 5¼" l $28.00
Erickson, smoky gray glass with bubbles, 7" l, between 1943 and 1961 . . . . $48.00

Row 2:

Black tall dish, three claw feet, beaded work on rim, 4" d $20.00
Black with match holder, black glass with brass rim & match holder, 3" d $18.00
Higgins, name signed on front rim, one rest, 5¼" sq, after 1964 . . . . $35.00
Blue round, blue opaline, etched rim, nice work, China, 3¼" d, very old $25.00
Italian black cup, paper label for Venetian Weil - Murano, marked Italy, 3½" l $38.00
Black glass in stand, brass legs, rim & rest across top, some moriage, 2½" h $45.00

PLATE 65

PLATE 66

ART GLASS ASHTRAYS – ITALIAN CLOWNS

One of the major glassworking centers in the world is situated on the Island of Murano, in Venice, Italy. Excellent glassware has been made there since the thirteenth century. During this century, Murano has become known for their contemporary designs. See Plate 62 and 66 for other Italian glass ashtrays.

The clowns, shown in Plate 67, may have originally been made on the Island of Murano. These have probably not been made in one of the better houses because they are not signed, but the craftmanship is excellent. They are fun to look at and fun to collect. There are some imitation ones on the market for $10.00 to $15.00, but if you know what to look for, you won't be fooled. First, study their hair. It is very similar in all the ones below. If they have hands, they are very much alike. Their faces vary, but not the workmanship. Also, most new clowns are hollow inside, while these are solid.

PLATE 67 (left to right)
>   **Row 1:**
>   **Sitting with pointed hat,** white gloves, they are the rests, 5¾" h $115.00
>   **Sitting with top hat,** no hands, two rests, 5" h . . . . $ 95.00
>
>   **Row 2:**
>   **Sitting or standing with flat hat,** great color work, two rests, standing 8" h $135.00
>   **Large sitting,** two rests, sturdy base, white gloves, 6½" h $120.00
>   **Sitting or standing with pointed hat,** two rests, 6½" h. . . . . $ 95.00

ART GLASS ASHTRAYS – VASELINE

Vaseline glass is yellow-greenish in color and tends to glow in good light. Although the color resembles the product Vaseline, hence the name, the actual shade may vary from piece to piece. Some will be more yellow, others more green. Under an ultraviolet light vaseline glass will fluoresce, and is very exciting to see. In Plate 68B, I have shown how vaseline glass looks under in ultra violet light.

The color is obtained by adding uranium oxide to the molten glass. It was very popular in Victorian times, usually produced as pressed glass, but then it lost its popularity. Some factories are still making vaseline glass in limited quantities.

PLATE 68A (left to right)   **All are vaseline glass.**
>   **Row 1:**
>   **Vaseline pitcher,** good for cigarette holder, birds on sides, nice, 3½" h $22.00
>   **Cigarette box,** by Boyd, Candlewick pattern, 5½" l $25.00
>   **Hat,** two rests, 1⅝" h $12.00
>   **Cigarette holder and ashtray,** 3" h $30.00
>
>   **Row 2:**
>   **Round with match holder,** three rests plus one in matchbox holder, 4" d, 1920 . . . . $25.00
>   **Large round,** four rests, 9" d $40.00
>   **Leaf,** pressed pattern, one rest, 5¼" l $10.00

PLATE 68B (left to right)
>   Same order as Plate 68A, but shown under black light.

PLATE 67

PLATE 68A (above), PLATE 68B (below)

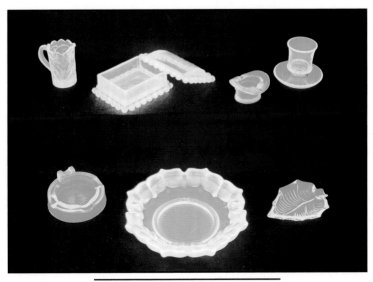

ART GLASS ASHTRAYS – FISH AND ANIMALS

While the artistic merits of the ashtrays in Plate 69 may not be very high, these animals are fun to collect. They are fairly easy to find on the market. Most are in bold, primary colors. These ashtrays are only a sampling of what I have seen. I have not seen any signed.

PLATE 69 (left to right)
    Row 1:
    Squirrel, 6" h $20.00
    Fish, 8½" h $40.00
    Cat, 6¾" h $25.00

    Row 2:
    Bird cigarette prop, no ashtray. $15.00
    Sailfish, 6¾" h. $40.00
    Elephant, 6" h $30.00

WOULD YOU BELIEVE – PEDESTAL ASHTRAYS?

These pedestal ashtrays fascinate me because I am not used to reaching up to put out a cigarette. And yet they are table models. Also, they are so unusual; truly unique. Some of them are quite old, while others are from the 1940s and 1950s. Notice the similarity of the blue glass ashtray on the pedestal to the Blue Capri triangle by Hazel Atlas in the Depression glass section. The green Fostoria ashtray is comparatively new, from the 1970s on. It has the original label.

The cut crystal one is probably old. The ashtray is deeply and nicely cut, and the tall stork holding an ashtray is quite unique. It also comes in a floor model.

PLATE 70 (left to right)
    Row 1:
    Large, smoky glass ashtray with crystal prisms, four rests, gold-tone pot metal base, 7" h $40.00
    Cut crystal ashtray, three rests, pedestal of gold leaf on flowers & leaves, 4⅛" h $17.00
    Stork, cast iron, glass insert into metal frame with two rests, Akro Agate base, 10¾" h. $50.00

    Row 2:
    Blue Capri, silver-tone pedestal, 3⅝" h $13.00
    Glass basket, two definite rests, 7¾" h. $25.00
    Fostoria pedestal, green, textured glass, 3½" h, paper label from 1957+. $30.00

PLATE 69

PLATE 70

METAL ASHTRAYS

I have divided this part into eight sections: brass, bronze and copper, chrome and aluminum, cloisonné, enameling, lead and pot metals, pewter, and sterling and silver plate. It is not always easy to tell what metal it is. I hope that my help has been correct. Let me know if there are errors, so they may be corrected. The following are some helpful terms for this section:

Cuprous metal: Copper and brass.

Embossed: Raised design made by hammering the metal from the under side so that the design is raised above the surface of the metal.

Enamel: Opaque composition applied to metal, pottery, or glass, usually for decoration.

Flashing: Applying a thin coating, usually brass or copper, over cheaper metal to make it look nicer.

Fret work: Cutting out patterns on surface of metal.

Ferrous metal: Iron, both cast and steel.

Hammered: Using a blunt object to knock a pattern into metal, particularly used on copper.

In relief: Term used to describe the surface when the decoration is raised above the surface.

Inscribed: To draw on metal with a tool that marks in the surface.

Patina: Surface changes brought about by exposure to air and age, usually darkening the metal.

Pot metal: A mixture of metals often used as a base to reduce cost.

Soldering metal: Used to join a seam.

Verdigris: A greenish blue pigment on the surface of brass, bronze, and copper over time

PLATE 71 (left to right)
Row 1:
Chrome fret work, chrome plate, machine cut out side, cobalt glass insert, Hong Kong, 4" d $25.00
Llama at side, sterling; cornucopia, tree, and llama embossed in center, llama on side, 3⅜" l,
    with golden tarnish that comes only in sterling patina, 1⅜" h, 1903 . . . . $42.00
Wood ball, chrome with ball which has two snufferettes, two rests, ball lifts up to drop any ashes
    into tray, Rookwood has a similar one in china, Art Deco style, 6" d $45.00
Leaf shape, blue enamel on metal, five rests on one side, 4⅛" l $10.00
Silver color ball on pedestal, etched designs, extended rest, 3" h $12.00

Row 2:
Brass flowers, flowers & leaves in relief around rim, some patina, darkening with age, 5¼" d,
    Art Nouveau style, early 1900s $75.00
Gold colored car ashtray, magnets on bottom so will attach to older car with metal dash, aluminum, 4" w . . $18.00
Copper square, incised markings around edge of rim, hammered decor, embossed leaves
    at one corner, 5" sides, almost square $20.00

PLATE 72 (left to right)
Row 1:
Dog on ashtray, good work, 2¾" h $25.00
Three swans, silver color metal, three rests, 3½" h. $24.00
Small blue, anodized aluminum, to clip on a plate, 2" w . . . . $ 5.00
1939 calendar, thin sheet metal, 4¼" w. $18.00

Row 2:
Round on three legs, top of round enamel, brown painted metal, 2⅞" h $15.00
Blue round, anodized aluminum top, painted alum. bottom, 1 rest, 3¼" d. . . . . $ 6.00
Copper man, German water carrier, Hummel on back, no relation to the Goebel Hummel, 2⅞" h. $20.00
Lavender round, anodized aluminum top, painted alum. bottom, 1 rest, 3¼" d . . . . $ 6.00
Buffalo, picture painted on thin gold color metal, 3⅜" sq . . . . $ 7.00

PLATE 71

PLATE 72

BRASS ASHTRAYS

Brass is an alloy of copper and zinc. It is easy to decorate by hand or machine or by engraving or relief work, as well as by making pierced patterns. American brass is expensive to produce. English brass is cheaper, and much of it is exported to the United States.

Brass will tarnish. Today the factories will sometimes lacquer the piece to prevent tarnishing. If this has been done, do not attempt to remove it. Wash only with water. However, many people prefer brass without this finish. New brass tends to turn red or gets a pink cast as it tarnishes; old brass will darken with age.

Older brass, from the 1800s, is heavier and thicker, and sometimes the soldering metal will show slightly in the seams. Beware of seeing a lot of identical items, as they are probably new.

Many of the brass ashtrays found today will show tavern drinking scenes. These are often from the early 1900s. But if the scenes are allegorical, the ashtrays might be from the late 1800s.

Note: Brass may be cleaned if it does not have a lacquer finish. Use only a good brass polish. Remember that usually the tarnish that comes with age is desirable. Be sure you know what you are doing before you polish.

PLATE 73 (left to right)   **All solid brass unless noted.**
Row 1:
Brussels boy, note swastika, 2¾" h $70.00
Cut out pattern rim, 1" rim, Forman Bros., 5⅞" d $10.00
Rabbit on dish, figure of long-eared rabbit, dish on pedestal, China, 3½" h, old $30.00
Candle, called bedside ashtray, six rests, 2⅝" h $15.00
Winged dog, holding tray in mouth for ashes, China, 3½" h, very old $32.00
Birds & animals on rim, shows some wear, 5½" d $14.00
Brussels boy, note cathedral where swastika was in first ashtray, 2¾" h $35.00

Row 2:
WWI soldier, brass finish, patented, glass insert, 6" l, 1916 .... $20.00
Octagon, raised center for pipe, inscribed decor, 5" w, on back "Don Shafer, Casablanca, 1943" $20.00
Zodiac dish, wide rim with embossed zodiac symbols, glass insert with snufferette, 7⅜" d, 1950s $18.00
Matchbox holder, tray with incised pattern, cut out pattern on match holder, China, 4" h, very old $30.00
Fold-down handle, embossed parrot designs, 4¼" d $14.00

PLATE 74 (left to right)   **All solid brass unless noted.**
Row 1:
Xochimilco, embossed picture of Mexican waterway, 6½" d, 1976 .... $14.00
Long horned goat, an old mark, made in Israel, 4⅜" l $12.00
Set, jar for cigars, nice inscribed work on tray, ashtray is 3⅜" d, probably the 1920s $30.00
Porcelain center, on three small legs, 7¼" d, old $16.00
Leaf shape, India, etched pattern of leaves, 3" l .... $ 8.00

Row 2:
Cigarette holder & ashtray, plastic holder, enamel black band, brass tray top, probably 1920s–1930s $14.00
Cut out pattern rim, bamboo & flower on rim, Taiwan, 4" d, recent $11.00
Globe cigarette holder & ashtray, brass finish, globe will also close, 6" d $55.00
Fighting scene, nice deep embossing, mark Germany, 4⅞" d, probably very old $20.00
Steer head, sitting on 3 feet, 5" l $25.00

Row 3:
Aladdin's lamp shape, animals & birds embossed on cup, not very good work, 2¾" h, old $13.00
Oriental, raised center for cigar, Oriental characters on rim embossed work, 4⅞" sq. $14.00
Chinese dragons on rim, inscribed work is nice, about 5" side, China mark, old $13.00

PLATE 73

PLATE 74

BRONZE AND COPPER ASHTRAYS

Bronze, an alloy of copper and tin, will not rust. However, it will show corrosion in the form of tiny black spots or powdery green areas which cannot be removed easily. Keep in mind that bronze will acquire a handsome mellow-toned appearance. The value of bronze is often determined by the amount of patina.

In the early 1900s, copper became very popular with the arts and crafts makers, who often hammered it or decorated it with other metals. Although stronger than gold, it is still soft and will tarnish. Some people lacquer their copper pieces, but most prefer the patina, a blue-green coating called verdigris, that comes with age. Carry a small magnet with you to test potential purchases for the presence of iron. Brass, bronze, and copper are not magnetic, but iron is.

PLATE 75 (left to right)
Row 1:
Sailfish, cast bronze, shows some patina, 5½" l, 4¼" h $30.00
Copper rectangle, marked Gregorian, nice coloring, 4¾" l $13.00
Set, bronze colored only with copper dancing figures, ashtray dump, Yugoslavia, 3" h $18.00
Silver crest, sterling decor on bronze, matchbox holder, 5" l $60.00
Elephant, solid bronze, white tusk, sand casting, 6¼" l $58.00

Row 2:
Indian arrowhead, copper plating has some wear, Indian inscribed in center, 5⅝" l $15.00
Coin dish, copper coins, brass center, Mexican 4" d, 1974 . . . . $ 9.00
Art Nouveau lady, solid bronze, lovely, nice patina, 6" l $65.00
Silver crest, large with matchbox holder, solid bronze, 6½" d, early 1900s $50.00
Hammered square, copper, heavy, 5¼" sq $18.00
Copper miner, plate, 3½" h $13.00
Indian rectangle, bird in corner, inscribed decoration on copper, 4⅛" l $12.00

CHROME AND ALUMINUM ASHTRAYS

Chromium is a base metal, used as a plating over another metal, often brass or copper. It became popular in the 1930s, particularly in the Art Deco style. The Chase Brass & Copper Company and the Farber Brothers Company have made many interesting pieces. Farber Brothers often would include a glass insert in their tableware. When the glass was red or cobalt, it made a very pleasing visual impact. See Plate 76 for examples.

The use of chrome plating, in 1932, gave people an easy-to-care-for product that needed no polishing to preserve its lustrous finish. By the 1950s, chrome had lost its appeal with the public, and silver recaptured the market, particularly silver plate used in household items.

Although aluminum is the most abundant metal in the earth's crust, originally it was more expensive to produce than gold or silver. Eventually by 1916, commercial smelting was perfected, and it helped lower price. In the 1930s, many aluminum tablewares were produced, including ashtrays. Spun aluminum was from the 1930s, but it gave way to hammered aluminum as a favorite type of decoration in the 1950s. Those well-made pieces are becoming collectible today.

PLATE 76 (left to right)
Row 1:
Chase, matchbox holder on handle, chrome plating/embossed on rim & under glass insert, 6" d, old $35.00
Chrome plate & extended rests, dish with glass insert, 4⅜" d $10.00
Aluminum on legs, tulips in relief in center, legs form rests on top, 5½" d . . . . $ 9.00
Anodized pink, aluminum, 4" l . . . . $ 9.00
Fish by Chase, chrome plating in shape of fish, 6¼" l $18.00
Chase, chrome plating with raised center to form cigarette rest, 3¾" d $13.00
Ruby glass lining, chrome plate with fret work on matchbox holder, 3¾" d, old $20.00

Row 2:
Bird figural, probably chrome plate, dish on pedestal, China, 3½" h $22.00
Chase, chrome plating over brass, small brass whale center as cigarette holder, 4¼" d $16.00
Aluminum w/cigarette holder, flowers in relief, Trade Continental mark, hand wrought, probably 1950s . . $12.00
Cobalt insert, cut out pattern of chrome plate with handle, 4¼" d $18.00
Chrome-like dish on pedestal, three rests, 4⅜" d . . . . $ 8.00

PLATE 75

PLATE 76

CLOISONNÉ ASHTRAYS

Cloisonné is enamel decoration in which the enamel is applied and fired in raised cells made from wires, usually brass or copper. In the ashtrays shown in Plate 77, silver, copper, and brass wires have been used to make the cells. I have never seen more than one metal used for the wires in any one item.

Note the small, cloisonné ashtray with all the brass cells raised above the enameling in Plate 77. This is unusual because the wires are raised from the metal surface. This leaves the enamel at a lower level with the brass cells raised; a very different effect.

PLATE 77 (left to right)   **All cloisonné.**
Row 1:
Round with removable rests, rests on brass ring which comes off, 3¾" d $35.00
Silver & cobalt, silver cells, visual impact, 3¾" sq $30.00
Ashtray with match holder in center, copper cells, dragons, China, excellent work, 4" h, old $60.00
Square, lots of white with silver trim, 4⅛" sq $38.00
Green inside, copper cells, multicolored flowers, China, 3⅞" d $20.00

Row 2:
White bowl, blue inside, China in red paint on bottom, 3¼" d, very old $18.00
Frog, brass cells, rest in mouth, lovely work, 3½" h $75.00
One-piece smoking set, copper cells, blue enamel interior, cigs, matches, ashes, striker, unusual, 6⅛" l. . . $80.00
Swivel top, top pivots on two extended rods so opens to expose bottom for ashes, 3¼" d. $34.00
Small with rust flowers, brass cells, probably China, 3¼" d $16.00

ENAMELED ASHTRAYS

Enameling is the application of an opaque composition by fusion to the surface of metal, glass, or pottery. Note the brass ashtray in Plate 78 with enameled tree flowers and birds made of lacquered paper maché. Hand-made in Kashmir, I have never seen another ashtray like this. The inside is lined in brass.

Another ashtray worthy of special note in Plate 78 is the set of copper with blue enameling. It is very old, very well done, and very lovely with its flower enameling on blue against the copper cut outs.

PLATE 78 (left to right)
Row 1:
Brass & bright blue, multicolored flowers, three brass rests, 5" l $15.00
Green enamel with birds, pink tree blossoms, heavy, hexagon, 4⅞" w $20.00
Blue enamel, jade handle with carved figures at end with frog at other end, China, 8" l, probably old $60.00
Small orange enamel, brass with bright orange, Germany mark, cen removes for cleaning, 2½" d $40.00
Green & orange enamel, Persian effect, sloppy work, 5" l. . . . . $ 8.00
Rare round brass bowl, lacquered paper mache, birds & tree blossoms, brass lining, Kashmir, lovely,
     very unusual use of materials, 3¼" d $55.00

Row 2:
Butterfly, copper, enameled work excellent, Holland, 3¼" d $30.00
Set with blue enamel, separate matchbox holder, copper cut out work, ashtray is 4" l, China, old $65.00
Green enamel, figure of small frog, jade handle, great, China, 5" w, probably old. $70.00
Solfatara, enamel dish supported by legs of three rearing horses of pewter, refers to covered shed in
     Iceland emitting sulfuric gasses, great detail in picture in the enamel dish, 1¾" l $42.00
Egg, pink enamel, brass trim, by Evans, 3¾" l. $26.00

PLATE 77

PLATE 78

LEAD AND POT METAL ASHTRAYS

Lead is a heavy, soft, bluish-white metallic element, seldom used in ashtrays. However it is a metal often used for soldering. Pot metal is an inexpensive metal often used as a base to reduce the cost of an item. Then it is coated with a layer of copper, bronze, silver, or sometimes painted.

PLATE 79 (left to right)

Row 1:

Alfred Dunhill, iron, black and green paint, serpent handle, swivel top spring loaded, 4⅝" h $40.00

Matchbox holder on top, lead with brass plating which is worn off, decor in relief & embossed, 2" h, 1910 . . $25.00

Indian dish, pot metal with copper plating, embossed Indian in center, 5" d $15.00

Lead dish with bird, brass used for decor center, two stones in top, probably China, 5" l $16.00

Ship with mermaid, pot metal, bronze finish, nicely done for its kind, 4¼" h $23.00

Row 2:

Heart, lead, center knob & handle used to knock pipe, handmade, 5" l $12.00

Devil, iron, possibly originally painted, 6¼" l, very old $95.00

Ivory rickshaw, pot metal, bronze finish, ornate rim, glass in center over lovely scene, 5⅝" d $25.00

Bowling, cast iron with bronze finish, "hurra for Batallon," very old, 5" l $45.00

Cowboy, pot metal with copper finish, Japan, 5" l $19.00

PEWTER

Pewter is a metal alloy of tin, copper, and lead. It has a silver-gray appearance without the shine of silver, and it does not tarnish. Many of the early good pewter products were melted down during the Revolutionary War to make bullets.

Britannia metal was a later type of pewter made with antimony as the major alloy with tin. This produced a lustrous, silver-like appearance, which was also more durable. To distinguish between the two, the mark "Genuine Pewter" was used.

PLATE 80 (left to right)

Row 1:

Prairie dogs holding up tray, American pewter, 3¾" h, old $35.00

Pewter-like, map of Americas and microscope, 7" d $11.00

Square, American pewter, 3½" sq $14.00

Cup on legs, Holland pewter, 1½" h $15.00

Pairpont pewter, picture of engraved ship on cigarette holder, match holder in front, 6" d $50.00

Row 2:

Squirrel, pot metal, bronze coating, sitting on log, 3⅛" h $20.00

Tile in center, pewter, lovely tile about grape harvesting, 4½" w $25.00

Pewter-like, Don Quixote on horseback with his squire, Sancho Panza, 8" d $12.00

Boat figural, Norwegian pewter, figural boat in center, 3½" d $25.00

Dog, figural for handle, American pewter, 3¾" h, old $28.00

FUNCTIONAL ASHTRAYS

PLATE 79

PLATE 80

FUNCTIONAL ASHTRAYS

STERLING AND SILVER PLATE ASHTRAYS

Sterling is a term that means that the item in the United States is 925 parts silver out of 1,000 parts metal. Usually the metal added to silver is copper, to give it strength. Sterling is a quality guarantee, used after 1860. It was used much earlier in England and Ireland, shown by a special mark. In Germany and the Scandinavian countries, solid silver refers to 830 parts/1000.

Silver plate is usually made of nickel or copper, with a thin coating of silver over it. Sometimes, it is marked quadruple plate, meaning four layers of silver have been added in the coating. Obviously, this will last much longer and will cost more. Sterling is lighter and thinner than plate.

Proper polishing of all silver products gives a beautiful appearance over the years. When tarnished, silver plate looks blackish, while tarnished sterling has a mellow, golden color. Sometimes, you can tell which is which by the color of tarnish. See Plate 81 to see tarnish on a sterling ashtray. Remember, sterling is difficult to identify, and if the price is too good to be true, it probably isn't sterling.

PLATE 81 (left to right)   **All sterling.**
Row 1:
Llama in center, sterling/tarnish, inscribed pattern with llama figural in center, ruffled rim, 3½" d $28.00
Triangular flat, drinking scene, Danish mark, three wide rests, 4" sides $23.00
Triangular, sterling, embossed elephants & patterns, three rests, 4¼" sides $30.00
Mexican square, marked sterling, 4" d, 1894 . . . . $25.00
Ashtray & cigarette cup, sterling set, cup is 2¾" h, ashtray directly below in Row 2, set price $28.00

Row 2:
Horseshoe, 2⅞" l $15.00
Plate with two rests, 1894 silver Mexican coin in center, marked, 4" w $25.00
Round with initial, weighted sterling, embossed pattern around rise, 4¼" d, 1950s $35.00
Ashtray from above set, three rests, 3¾" d, price of set, see above
Enameled shield, sterling, embossed pattern around wide rim, shield in center, 3¼" d $18.00

SILVER PLATE ASHTRAYS

Note: If the silver is dusty or dirty, be sure to wash first with only soap and water so that the dirt does not scratch it while polishing. Silver may be safely cleaned with a paste cleaner, never a liquid. Then store the ashtray in tarnish-preventive cloths. Frequent polishing of silver plate may eventually cause plate to show wear.

PLATE 82 (left to right)   **All silver plate.**
Row 1:
Coaster & ashtray, plate, Napier, ashtray swings out from underneath, 6¾" l when extended $12.00
Holland round, plate, set matchbox, embossed drinking scenes, Dutch, 5¼" d $22.00
Cigarette cup, drinking scene on sides, 2¾" h $20.00
Holland square, plate, matchbox holder, embossed scenes, lovely work, International, 7" sq, early 1900s . . $85.00
Matchbox cover, drinking scene $18.00
Drinking scene, plate, deep embossing, European, 5¼" d $55.00
Bird with wishbone, heavy plate, Forbes Silver Co., not polished, 7¼" w $45.00

Row 2:
Silver holder over glass insert matchbox holder, two wide rests, embossed ships, animals,
   people, Dutch, 8" l $60.00
Unusual shape, plate, embossed people, rests on sides, hole for ashes, Dutch, 4½" h, old $90.00
Round with center matchbox, worn plate, embossed scenes of animals, houses, people, 6¼" d $48.00

PLATE 81

PLATE 82

ASHTRAYS MADE FROM
PLASTICS, MARBLE, SOAPSTONE, AND WOOD

The term "collectible plastics" refer to those items manufactured from the late 1800s to the end of the 1950s. The earlier plastics were highly inflammable, and many would yellow with age. Bakelite was invented in 1908, and was widely used in the late 1920s and 1930s. The Art Deco style was popular then, and it lent itself beautifully for decoration with plastics.

In the early 1940s and 1950s, many household items, including ashtrays, were made of plastics. Remember the radios, telephones, dishes, lamps? Note the red and black ashtray in Plate 83. It was probably made in the 1950s. It has a lighter in the center, and three removable trays.

Marble is limestone that is more or less crystallized, ranging from granular to compact in texture, and is capable of being highly polished. The fact that marble is often used in architecture, is reflected in the massive look that marble ashtrays often have. These ashtrays were also popular in the Art Deco period.

Soapstone is a soft stone having a soapy feel. It was often used in carvings in many countries during the nineteenth and twentieth centuries. Most of this work that is found today is Oriental. One of the ashtrays in Plate 84 is really a imitation ivory, intricately carved.

Wooden items have been used in all areas of the house. People have carved wood for many centuries, and it is often part of our folk art. Oriental people have shown great proficiency at carving wood and ivory.

Note: Keep wooden items away from sunlight. It dries out the wood, and is harmful to the finish.

PLATE 83 (left to right)

Row 1:
Off-white marble, gray markings, 7" d $17.00
Metal peacock, brown plastic base, Orfear, France, nice, 1¾" h $14.00
Wine plastic, bottom magnetic, good for cars, slide to empty & clean, 2⅞" d $13.00
Dark gray & tan marble, lovely markings, great deco piece, very heavy, 6" square $35.00
Green plastic, speckled, three rests on rim, 4" d . . . . $ 6.00
Red plastic ashtrays with cigarette lighter in center, black plastic base, 7½" d $20.00

Row 2:
Yellow marble, gray markings, heavy, nice, 4½" square $18.00
Black round, small, high rise to protect cigs from wind, Island Ashtray, 3⅜" d, patented, 1973 . . . . $ 5.00
Black plastic with match holder, Hotel Peabody, Memphis, 7" d, typical style of 1930s $12.00
Yellow plastic, chrome plate rim, one rest, Japan, 2⅞" d . . . . $ 7.00
Brown smokador, raised bump in center to knock off ashes, lift top up & ashes go to bottom, 4⅜" d $15.00

PLATE 84 (left to right)

Row 1:
Soapstone square, shades of gray, pie crust rim, lotus bud & pods, 5" sq $28.00
Polynesian type, hand carved, two rests, match holder, nice, 6" h $40.00
Green soapstone leaf shape, two rests at wide end, China, 4¾" l $12.00
Ivory carving, good work, sterling top, lining & three rests, 2½" h $60.00
Wood gnome, hand work, copper ashtray, note gnome smoking pipe, 8" l $55.00
Soapstone elephant, figural on back rim, shades of gray, 4¼" l $35.00

Row 2:
Green soapstone lotus pods, two rests, heavy, 5½" l $38.00
Molded plastic or composition, Spanish dancers in relief, cheaply made, 6" l . . . . $ 7.00
Imitation ivory, very fine Oriental carving, nicely done, 4¾" sq $30.00
Bird figural, ashtray and bird made from horn, 5⅛" l $15.00
Soapstone dish, shades rust & gray, carving of flowers & leaves, one rest, 5¼" l $18.00
Lacquered wood, metallic gold fish, copper lining ashtray, Oriental, very nice, 4½" d $35.00

PLATE 83

PLATE 84

ADVERTISING ASHTRAYS

Although cigarette smoking started to become popular for men in the United States toward the end of the nineteenth century, and ashtrays were used, advertising ashtrays did not appear on the scene until well into the twentieth century. However, the stage was set for their appearance long before that.

In the 1880s, the Industrial Revolution was well under way and mass production was thriving. Hawkers and manufacturers sought ways to inform people about all the products being produced. The era was bursting with information waiting to be communicated. Advertising, with its purpose of informing, exciting, and igniting desires of customers, became very important in this age of inexpensively produced products for the masses. One historian observed that wherever there was a blank space to be found, soon it was filled with "advertising."

Where do advertising ashtrays fit into all this? Well, eventually someone looked at ashtrays and thought they were a "space" on which one could advertise, a space that went into many people's homes, stores, and taverns. Advertising on ashtrays would be a simple and effective way to keep a company, product, or any name before people's eyes.

This did not happen until smoking became even more acceptable and ashtrays were commonly used. Advertisers then started to use ashtrays as another means to reach more people. Probably by the late 1920s, manufacturers began to put their ads on ashtrays and give them to stores for people to see. Soon local pubs and other establishments had ads for their products on their ashtrays too. By 1950, smoking had become so popular with men and women that advertising ashtrays could be found almost everywhere, even in doctors' offices and schools.

As early as the beginning of this century, company logos and advertising characters were created to help people remember the product's name. Nipper, one of the oldest advertising logo characters, started life as a trademark for Victor in the early 1900s. In 1929, RCA purchased Victor and Nipper became a very familiar trademark for RCA. Eventually Nipper's picture appeared on ashtrays used for advertising.

Mr. Peanut of Planters Peanuts, who also started life early in the 1900s, was taken from a child's drawing. He has since become one of the most collectible advertising characters of all time. An advertising ashtray of Mr. Peanut was made for Planters Peanuts' fiftieth anniversary in 1956. However, there were also earlier ashtrays manufactured with Mr. Peanut on them.

Until 1936, Howard Johnson Ice Cream Shops and Restaurants used Simple Simon and the Pieman as their trademark. The old glass ashtray in Plate 115 with the orange Pieman was made before 1936 (white paper has been put under the ashtray to show the trademark more clearly). There are many more advertising characters, including Kools' penguins, Ronald McDonald, and Joe Camel. If you know some history of trademarks and advertising characters, it helps to establish the date, and high prices are often paid for these ashtrays.

The United States has become one of the largest consumer nations in the world, thanks in part to competitive advertising. Today, the purpose of advertising remains the same. All that has changed is the means of spreading the information: newsprint, radio, telephone, television, and now computers. Advertisers have had to change and develop new ways to catch the consumer's eye, or ear.

As more foreign goods were imported and price competition increased, many businesses found it too expensive to make the elaborate advertising ashtrays of the 1930s through the 1960s. Many companies, concerned about negative public opinion, stopped putting their name on ashtrays when smoking was determined to be a health hazard. Also, with the increase of the smoke-free environment, advertising ashtrays were not seen by as many people, and companies that used to make them have seen their sales drop sharply. If any were made, they were usually glass or plastic, very plain and simple, and definitely not as interesting and unusual as the older ashtrays. Those advertising ashtrays have become part of the past smoking culture in the United States.

I have devoted many pages to advertising ashtrays because now they are plentiful on the market and many collectors and dealers are very interested in them. Now, all types of ashtrays should become increasingly collectible and prices on ashtrays will rise. One thing is certain — they don't make them like they used to!

ASHTRAYS ADVERTISING BEERS

Ashtrays advertising beers are more plentiful than any other kind. The older ones are harder to find but often are very interesting, with more colors, hand work, better materials, and sometimes a figure.

Beer was processed in bottles in the 1890s, and before that it was sold in kegs. Beer cans were not used before 1935. Interestingly, most figural ashtrays in this area are of bottles, not cans.

In Plate 85 there is one ashtray of Coors, ceramic, a pale cream round with a plain center, found in almost every mall. There are ashtrays just like this but yellow, or with a different shape in the center, or the same shape with a verse in the center. The last two ashtrays are very hard to find and are priced much higher. The verse in the center of one reads, "Our forefathers thought nothing of working 15 hrs. a day. We don't think much of it either!" It is not pictured here but is priced in the non-illustrated price guide at the end of the book.

PLATE 85 (left to right)
Row 1:
Schlitz, tan ceramic, brown logo & picture, 5¼" d $20.00
Colt 45, blue plastic, by National, 6½" sq . . . .$ 9.00
Coors, red plastic, white letters around wide rim, 5½" sq . . . .$ 5.00
Tuborg Lager, gold crown in green center, white & green letters, plastic, 6" d . . . .$ 5.00

Row 2:
Coors, red & gray letters, *America's Fine Light Beer,* cream, 5⅞" d . . . .$ 6.00
Miller High Life, picture of girl on moon, *If you've got time — we've got the beer,* plastic, 4¾" sq $35.00
Blatz Pilsner, glass figural of Blatz bottle 4" h, pressed pattern in center of ashtray, 5" l $30.00
Miller High Life, name & logo center in red, amber glass, 6½" d . . . .$ 6.00

PLATE 86 (left to right)
Row 1:
Heineken, *Beer,* cup shape, name in green letters around top, cream ceramic 3⅝" w, 2" h . . . .$ 9.00
Michelob, name & logo in black & red on rise, cream plastic, 3¾" d . . . .$ 5.00

Row 2:
Tennent's Lager, red glass, white letters, 5½" d $10.00
Bud Light, dk blue letters on wide rim outlined in red, cream ceramic, 5¼" d . . . .$ 6.00
Grain Belt, actual beer bottle in center, 9½" h, gold metal ashtray, 7½" sq $21.00
Carling's, black enameled metal, red letters on rim, *Lager, Red Cap Ale, Stout,* 6"x4¾" $22.00
Falstaff, amber opalized glass, logo in center, 5¼" d . . . .$ 5.00

Row 3
Pabst, logo & name in white on rise, *Pabst Blue Ribbon,* blue plastic, 4" d, 1½" h . . . .$ 7.00
Budweiser, red letters on rim, *Budweiser King Of Beers,* cream ceramic, 5¼" d . . . .$ 6.00
Carling Black Label, bronze metal with chrome strip across, *Hey Mabel,* oval, 5¼" w . . . .$ 8.00
Heineken, black picture of town and river in center, name on rise, cream ceramic, 7" sq $15.00
Hamm's, red name at top, *Born in the land of sky blue waters* in blue, cream ceramic, 6¾" d $10.00
Pabst, copper, letters etched on rim & center, *Pabst Blue Ribbon Beer Milwaukee,* 4⅞" d $20.00
Andeker, gold letters on rise, black plastic, *The Beer Supreme, Pabst,* 3¾" d . . . .$ 5.00

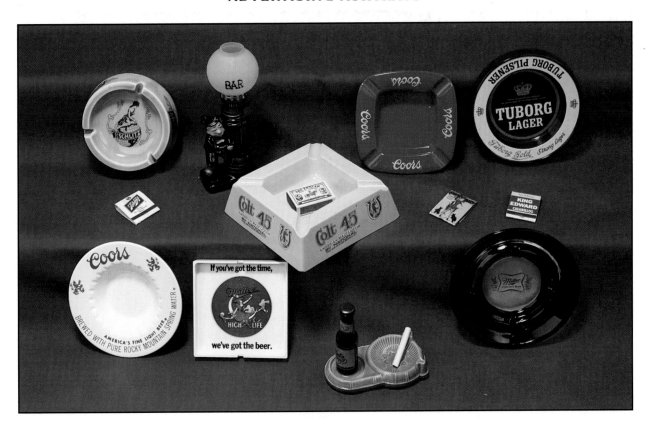

PLATE 85

PLATE 86

ASHTRAYS ADVERTISING BEERS

PLATE 87 (left to right)

Row 1:

Skol Lager, yellow glass, name in red along rise, picture of two beer mugs on rise, 6" d . . . . $ 6.00

Tennent's Beer, tan stoneware high sides, 4" d $12.00

Molson's Ale-Porter, navy blue porcelain, three rests, 6¾" w $30.00

Lowenbrau, glass, red & black name on rise, *Swiss Beer, Zurich,* 3⅞" d . . . . $ 6.00

Kirner Bier, tan keg figural, blue letters, German beer, white ceramic, 6½" sq $30.00

Courage, rooster in relief in center, white name on rim, English, glass, 6¼" d $12.00

Hackerbrau, picture of girl in center, red edge, 4" d. $11.00

Schrempp Bier, raised picture of bird drinking beer in center, ceramic, German, 6½" d, old $13.00

Kirin Beer, knob in center with bottle cap, Japan, ceramic, 4¾" d $12.00

Row 2:

Jax Beer, brown ceramic, Jackson Brewing Co, New Orleans, LA, 6¾" w $17.00

Bass, *Export Ale,* picture of beer being poured, plastic, 6" d. $11.00

Tucher Bier, picture of black boy in center, red letters, *Nurnberg,* ceramic, 6½" x 5½" $20.00

Hackerbrau, blue letters on rim, crossed hatchets in center, ceramic, 8" d $11.00

Busch, *Bavarian Beer,* white center, red & blue name & logo, glass tri, 3½" sides . . . . $ 5.00

Zywiec, colorful Polish dancers in center, four rests at each end, ceramic, 6⅜" x 3¼" . . . . $ 8.00

ASHTRAYS ADVERTISING WINES

When smoking was the "in thing" and advertisers gave away ashtrays as a popular marketing tool, wine was not as popular a drink as other alcoholic beverages in our country. This is probably the most important reason why wine ashtrays today are not as easy to find as those for liquors and beers. Wine ashtrays might be easier to find today in Europe. Liquore Galliano, Pernod, Dubonnet, and Ricard Anisette Liquor are all European aperitifs.

The advertising ashtrays in European bars today are very plain. They are usually glass, round, and stacking, and have the name printed around the outside.

PLATE 88 (left to right)

Row 1:

Liquore Galliano, triangle, name in red on sides, Italian, white ceramic, 5½" sides $10.00

Ricard Anisette Liquor, yellow glass, name on rise on black & red area, 5" sides . . . . $ 6.00

Alianca, picture in center of rose wine & glass, Portugal, pale amber irid glass, 5¼" d . . . . $ 7.00

Aristocrat Brandy Ambassador Vermouth, white letters on rise of black amethyst glass, 4½" d $10.00

Martini, cobalt glass, name on four sides, 5" sq $25.00

Bigi Orvieto, Chianti bottle shape raised up in center & painted, white ceramic, 4¼" l $18.00

Row 2:

Cinzano, rests in center on raised area, name on rise, cream ceramic, 6½"x5¾" . . . . $ 9.00

Noilly Prat, dry, sweet vermouth, 7" sq $20.00

Hennessy Cognac, Limoges cream china, gold letters, 4" d . . . . $ 9.00

Harveys Bristol Cream Sherry, triangle, green letters on sides, *Imported,* ceramic, 6" sides. . . . . $ 9.00

PLATE 87

PLATE 88

ASHTRAYS ADVERTISING WINES

Note the two Martini & Rossi ashtrays in Plate 89. The one with the red circle on the rise is china, and the one with the green circle is milk glass. The ceramic ashtray is older and harder to find, and I have only seen it with the red circle. Both come in milk glass and are seen frequently in malls and flea markets.

PLATE 89 (left to right)

Row 1:

Benedictine, green bottle cut in half, made into ashtray, labels still on bottle, 7½" l $18.00

Martell, dk blue ceramic, gold & white logo on rise, 4¼" sq. . . . . $ 8.00

Dubonnet, picture in center of woman & bottle, *Red & Blonde,* milk glass, 5½" sides $14.00

B&B, Brandy & Benedictine brown bottle cut in half, made into ashtray, labels still on, 7½" l $18.00

Row 2:

Dubonnet, match holder with striker surface, 3" h $10.00

Martini & Rossi, triangle, black & green logo on side, *Extra Dry Vermouth,* milk glass, 4½" sides . . . . $ 9.00

Texier Wine, white ceramic with blue letters, 7" d . . . . $ 6.00

Martini & Rossi, triangle, black & red logo on side, name only, white ceramic, 4½" sides . . . . $ 9.00

Pernod, yellow-green glass, blue letters, 5½" d $14.00

ASHTRAYS ADVERTISING LIQUORS

In Plate 90 there is a Glenmore Whisky chalkware ashtray. Because of its composition, it is usually hard to find in good condition. I also found a bronze colored one. I looked closely at the color application, and I do not believe that someone just painted it bronze. If anyone knows more about this, I would appreciate hearing from you.

The Carstairs White Seal ashtray was a find. I have seen only one of these. Black and White Scotch is another hard-to-find ashtray of the same type. You can see the Carstairs ashtray in Plate 90, and the Black and White Scotch ashtray in Plate 92.

PLATE 90 (left to right)

Row 1:

Glenmore, figural man, pale yellow chalkware, black center, *Ky's Finest Whiskies,* 5" d, 1930s $45.00

Johnnie Walker Scotch, picture of man in center, *Born 1820 – Still Going Strong,* 5" sq $12.00

Carstairs White Seal, scotch, black plastic, *For the man who cares,* white seal/red ball, 9¾" d $50.00

Early Times, name in red, *Kentucky Bourbon* in black letters, 5¼" d . . . . $ 5.00

White Horse Whisky, white ceramic fig horse, 4" h $25.00

Row 2:

Schenley Red Label, bottle figural, *Light Bodied Blended Whisky,* gold metal ashtray, 6" d $22.00

Squires, *London Dry Gin,* green ceramic, white center, black letters & picture of man hunting, 8" l $10.00

Old Hickory Burbon, decal center w/picture of man & name, pale amber irid glass, 4⅜" d $10.00

Flowers Best Bitter, picture of man in center in red & black, *Flower & Sons,* white ceramic oval 9" l $13.00

Old Taylor, yellow center with picture & name, *Ky. Bourbon Whiskey,* stoneware, 5" sq $12.00

Glenmore Vodka, triangle, red center, yellow letters, glass, 3" sides . . . . $ 6.00

Johnnie Walker Scotch, old style ceramic, logo & name on high rise, 4" sq, 2½" h $15.00

PLATE 89

PLATE 90

ASHTRAYS ADVERTISING LIQUORS

Plate 91 shows three ashtrays made by Wade, an English porcelain company. There are the Beefeater Gin, the J&B Scotch Whiskey, and the Tanqueray Gin. Wade also made other ashtrays and there are several excellent books about their excellent products. Their pictured trademarks make it easy to date their ashtrays.

In Plate 92 there is a favorite ashtray of many people, the two dogs in the Black and White Scotch ashtray. The Gordon Gin ashtray is also great! It is clever and has a catchy color combination.

Although manufacturers continued to make ashtrays for different kinds of alcohol for many years after they made these great ones, the ashtrays began to be simpler and plainer. Other advertising methods were becoming important; newspapers and magazines, for example, soon had more influence.

PLATE 91 (left to right)
Row 1:
Beefeater Gin, name & men in red/black, almost red, by Wade, 5½" d, 1970–1980 . . . . $18.00
Jim Beam Bourbon Whiskey, red rim, white center with picture of bottle, metal, 4½" d . . . . $ 6.00
Pimm's, white ceramic, name on rise, picture of polo players on inside, 4⅛" d . . . . $ 8.00
Seagram's VO Canadian, cobalt ceramic in VO shape, gold letters & rests, 8" w. $15.00
Bonded Beam, metal, yellow center with picture of bottle, brown rim, *Bourbon Whiskey,* 4½" d. . . . . $ 7.00
Jim Beam Bourbon Whiskey, picture of bottle, *Worthy — Trust,* red, white, black on metal, 4½" d . . . . . . $ 6.00
Smirnoff (vodka), name in red, *on the rocks* in blue, white ceramic, 3½" sides . . . . $ 8.00

Row 2:
Teachers Scotch Whisky, pale green bottle made into ashtray, label & top wrapper show, 8" l $12.00
Calvert Dry Gin, gold flowers, green leaves, black letters, crackled glaze, 7⅜" sq. $10.00
Plymouth Gin, brass, raised letters around rim, Original Coates & Co's, 4½" sq $20.00
J&B Scotch Whisky, name on rise, olive ceramic, by Wade, 6" l, 1970–1980 . . . . $17.00
Tanqueray, letters in black, *English Gin,* green ceramic by Wade, 6" d $20.00

PLATE 92 (left to right)
Row 1:
Booth's Dry Gin, by Carlton Ware, hexagon, six rests, yellow on rise, 7" w. $26.00
Gilbey's London Dry Gin, by London & Stoke, picture on rise, 2½" h. $30.00
Black & White Scotch, ceramic, two Scotty dogs figurals in center, 9" d $55.00
Seagrams Scotch – 100 Pipers, brown, gold rim, triangular, 2⅛" h. $11.00
Gordon's, *the Heart of a Good Cocktail,* yellow ceramic, black letters on white rim, 5½" w $40.00

Row 2:
Imperial, milk glass, black letters rim, *Whiskey By Hiram Walker,* 5¼" d . . . . $ 6.00
Ambassador, Deluxe Scotch, by Wade, black letters & trim, high rise, 5¾" d. $27.00
Canadian Club Whisky, ceramic, green letters sloped rise, 5½" d $20.00

PLATE 91

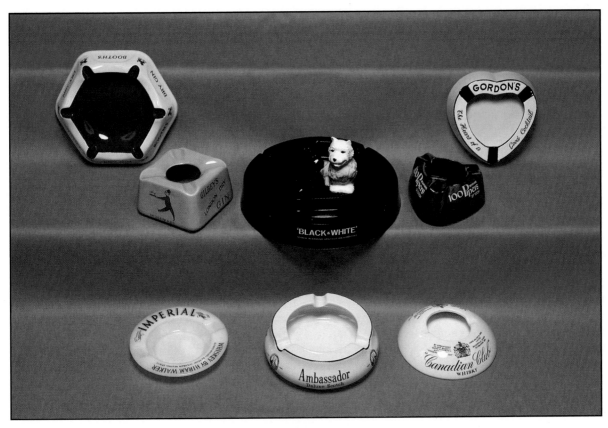

PLATE 92

ASHTRAYS FOR CLOTHING AND COMESTICS

With the exception of the hats, I have not seen many ashtrays in this category. The cobalt blue glass hat is very common, but it usually has a plain bottom. This one has an advertisement for "Lowell Hand Cream, Deodorant, Blue Gem Cream, Piqua, Ohio." The black glass hat has Dobbs on the brim, the name of a hat manufacturer. None of these products is being made today, which makes these hats fun to collect.

The square tan stoneware ashtrays show pictures of advertisements of products that might have been used around the turn of the century. Unfortunately, these ashtrays shown here are not that old.

The ashtray with the blue center, in Plate 93, is made by Limoges for one of the leading department stores in Paris. It, or a similar one, may still be used at the store, since smoking is prevalent throughout Europe.

PLATE 93 (left to right)

Row 1:

Curlique – Make Hair Curl, tan stoneware, black picture & letters in center, 5⅜" sq. $15.00
Aqua Velva, glass with blue decal on bottom, 3¾" w. . . . . $ 7.00
Jockey Underwear, picture in center of a jockey, *100 year anniversary – 1976,* 8¾" d. $12.00
Galeries Lafayette, cobalt blue center with gold emblem, name on rim gold, Limoges, 4" d. . . . . $ 8.00
Childs's Cash Shoe Store, tan stoneware, black picture & letters in center, 5⅜" sq. $15.00

Row 2:

Resistol Hats, brown plastic, ad on top of brim, 4¾" l. $16.00
Campbell Kid, Dry Goods Store, Campbell Kid painting sign, hexagon, cream ceramic, 6" l. $25.00
Lowell Hand Cream, Deodorant, Blue Gem Cream, name on bottom, cobalt glass hat, 2½" h. $25.00
Du-Flex Soles, Avon Sole Co., Avon Mass., copper over metal, 5½" d, old $14.00
Dobbs (hats), black amethyst glass hat shape, name in relief on brim, 2" h. $28.00
Elgin Watches, tan ceramic, wine letters, 5⅜" d. $12.00
Florsheim Shoe, brown chalkware, one rest at heel, name on bottom, 5½" l. $26.00

ASHTRAYS FOR EDUCATIONAL FACILITIES

Shortly after I started collecting ashtrays, I found one from a local high school. Knowing what we know now about the dangers of smoking, I found this surprising. Intrigued, I decided to see what was available in the field of education. As you can see, education was provided in many different types of institutions, from a dog training school to Oxford University, and they all had their own ashtray.

PLATE 94 (left to right)

Row 1:

Massachusetts Institute of Technology, red & black seal in ceramic, 7¼" sq. . . . . $ 8.00
Museum of Science & Industry, name & logo impressed in center, *Chicago,* aluminum, 5" d. . . . . $ 8.00
Wisconsin Telephone Technical Training Center, green center with yellow name, amber glass, 6" d. . . . . . . $ 5.00
Oxford University, enameled seal in blue, yellow & silver at top, chrome, 4" d. $20.00
Lakeland College, black picture of building in center, *Old Main,* ceramic, 7½", 1960s. . . . . $ 5.00

Row 2:

Dog Training Club – Queen City, red dog & name in center, *Cincinnati,* 5¾" d. . . . . $ 5.00
University of Michigan, cream china by Wedgwood, 4⅜" d $11.00
Yale University, blue letters and seal in center, ceramic, 4⅝" d $10.00
Corning Glass Center (a museum), blue name with logo in center, 3½" sq . . . . $ 7.00
Northern Michigan University, yellow center with green name & torch, 4½" d . . . . $ 8.00
Carleton College, picture of Willis Hall in black & blue in center, ceramic, 4½" d . . . . $ 6.00
Princeton, orange & black seal in center with name, 3½" sq $11.00
North Carolina State University, cream ceramic, picture in center, 5¼" d . . . . $ 6.00
University of Virginia, tan ceramic, brown picture in center, 4½" d . . . . $ 8.00

PLATE 93

PLATE 94

ASHTRAYS FOR ENTERTAINMENT AND CASINOS

The Gun & Rod Club ashtray from Bad Hersfeld was made by Royal Bayreuth before 1919. The opalescence is quite pronounced, and looks lovely with the fish and seaweed. It is in mint condition, even in the center, which often has nicks made by pipes.

The Yamaha ashtray, shaped like a helmet, has a drawing of a motorcycle inside it. It is in black, like an etching. Unfortunately, this does not show up very well in Plate 95.

In the bottom picture is an Evinrude motor figural ashtray, which I was delighted to find. But when I looked up the patent number on the bottom of the tray, I was disappointed to discover that someone had taken off the original figural and substituted the motor figural in its place. Although I still like it, it cannot be considered a manufactured ashtray. Unfortunately, I had paid $55.00 for it.

The Playboy Club ashtrays are easy to find. See Plate 96. There is an orange glass one, just like the yellow one pictured, and it is seen more frequently than the yellow one. This same design also comes in black and white. They were made in the 1960s. The same mold also comes with just a small picture of a bunny head. See the price guide in the back of the book for information on these and other styles from the Playboy Club.

PLATE 95 (left to right)
Row 1:
Yamaha, ceramic helmet, white top with red name, blue bottom, two rests, picture of cycle inside, 5" d . . . $25.00
Milwaukee Athletic Club, blue & white stylized picture of man exercising, ceramic, 4½" d. . . . . $ 5.00
Brunswick Corp. (bowling balls), orange center, black picture of man holding ball, local ad, 3⅝" sq . . . . . . $ 8.00
Indianapolis 500, red & black name in centered, *74th May 27, 1990,* ceramic, 4½" d $13.00
Derringer – Famous Antique Firearms, brown gun on back rim *.41 Caliber–1850,* ceramic, 3½" sides . . . $12.00

Row 2:
Wilson Staff, (golf ball) white center, gold ball, *Win With Wilson* in black, 3⅝" sq $10.00
Rod & Gun Club – Bad Hersfeld, white opalescent china, name on rim, four fish & seaweed
    painted in center, lg gold rests, Royal Bayreuth mark, 8¾" d $30.00
National Campers & Hikers Assoc., yellow & green decal center, *NCHA,* glass, 4¼" sq. . . . . $ 8.00

PLATE 96 (left to right)
Row 1:
Atari (video games), black center, gold logo & name in center, 4½" d $10.00
Havana Club, in Cuba, plastic, picture in center, 5½" d $10.00
Evinrude (boat motor), figural of boat motor in center, black plastic ashtray, 7" d (See notes above) $30.00
Sea World, picture in center of penguin in black, yellow, white, name in black, 4⅛" sq, 1985. . . . . $ 9.00
Busch Gardens, name & picture in white on rise, cross-hatched bottom, dk amber glass, 3½" d . . . . $ 8.00

Row 2:
Disneyland, pink & blue picture of Magic Kingdom & Tinker Bell in center, ceramic, 5" d $15.00
Lido de Paris (famous nightclub), black plastic hat, also ad Moet & Chandon champagne, 2¼" h $25.00
Playboy Club, yellow glass, Playmate in center holding key, name in black in circle, 4" sq, 1960s. $20.00
Walt Disney World, gold, orange & brown buildings in center, orange name on rim, ceramic, 5" d $12.00

PLATE 95

PLATE 96

ASHTRAYS FOR CASINOS

The casino ashtrays are easy to find. The black amethyst are seen more frequently, and they usually sell for $4.00 to $6.00. If the ashtray comes from a casino that no longer exists, it may be worth more, but rarity and demand also enter into the price. For more detailed reading, consult *Casinos and Their Ashtrays* by Art Anderson.

PLATE 97 (left to right)

Row 1:

Sands Hotel, yellow center, brown name & picture of hotel, *Las Vegas, NV,* smoke glass, 4" d . . . . $ 7.00

Mapes, white center, orange name with picture of two cowboys, *Reno's Motor Hotel,* 3½" sq . . . . $ 6.00

Riviera, red & white center, *The Magnificent, Las Vegas, NV,* smoke glass, 4" d . . . . $ 6.00

Harrah's, orange center, white letters, *Reno and Lake Tahoe,* crystal glass, 3⅝" sq . . . . $ 5.00

Desert Inn, black & white plastic, shape of roulette wheel in center, *Wilbur Clark's, Las Vegas,* 5" d $10.00

Sahara, yellow center, red name & logo, *Del Webb's Hotel,* amber, 3½" sq . . . . $ 8.00

Silver Slipper, green glass with lt green center; blue slipper & name, 3¾" d . . . . $ 9.00

Mint, orange center, black name & picture of the Mint, *Del Webb's, Las Vegas,* amber glass, 3½" sq . . . . . . $ 6.00

Golden Nugget, yellow center with red name, *Gambling Hall,* amber glass, 3½" sq . . . . $ 6.00

Row 2:

Desert Inn, green glass, name, sun & cacti on rise, *Wilbur Clark's,* 3½" d $10.00

Fabulous Flamingo, red flamingo in center, *Las Vegas, Nevada,* glass, 4" d . . . . $ 8.00

Tropicana Hotel, fountain & letters in center, *Las Vegas,* amber glass, 4½" d . . . . $ 6.00

Landmark, blue center, gray logo & name, *Las Vegas, NV,* smoke glass, 4½" d . . . . $ 8.00

MGM Grand Hotel, white center with red lion & letters, 4½" d . . . . $ 8.00

Riverside, white letters on rise of blue glass, *Pick Hobson's Hotel, Casino, Reno,* 3½" d . . . . $ 7.00

ASHTRAYS FOR FINANCE & INSURANCE COMPANIES

I was able to find many different kinds of ashtrays for this category. Of the banks pictured in Plate 98, the ashtray from the First National Bank of Pekin is probably older than the one from Kenosha because the perimeter shape and the cigarette rests are much more complex. Also, notice the clock tower, which has a lot of detail and is in relief, along with the letters in the center.

PLATE 98 (left to right)

Row 1:

Financial Analysts Federation, blue name & logo in center, Chicago, 5¼" d, 1963 . . . . $ 7.00

1st National Bank, red & blue shield in center, name in red, *Kenosha, WI.,* 7" d . . . . $ 6.00

Kellogg's Federal Credit Union, blue & red letters in center, green wheat, *10th Anniversary,* 7¾" w . . . . . . $ 8.00

Lutheran Brotherhood (insurance), green picture in center of building, *Minneapolis, MN.,* ceramic 7½" d . . $ 7.00

Aetna Bonds (insurance), blue & red picture in center, *The Sky's The Limit,* 5¾" d . . . . $ 6.00

Row 2:

Brewery Worker's Credit Union, white center, picture of house in black, 4¼" sq . . . . $ 5.00

Pekin 1st National Bank, green ceramic, letters & clock raised up in center, 5½" d, old . . . . $ 9.00

Eurocard – MasterCard, name & logo in center & around rise in red & black, 4⅛" d . . . . $ 5.00

American Express, green & blue stripes & logo name in center, 3¾" sq . . . . $ 6.00

Occidental Life – California, 50th anniversary, blue letters & logo in center, 5¾" sq, 1956 . . . . $ 7.00

Catholic Aid Association, *Minn,* blue letters & logo of cross in center, started in 1878, glass, 4⅛" sq . . . . . . $ 5.00

PLATE 97

PLATE 98

ASHTRAYS FOR NON-ALCOHOLIC BEVERAGES AND FOOD

Food advertising ashtrays are not as easy to find as some other categories. However, collecting Coca-Cola items is extremely popular, and there are several good books that are illustrated, and show dates and prices. There are more elaborate ashtrays pictured in these books that are very interesting. I have selected four for the top picture, and there are more in the non-illustrated price guide at the end of the book.

Around the turn of the century, some companies became aware that if they personified their product, it would be a great advertising tool. Although most advertising characters did not come into existence until the 1930s, there were some notable exceptions, including Mr. Peanut and the Campbell Kids.

Mr. Peanut was developed in 1916, updated in 1927, and stylized in 1962. His figural ashtray is in Plate 100. He has become one of the world's most recognized advertising characters, and he is still being used! One of his ashtrays celebrates Planter's 50th anniversary.

PLATE 99 (left to right)
Row 1:
Néscafe, ceramic shape of half coffee bean, 4⅝" l $20.00
Moxie, copper, 5½" d, old $40.00
Old Judge Coffee, metal can with red paint, two rests, match holder, 3¾" h, old $95.00
Schweppes, colorful coat of arms in center, cigarette rests in circle near center, 8½" d $20.00
7-UP, green bottle in ashtray shape, red & white label, 8" l $10.00
Herva, alcohol-free drink, German, 4⅝" h $12.00
50-50 Grafs, gold metal, center rise with red & green letters, 5½" d $10.00
Squirt, red cardboard with silver inside, *Fine Dry Flavor,* 3" sq, 1962 . . . . $ 5.00

Row 2:
Coca-Cola Bottling Co., black plastic, 5½" l $20.00
Coca-Cola, white letters in center, *Enjoy,* red metal, 5½" d $10.00
Grafs, red letters in center, glass, hexagonal, *Carbonated Beverages,* 4" across . . . . $ 7.00
7-UP, plastic, *The International Drink,* 5½" sq $10.00
B1 Lemon Lime Soda, red center, white letters, 3½" sq . . . . $ 6.00
Sanka, orange center, *97% Caffeine Free,* 4" sq . . . . $ 5.00
Coca-Cola, ripple rim, *Drink Coca Cola,* red aluminum, 4½" d, 1950 . . . . $13.00
Coca-Cola, red circle in center, matchbox holder & match pack holder back rim, ceramic, 5" d, 1950s $45.00

PLATE 100 (left to right)
Row 1:
Purina Chow, red & white checkerboard center, glass, octagon 4½" across . . . . $ 4.00
Jello, picture of dessert in center, *Now Ten Delicious Flavors,* 7½" sq, 1940s $12.00
Wonder Bread & Hostess Cakes, red & blue logo in center, 3½" sq . . . . $ 6.00
Planters Peanut, *1906–1956,* at base of figural, gold metal, 5¾" d $55.00
Stokely's Finest, *Frozen Foods,* frosted glass with picture, 4½" l $15.00
Reed's Butter Scotch, black jar lid to be used as ashtray, 2½" d $10.00
Post Cereals, black center, red letters, glass, 4" d, late 1930s $35.00
General Mills, picture of logo & general office in Minneapolis in center, ceramic, 7½" sq $12.00
Hershey's, brown logo in center, heavy glass, 4" d $10.00

Row 2:
Kraft Foods Company, *Golden Anniversary 1903–1953,* 4⅝" l $15.00
Slim Jims, *All Beef, Make Your Next Drink Taste Better,* gold tin, 4½" d . . . . $ 6.00
Pepsin Tutti Frutti, Victorian picture in middle, red & beige tin, 8" d, not old $12.00
Slim Jims, *Ready-To-Eat Meat Snacks,* red tin, black letters, 4½" d . . . . $ 8.00
Bryers Ice Cream, logo red & green in center, ceramic, 5½" d $15.00

PLATE 99

PLATE 100

ASHTRAYS FOR FRATERNAL AND SERVICE ORGANIZATIONS

Benevolent and secret societies have a long history in the United States, starting in the eighteenth century. They were originally formed as social clubs that would help their members in times of need. But times changed; secret and discriminatory practices were frowned on. Also, members did not need as much help in the twentieth century. Many organizations closed local chapters, and those that remained changed their purpose to helping others in need.

During this century, other service clubs were formed, such as the Rotary and Lions. Their emphasis is on service, and the ashtrays of these groups have no history as secret societies. Perhaps this makes them less interesting. Whatever the reason, they are not considered very collectible now, but they may be more collectible in the future.

PLATE 101 (left to right)

Row 1:

Shrine, *Mohammed Temple,* cast solid bronze, symbols raised in cen, on back – *Illustrious Potentate - Clayton W. Burress,* 1934, 5¼" d $25.00

Shrine, glass with silver rims with sword, moon, star, and Egyptian face in center, 6" d $30.00

Masonic, *Waldeck Lodge, 75 Anniversary,* silver metal, 5" sq. $15.00

Row 2:

Shrine, white ceramic with figural of fez at back, gold symbols on hat & star in ashtray, 4" h. $30.00

Loyal Order of Moose, cast aluminum, raised moose in center, wide rests for cigars also, 4¾" d, 1930s . . . $15.00

Order of Eastern Star, (women's part of Masons), star emblem center, triangular, Lefton china, 4½" sides . . $ 8.00

Knights of Khorassan, *D.O.K.K.,* cast metal with symbols in center & camels around rim, 6" d. $10.00

Masonic, gold compass & square in center, ceramic with gold design around rim, 5" d, 1963. . . . . $ 8.00

Row 3:

Masonic, glass with blue center, *Excelsior Lodge, 75th Anniversary, 1869–1944,* 4⅛" sq $10.00

Loyal Order of Moose, cast metal diamond, raised moose in center, *75th anniversary, 1901–1976* $14.00

International Organization of Odd Fellows, brass, three rests, 4¼" across, old $20.00

Masonic, glass with lt blue center, gray letters, *Centennial 1857–1957,* 4⅛" sq $15.00

PLATE 102 (left to right)

Row 1:

American Legion, *Grandpromenade-Chicago,* stamped metal, seal in center, 4" d, 1952. . . . . $ 8.00

Knights of Columbus, chrome , figural of K of C emblem painted red, white, blue, 5⅝" d, 1950s $11.00

Eagles 995, center pic of chapter house in relief, 1966, white ceramic, *61st Anniv. 1905–1967,* 7¾" d . . . . $ 7.00

Rotary, *District Conference, Sheboygan, WI,* stainless steel, 5⅞" d, 1957 . . . . $10.00

Rotary International, blue & gray center with cogwheel emblem & name, glass oval, 5" l $10.00

Row 2:

Lions International, copper bottom & rests with logo center, crystal glass insert, 4¼" d. $11.00

Lions International, white plastic, trademark of two lion heads & name in center, 9" d. $10.00

Lions International, yellow & green trademark of two lion heads in center, glass, 3½" sq. . . . . $ 8.00

Rotary International, blue & yellow center with cogwheel emblem & name, glass, 5" d $10.00

PLATE 101

PLATE 102

ASHTRAYS RELATING TO THE HEALTH FIELD

Since there are few ashtrays in this category, collecting them is a challenge. When you find one, such as the arsonic powder advertisement, it makes you think of old-fashioned drugstores. The pestle of the Sharp & Dohme mortar and pestle ashtray is hard to find, regardless of condition. I think this is one of the nicer ones. The ceramic bedpan advertises Abbey Rents, the chain stores. They really rent many types of items, but since some stores handle medical equipment, I included this ashtray here.

PLATE 103 (left to right)
Row 1:
Arsonic Powder, black & yellow picture, bottle in center, *Dr. Mayfield Laboratories,* 5⅝" d $12.00
Wyeth (Drug Co.), name in white, green & white, picture of Hippocrates center, black glass, 4¾" l $10.00
Rexall Drugs, orange center, blue letters, local ad, *Famous For Prescriptions,* 3½" sq . . . . $ 8.00
Pfizer (Drug Co.), picture of calendar months around rise, black plastic, 7¾" d, 1960. . . . . $10.00
Napril, *Marion Labs,* presenting its drug Napril, clear glass, black & white center picture & letters, 3¾" sq.. $ 9.00
Tums, red letters in center, *Always carry TUMS for the Tummy!,* 3½" sq $11.00
Irish Hospitals Sweepstakes, ceramic oval, 5⅛" w $16.00
Central Drugs Anniv., *Prescription Specialists, 65th,* 5⅜" d $13.00

Row 2:
Abbey Rents, bedpan, black pic in center of people using wheelchair & walker, ceramic, 4½" w $15.00
Community Hospital, high rise with white letters, name & local ad, brown plastic, 4¼" d . . . . $ 6.00
Dentistry, gold seal in center, two rests curl up over bottom, Lenox mark, 5⅜" d $18.00
Rexall, *Cousins-Harris Pharmacy,* amber irid glass, 3½" d . . . . $ 8.00
Sharp & Dohme, blue picture of old apothecary on sides of mortar, on rim Charles Lamb's quote –
   "The Good Things Of Life Are---To Us With A Mixture," name on pestle, ceramic, 2⅛" h. $65.00
Lilly (Drug Co.), pic of green & white pill in center, two rests – one for cigs, one for cigars, Ultran, 5" w . . . $ 9.00

ASHTRAYS FOR HOME PRODUCTS

Ashtrays were also made to advertise products found in the home. One of these ashtrays, in Plate 104, contains the figural of the Iron Fireman. This company made furnaces that were popular in the 1930s and 1940s. The furnaces burned coal, which had to be shoveled into the furnace, hence the name and the figural. I have seen two styles of this ashtray; the other one does not have cigarette rests.

Five ashtrays, pictured in Plate 104, have a metal base covered with porcelain enamel — Wagner fry pan, Western Holly, Whirlpool, Hardwick, and Magic Chef. Porcelain enamel gives a protective surface.

PLATE 104 (left to right)
Row 1:
Griswold Quality Ware, cast iron, match pack holder, marked 00, Erie PA. 570, Griswold TM, 6⅝" l $56.00
Western-Holly, pink enamelware, *Gas Ranges,* 6½" d. $25.00
Herbert Coal & Ice, *Columbia, PA,* plastic bucket, 1¾" h. $10.00
Magic Chef, green enamelware, *American Stove Co.,* 4¾" d. $15.00
Iron Fireman, figural for furnace manufacturer, nickel plated, 4½" h, 1930s. $60.00
Whirlpool, gold enamelware, logo in center, 7¾" d. $30.00
Wagner Ware, black cast iron skillet, mark on back with name & #1050, 6⅛" l $22.00
Hardwick, *Speedi-Baker,* enamelware, 5½" d, old $30.00
Wagner Ware, black & red enamelware, mark on back with name & #1050, 6⅛" l $24.00

Row 2:
Reynolds Aluminum, gold aluminum, 4½" sq $12.00
Thermador, ovens & ranges, stainless steel, logo man in relief in cen, 4¾" d $15.00
Maytag, *Gas Ranges,* shape of gas burner, white enamelware & chrome, 6" d. $17.00
Westinghouse Stove Unit, picture of red burner coil, *Red Hot in 30 seconds,* 4¼" sq $12.00
Monarch, ovens & ranges, chrome, logo name in center, 5" d $13.00
Hotpoint, kitchen range, stainless steel, *Select A Heat-Calrod Unit,* 5" d $15.00

PLATE 103

PLATE 104

ASHTRAYS FOR HOME PRODUCTS

The yellow Alexander Smith ashtray, in Plate 105, is very interesting. The Good Housekeeping Guarantee is printed underneath the rug company's name and guarantees that what the company said about its rugs on the ashtray ad is true. Also note the cigarette rests. They were designed so that the cigarette will snuff out at the edge of the rest, instead of falling out while still burning.

The Panasonic Matsushita ashtray is very small and designed to be held in your hand. When opened, the cigarette rest swivels out and there is room for ashes and a cigarette butt. This is one of only a few hand-held advertising ashtrays that I have ever seen.

On the RCA Victor ashtray in the top picture, you will see the dog, Nipper, one of the older advertising characters. The drawing of Nipper originally belonged to Victor. In 1929, RCA purchased Victor and Nipper was used as the trademark for RCA Victor.

In Plate 106, there is a gold-painted metal ashtray with the Dutch Boy trademark in the center. In 1907, the National Lead Co., a group of white lead manufacturers, looked for a common trademark. They chose a Dutch theme because white lead was made from a Dutch process and the Dutch kept their buildings immaculate with white wash. That is how the Dutch Boy advertising character started life in 1907 with the National Lead Co., the forerunner of the Dutch Boy Paints and their logo. See Eagle paint can in Plate 106.

PLATE 105 (left to right)

Row 1:

Monsanto, name on rise, *Wear dated, 1 year guarantee,* ceramic, 5½" sides $10.00

Alexander Smith, rug co., *Guaranteed by Good Housekeeping,* bottom – Safety ashtray, 3⅝" w $14.00

RCA Victor, Nipper ™, *"For Color So Real — You Are There,"* ceramic, 7¾" d, 1978 . . . . $20.00

Nora Radio manufacturing co., picture of radios, white ceramic, 5¼" d, German, 1935. . . . . $ 8.00

Black & Decker, logo in center in relief, *Portable Electric Tools,* aluminum, hexagon, 5" across . . . . $ 9.00

Row 2:

Holophane Co. Illumination Service, frosting on bottom, match holder back rim, 5" l, 1920s $35.00

Panasonic, Matsushita, hand-held metal with enamel top, opens & rest swivels out, 1½" sq $15.00

Anchor Hocking, *75th Anniversary 1905–1980,* shows different trademarks & their dates, box, 5½" d $16.00

Holophane Co, manufacturer of glass lamp shades, two wide rests for cigars & pipes, 5⅞" w, 1920s $20.00

PLATE 106 (left to right)

Row 1:

In-Sink-Erator, nickel-plated metal, *ISE Disposer,* 4½" d, 1½" h. . . . . $ 8.00

Anchor Hocking, amber glass, blue decal in center, picture of glass blower, 64th anniv., 7¾" d $10.00

Pert Napkins, pottery with cigarette holder back rim, some glaze cracks, 3⅝" h, 1956 . . . . $20.00

Row 2:

General Electric, *75th anniversary 1878–1953,* both cigar & cig. rests, 5½" d. $15.00

IBM Personal Computers, white ceramic, picture of Charlie Chaplin-type man in chair in center, 4" d. . . . $13.00

J.C.Penney Co., white ceramic, yellow & black letters, 5¼" d $25.00

Kohler of Kohler, nickel-plated metal, octagon, 5" d, *N.A.M.P. June 26, 1931*. $11.00

Row 3

Rubbermaid, dustpan shape, *1934–1959, 25 anniv.,* 5" w. $20.00

National Lead Company, Doehler Jarvis Division, Dutch Boy trademark in center, 3¼" d, 1920s $22.00

Sears Paint, picture of two cans of paint in center, ceramic, gold edge, 5½" d . . . . $ 8.00

Eagle Paint Can, *Pure White Lead, Old Dutch Process,* metal, painted stripes, 2½" h, early 1900s. $20.00

Polar Ware, enamelware with black letters & picture of bear, 4¾" d, 1928 . . . . $75.00

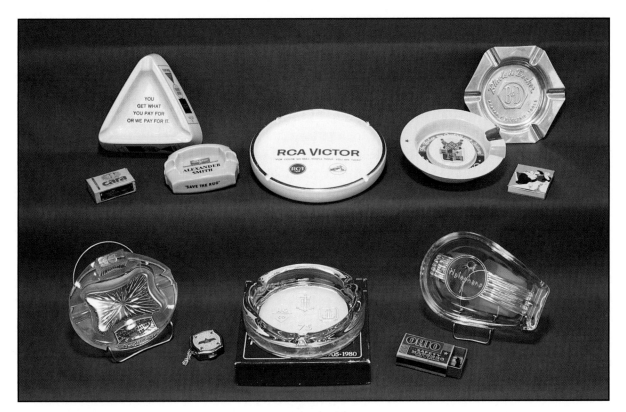

PLATE 105

PLATE 106

ASHTRAYS FOR HOTELS AND MOTELS

In Plate 107, there is a Palmer House ashtray made by Hall China Co., known for its restaurant-type dinnerware lines and teapots. Because of their high-quality china, their ashtrays are usually in good condition. The ashtray for the Radisson Hotel chain, found in Plate 108, has a match holder that exposes the striking surface, common in the 1920s, and a backstamp from the teens to late 1920s. The Palmer House ashtray backstamp is from the 1930s to 1970, but the style is more like 1930s and 1940s.

Many of the ashtrays pictured opposite are from hotels that no longer exist. They are more difficult to find, and should cost more. They are still available, however, and should be purchased only in excellent or prime condition. The ones with decals on the back are more recent.

PLATE 107 (left to right)

Row 1:

Statler Hotel, green ceramic, match holder in center, name in relief near edge, 5⅛" d $12.00

Ritz Carlton, white with gold lion & name in center, 4⅛" d $12.00

Palmer House Hotel, logo in gold, match holder & two cigarette rests, bottom – Chicago,
Hall, 5½" d, 1930s $16.00

American Club, white ceramic, 4⅛" d .... $ 8.00

Statler Hotel, match pack holder on back rim with logo S in front, yellow china by Onondaga, 5⅜" d..... $30.00

Row 2:

YMCA Hotel, *Chicago,* red center, black picture of building & name, 3½" sq $14.00

The Royal Orleans, hotel in New Orleans French Quarter, black center, logo in gold, 4¼" d............. $ 8.00

Broadmoor, hotel Colorado Springs, by Francoma, 5½" d $15.00

Claridge's, silver plate, seal & name in center, 4½" d $15.00

Mayflower, black china, deco shape, name in relief in center, 3¼" l................................ $ 8.00

Hotel Andalucia Palace-Sevilla, Spain, ceramic with brown picture in center, mark Pickman, 4" sq ...... $ 6.00

PLATE 108 (left to right)

Row 1:

Town & Country Motel, cream ceramic with picture of Selden's 1877 green motor wagon in center, 5¼" d.. $ 7.00

Blackhawk Hotels, Indian artifacts in relief in center, ceramic, 5" l................................ $10.00

Radisson Hotel, green ceramic, match holder center, logo in gold, back stamp Hall in gold, 5¼" l, 1920s .. $12.00

Mayfair Regent, *Chicago,* 3" d .... $ 8.00

Hotel Times Square, *In The Center Of N.Y.,* white decal with brown in center, match holder at end, 5⅛" l.. $18.00

Esso Motor Hotel, cream china, black coach light in center with name in red, by Rosenthal, 5⅝" d $15.00

Row 2:

Ambassador East, *Dunfey Classic Hotel, Chicago,* white ceramic, green name in center, 4" d .... $ 7.00

Omni, hotel chain, glass with wine & gold center, thick rim, 4½" d .... $ 5.00

Fontainebleau, *Miami Beach,* blue with white logo in center, by Harker, 5¼" d...................... $ 7.00

Arthur L. Roberts Hotels, black ceramic, 3¼" l .... $ 6.00

Radisson Hotel, black glass, white letters on rise, 4½" d .... $ 8.00

Hilton, hotel chain, logo H impressed in center, glass, ridges on bottom of rise, 4½" d................ $ 7.00

Fairmont Hotels, ceramic, gold & black logo in center, gold edge, 4½" d........................... $ 8.00

PLATE 107

PLATE 108

ASHTRAYS FOR HOTELS AND MOTELS

Motel and beer ashtrays are the easiest to find of all ashtrays. The fun is to find the older of these ashtrays. There are quite a few with different logos, from fancy to more plain. I have shown two each from three different motels, and there are even more from these same motels listed in the price guide section at the end of the book.

Howard Johnson built its first motor lodge in 1954, and in 1966 changed their logo to a stylized building with a spire. Therefore, the ashtray with the lamplighter logo is between 1954 and 1966. See Plate 109.

Also shown, in Plate 109, is a blue glass ashtray from Travelodge. In the early 1950s they formed a small motel chain in California and wanted a mascot. They chose a bear because it was part of the state emblem, and had him sleepwalking in a nightgown. In the 1970s he was modernized.

PLATE 109 (left to right)
Row 1:
Hyatt, *Lodges, Coffee Shoppes,* black center with red letters & outline U.S., smoke glass, 4½" d . . . . $ 6.00
Friendship Inns, *America's Friendliest Hosts,* white center, red letters, 3½" sq. . . . . $ 5.00
Motel 6, logo in center in green and orange, 4¼" sq. . . . . $ 5.00
TraveLodge, blue glass with green center, sleepwalking bear, *Highway Hotels,* 3½" sq, 1950s $15.00
Best Western, black & clear logo, amber glass, *Independent Worldwide Lodging,* 4" d . . . . $ 6.00
Holiday Inn, yellow center with green logo sign, *Nation's Innkeeper,* glass, 4¼" sq. $13.00
Quality Choice, crystal glass, blue logo center, 4" d . . . . $ 5.00
Thunderbird Motor Inns, 5" d . . . . $ 7.00

Row 2:
Comfort Inn, crystal glass with ripple rim, blue & white logo in center, 4½" d . . . . $ 6.00
Ramada Inn, *Welcome Home,* orange letters in center, glass, 4" d. . . . . $ 8.00
Howard Johnson's, Motor Lodges, blue name & lamp lighter in center, 3¾" sq, late 1950s $19.00
Executive Inn, blue center in crystal glass, 3¾" sq. . . . . $ 5.00
Holiday Inn, black ceramic, gold outline of logo sign, *World's Innkeeper,* hard to find, 3½" d. $18.00
Best Western, Best Eastern, amber irid glass, yellow center, hexagon, 3¾" across . . . . $ 8.00
Hampton Inn, blue area in center, name in clear glass, 4⅛" d . . . . $ 6.00
Howard Johnson's, *restaurants, motor lodges,* orange building & name center, 4½" d, 1966–1985. . . . . $ 7.00

ASHTRAYS FOR INDUSTRIAL COMPANIES

This category is a favorite of many collectors because many of the ashtrays have such interesting and unusual figurals. The prices often vary greatly from mall to mall, and some specially desired figurals sell for more than $200.00. Ashtrays as a collectible are a new area, and prices are still seeking acceptable levels with collectors.

The blue General Electric ashtray, in Plate 110, has a motor figural. Late in the 1920s, GE made the first affordable electric refrigerator, and might have used a motor similar to this. After the Depression years, they made washing machines and many industrial products which used motors.

The steam roller figural, also in Row 2, was made for the heavy equipment manufacturer, Galion. Today, the Komatsu Dresser Co. is the parent company, still making heavy equipment but not ashtrays like this.

PLATE 110 (left to right)
Row 1:
U.S. Pump – Western Land Roller Pumps, green ashtray with gray pump figural, 7⅞" x 6¼" $40.00
U.S. Motors Corp., figural of stand-by generator, bronze-plated metal casting, 4⅞" h. $55.00
Stockland Hydro Scoop, cast brass, very heavy, top pivots to dump ashes, 3" x 3" x 4⅜" h $38.00
U.S. Syncrogear, gray motor figural, rests inside ashtray, 7½" x 6½" $34.00

Row 2:
Jaeger Hi-Dump, *ready mix concrete,* cement mixer truck, brass plating, 8" l. $50.00
General Electric, motor figural in dk green, GE logo raised up in center, blue, 5⅜" d $48.00
Galion, heavy equipment, etc., figural steam roller, copper plating, 8" x 6½" $62.00

PLATE 109

PLATE 110

ASHTRAYS FOR INDUSTRIAL COMPANIES

The Detroit Diesel ashtray, in Plate 111, was hard to find in good condition. Perhaps there are more around Detroit. It seems to be a favorite among advertising collectors and they are willing to pay high prices for this ashtray.

In Plate 112, there is a cream plastic ashtray with a metal Cutler-Hammer tag on the front. Evidently, this was also made in a brown and black plastic. I recently saw someone trying to sell it as an Art Deco ashtray, having removed the metal tag. But note the three ridges in the center on the back end of the rectangle. These, plus two small holes left in the front, were a dead give away.

At least two ashtrays can be found for the Robinson Clay Product Co. They are both alike, except the one pictured in Plate 113, on the next page celebrates one hundred years of quality and service, while the one not pictured does not. Of course, the anniversary model brings higher prices. Actually, the company was sold to Clow Corporation in 1969, after one hundred thirteen years of business.

PLATE 111 (left to right)

Row 1:

Henry Kries & Sons, *Steam & Mill Supplies,* cartoon about price cutting, 5½" l.................... $ 9.00

FMC Corporation, *Mining Equipment,* cream ceramic, red letters, 6¾" d........................ $ 8.00

Detroit Diesel, brass over pot metal, both cigarette & cigar rests, very heavy, 5" h $45.00

General Motors, *Electro-Motive Division,* cream ceramic, picture of train, 8⅝" d $11.00

DuPont Nylon, *25 Anniv. 1939–1964,* chrome, 7¼" l................................. $18.00

Row 2:

AMP, electronic connectors, ashtray & lighter set, silver metal, 4¼" d $40.00

General Motors, *Electro-Motive Division,* smoky glass, blue center with picture, 6¾" l............. $ 8.00

Westinghouse, blue & orange center with white letters, heavy glass, 5" d...................... $13.00

PLATE 112 (left to right)

Row 1:

Allen Bradley, black & white plastic in shape of Q, logo *A-B Quality* in small circle on rim, 4½" w $13.00

Cutler-Hammer, *Motor Control,* plastic, Art Deco lines, metal name in black, red, silver, 6" l........... $14.00

Milwaukee Gear Co., picture of building in center, *50th anniversary 1918–1968,* ceramic, 6¾" d .... $ 7.00

Delco, *Dry Charge Batteries,* gray painted metal, black picture & local ad in center, 4" sq .... $ 8.00

Ohio Battery Terminals, with two figurals of battery terminals, letters in relief center, 2½" h $18.00

Row 2:

Allen Bradley, anodized metal in green, *A-B Quality* logo in relief in center, 6⅝" l .... $ 7.00

Sperry Univac (computers), blue & black name in center, ceramic, 4" d........................... $ 8.00

Spray Deflector-A-Pendant Co., chrome with red paint rim, figural of fire sprinkler, 6½" d, 1953 .... $35.00

Jones Metal Products, bedpan shape, name also in relief in center, 3½" l......................... $10.00

Allen Bradley, anodized metal in blue, *A-B Quality* logo in relief in center, 6⅝" l .... $ 7.00

PLATE 111

PLATE 112

ASHTRAYS FOR INDUSTRIAL COMPANIES

In Plate 113, there are three ashtrays for United States Steel, incorporated in 1901. In 1938, Benjamin Fairless became president and pulled United States Steel through the recovery years following the Depression. A new plant was built in Pennsylvania, in 1949, designed to compete with Bethlehem Steel. Finished in 1952, it was named Fairless Works after their president. Pennsbury Potters made this ashtray, celebrating the naming of the plant. They also made the one with the figural of the crucible, which is used to pour molten steel.

In 1986, USS became USX Corp., which in 1991 became USX-Marathon. So any ashtray with USS alone on it would have to date before 1986.

Owens-Illinois was incorporated in 1907. This company is interesting because today Owens-Illinois is the world's largest manufacturer of glass bottles and other glass products such as television tubes. I see that they made their ashtrays of glass, too.

PLATE 113 (left to right)
Row 1:
Kurth Malting Co., brown metal, plastic plunger opens space to drop ashes, 5" d $17.00
Hartland-Verona Gravel Co., heavy manufacturing equipment in relief on rise, silver color,
    grid across top, 4¼" d .... $ 9.00
Fairless Works (USS), picture center in relief of molten steel being poured, one rest, by Pennsbury, 7" l.. $19.00
Robinson Clay Product Co., *Akron, Ohio, 100 years, 1856 to 1956,* by Roseville, 4½" d $25.00
U.S. Steel, *Open House - Boston,* figure of crucible for molten steel, by Pennsbury, 4¼" h............. $50.00

Row 2:
Hanna Coal, Northwestern, red name & map in center, 4⅛" sq .... $ 8.00
W.H. Pipkorn Co., glass over red paint center, silver metal, figural thermometer still accurate, 4" h, old .. $45.00
United States Steel, stainless steel, etched name & initial USS logo in center, 4⅜" sq................. $13.00
Owens-Illinois (glass manufacturer), name and logo in center in black, smoke glass, 4½" sq............ $ 8.00

PLATE 114 (left to right)
Row 1:
Western Rubber Co., *Products For Industrial Trade,* painted hardened rubber compound, 6" $10.00
Grinnell Spray Sprinkler, *founded 1850,* fire heat breaks liquid in vial, chrome, 5½" d............... $60.00
Twin Disk Clutch Co., white name on rim, black painted iron, 6⅝" d............................. $ 9.00
Combustion Engineering, figural of heat exchanger tube section, chrome, 5¾" d...................... $18.00
Vactor Jet Rodder, *Peabody Myers,* picture of sewer cleaning vacuum truck, ceramic, 6½" d........... $ 9.00

Row 2:
Bradley Washfountain, glass liner over cement composite used for wash area, 4" h.................... $65.00
Allegheny Ludlum Steel, *Forging & Casting Div.,* plated steel, four rests, two snufferettes, 5" d $12.00
South Bend Lathe Works, gold, red & black logo in center, glass, 5⅞" sq........................... $ 8.00
Koehring Heavy Duty, match holder at side, top pivots to dump ashes, painted metal, about 1925, 2½" h.. $15.00

PLATE 113

PLATE 114

ASHTRAYS FOR RESTAURANTS

The first Howard Johnson Ice Cream Shop & Restaurant opened in 1925, and the second followed in 1929. Their ashtray, in Plate 115, shows one of their first trademarks, Simple Simon & the Pieman in orange. This trademark was not used after 1936, and now this ashtray is hard to find.

The Marc's Big Boy Restaurant was part of a chain started in California in the late 1930s as Bob's Big Boy. The other franchises continued to use the chubby boy with checkerboard overalls, pompadour hairdo, and big hamburger as an advertising character. See Plate 115.

The Pizza Hut, founded in 1958, shows Pizza Hut Pete on one of their ashtrays. He was an early character trademark used on their ashtrays in the 1960s. This advertising character is pictured in Plate 115.

In Plate 115, Coon Chicken Inn, with its caricature of a black face, is a very collectible ashtray. The chain opened in 1924, mainly in Washington, Oregon, and Utah. It went out of business in 1957.

The Original Brown Derby ashtray, in Plate 116, is from the famous restaurant on Wilshire Blvd. in Los Angeles. After being in business for 56 years, they closed their doors in 1985.

PLATE 115 (left to right)
Row 1:
International House of Pancakes, amber glass, brown letters in center, 3½" sq . . . . $ 7.00
Burger King, logo of king with crown, name in center in red, glass, 4½" d, about the 1970s . . . . $ 8.00
Wendy's, black letters, *Wendy's Old Fashioned Hamburgers,* crystal glass, 4" d . . . . $ 7.00
IHOP, logo/restaurant & sign holder, *International House of Pancakes,* blue glass, 3¼" sq $10.00
McDonald's, cream ceramic, golden arches logo in center with name superimposed in black, 6⅝" d $20.00
Arby's, yellow center with brown hat logo, *Arby's Roast Beef Sandwich is Delicious,* triangle, 3⅜" side . . . . . . $ 8.00
Marc's Big Boy, picture of mascot with big hamburger, smoke glass, 4" d $15.00
Big Boy, crystal glass, brown center, picture of mascot, 3½" sq $12.00
Shakey's Pizza Parlor, red picture of old fashioned men with mustaches in center, glass, 4¼" d $14.00
Denny's, gold decal center, red letters, *Denny's Fine Foods Satisfies – 24 hr's day,* amber glass, 3½" sq . . . . . . $ 7.00

Row 2:
Pizza Hut, red letters & Pizza Hut Pete logo, *Quality Reigns Supreme,* 4" sq, 1960s $14.00
TGI Friday's, crystal glass, logo in center, 4¼" sq $10.00
McDonald's, brass plate over metal, arches & name in relief in center, one of their older ashtrays, 4" sq $20.00
Pizza Hut, current logo centered on red roof with black letters, 5" d . . . . $ 6.00
Country Kitchen, center picture of farm boy with big sandwich in red, yellow & brown, 4¾" sq . . . . $ 7.00
Howard Johnson Ice Cream Shops & Restaurants, orange name & Simple Simon logo, 4⅛" sq, early 1930s . . $35.00

PLATE 116 (left to right)
Row 1:
Stork Club, beige ceramic, blue letters & stork, 7¼" d $30.00
Karl Ratzsch's Milwaukee, brown letters & glass in center, gold edge, ceramic, 4½" d $10.00
Coon Chicken Inn, smoke glass, black face with red hat in center, dk blue letters, 4" d, prior to 1957 . . . . $45.00
Al Capone, Gaslight Club, black plastic white letters, 4¾" d $13.00
Cheers, *Boston,* white decal with black letters, 4½" d $15.00
Bookbinder's, picture center of orange & black restaurant & horse drawn carriage, white ceramic, 4" x 3" l . . . $ 5.00
Buchow's NYC, figural of beer stein in center, base cream ceramic, blue rim & rise, 7" d $30.00

Row 2:
Harry's Bar Venice (famous bar in Italy), peach pottery, bartender in center, 6½" l, current $15.00
Sardi's, crystal glass, wine colored comedy & tragedy masks and name, 3¾" d $15.00
Dietze's Bavarian Wurst-House, colorful center of flowers & dancers, by Waldershof, 6⅝" d $15.00
Brown Derby The Original, brown picture of restaurant & letters in center, glass, 4" d $18.00
Toots Shor, wine ceramic, gold edging and name, 2¼" h $14.00

PLATE 115

PLATE 116

ASHTRAYS FOR TOBACCO PRODUCTS

American Brands and R.J. Reynolds tobacco companies started their businesses about the end of the nineteenth century. Liggett & Myers was a spin off from American Brands in 1911. Reynolds successfully launched Camel cigarettes with its Camel trademark in 1913. American Bands answered with Lucky Strike, Liggett & Myers with Chesterfields. All three brands were dominant in the field, but by 1935, Camel was the leader.

The Joe Camel ashtrays are recent designs, and he has became a popular advertising character. They may become very collectible in the next decade, and now is a good time buy. If all cigarette advertising becomes prohibited, even this type of ashtray will be obsolete.

The Abdulla Cigarette was made in England, using Egyptian blend tobacco, in the early twentieth century. Fatima, a popular Turkish blend cigarette produced by Liggett & Myers, was their answer to America's desire for foreign blend tobacco. The cigarette was popular in the teens. Now the ashtray is very collectible but difficult to find in good condition because of its age and use.

PLATE 117 (left to right)

Row 1:

Joe Camel, Joe Camel & friend in car, cobalt glass, turn over for back scene through window, 6" w $30.00
Joe Camel Lights, Joe Camel playing billiards, plastic, 7⅜" l, early 1990s. $11.00
Camel, polished gray marble with name on rise in gold, 6" d $25.00
Camel, pocket ashtray in metal with snap-out rest, also outside carton, 2¼" x 1½" $35.00
Camel, half circle shape of cobalt glass, name in yellow with green leaves in center, 8" l $31.00

Row 2:

Camel, crystal glass, blue camel & name, 3⅜" side . . . . $ 8.00
Joe Camel, *Smokin' Joe's Racing,* white ceramic, letters gold, 5" d $15.00
Camel, silver tin, camel in relief in center, *Camel – A Real – Cigarette* in relief on rim, 3½" d . . . . $ 5.00
Camel, *Special Lights,* cobalt diamond shape glass; name, palm trees & small camel in center, 4½" w $15.00
Camel, gold tin, *Camels Are Mild,* camel in relief in center, 3¾" d . . . . $ 8.00
Joe Camel, *Joe's Garage* logo in center, one rest for cigars, one for cigarettes, smoke glass, 3¼" x 5" $14.00
Camel, yellow plastic, eight rests, blue letters, 4" d $12.00
Joe Camel, *Tell 'em Joe Sent You,* letters in wine, 3⅜" side, 1992 . . . . $10.00

PLATE 118 (left to right)

Row 1:

Winston Filter Cigarettes, white name repeated on rise, pink anodized alum, 5¼" d . . . . $ 6.00
White Owl, cigars, white owl logo in center with cigar on blue background, 3½" sq $13.00
Cavalier, *Flavor, Mildness,* bronze tin, 3⅝" d . . . . $ 8.00
Benson & Hedges 100's, *Amer's Favorite Cigarette Break,* gold letters, unique shape, 7¼" l . . . . $ 7.00
Lucky Strike, crystal glass with white decal & pack of cigarettes picture, 3½" d $18.00
Salem, *Menthol Fresh,* Salem cigarette pack in relief center, silver tin, 3½" d . . . . $ 5.00
Lark, white ceramic, hi-rise, picture & letters in red, 2¼" h $10.00

Row 2:

Abdulla Cigarettes, name, sign with Bond St. (London) & Turkish-type soldiers in center, 1920s . . . . $ 65.00
Viceroy, *Smoke Viceroy for that Real Tobacco Taste,* blue letters, 5¼" d, 1940s . . . . $ 10.00
Fatima, *Turkish Blend Cigarettes,* large matchbox holder, some glaze cracks, Liggett & Myers Co., old . . . $110.00
Winston, impressed name in center might have been red at one time, aluminum, 8½" l . . . . $ 9.00
Zuban, Germany, white ceramic picture & name in red & black, 6" l, old . . . . $ 35.00
Lucky Strike, small cigarette box with snap-out rest on inside, with outer carton, 2⅝" l . . . . $ 25.00
Viceroy, gold ceramic, words on rim & name in center in relief, 5½" d . . . . $ 9.00
Player's, *Please,* heavy polished silver metal, 4½" d . . . . $ 10.00
Benson & Hedges, gold, red & blue logo in center with black name, ceramic, 4" d . . . . $ 5.00

PLATE 117

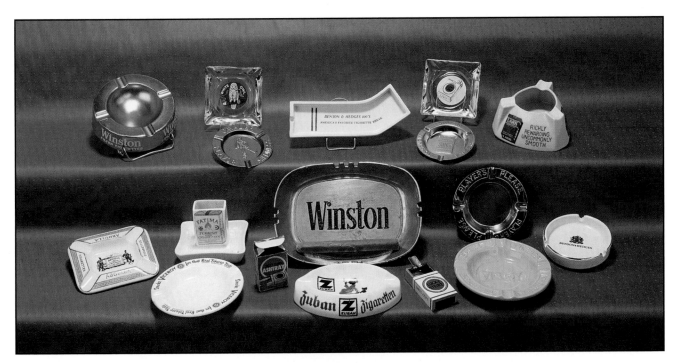

PLATE 118

ASHTRAYS FOR TOBACCO PRODUCTS

Most of the ashtrays, in Plate 119, are advertising more recent cigarette brands. The Kools' penguins were first used in 1933, and in 1940, they were given gender, named Willie and Nellie. The penguins were retired in the late 1950s. This enables you to narrow the date of the ashtray to a twenty-five year period.

R.J. Reynolds presented Winston cigarettes in 1954 to introduce filter tips to the industry. Note the eye-catching anodized pink ashtray carrying the new advertisement, in Plate 118 on the previous page.

Philip Morris introduced Marlboro about the same time, in the mid-1950s, and Marlboro struggled through the 1960s. Now it enjoys its leadership thanks to the enduring advertising appeal of the Marlboro Man. Their ashtrays are hard to find. See a small plastic one in Plate 119.

Plate 119 (left to right)

Row 1:

L&M, *Quality Cigarettes,* tri shape with high rise, picture of cigarette pkg on each side, tri, 5" sides...... $11.00
Prince Albert, letters in center in relief, gold tin, painted red bottom, 3⅝" d......................... $ 5.00
Navy Cut Cigarettes, lg metal tin with pictures in blue & cream, top has many rests, 5½" d............. $15.00
R.J. Reynolds Tobacco Co., *100th Anniversary,* picture of man, tobacco leaf & barn in relief, 3½", 1975 .. $16.00
Chesterfield, *Chesterfield Filter* on rise on back side & picture of red pack, 6¾" d at base.............. $24.00

Row 2:

Marlboro, name in white letters repeated on rise, red plastic, 3¾" d................................... $12.00
Kools, ceramic, green letters on rim, newer than the ashtray with the penguins, 5" d.................. $10.00
Old Gold, brass, eagle & shield in relief in center, name in relief on rim, 5½" d....................... $25.00
Dunhill, *London–Paris–New York,* black with wine sides, four rubber pads bottom, Wade, 4¾" sq....... $12.00
Chesterfield, red tin, white picture of cigarette pack in center, 4½" d................................ $10.00
Kools, *Smoke Kools for the Clean Kool taste,* penguins trademark, grayish milk glass, 5¼" d, prior 1960 .. $20.00
Chesterfield, *They Satisfy* & name in red & blue letters on rise, white ceramic tri, 4¼" side $22.00

ASHTRAYS FOR AIRLINES

British Air incorporated in 1924. They started out mainly with service across the English Channel and soon added India to their destinations. In 1974, they merged with BEA, and were named British Airways. The ashtray in the picture is British Air and was made before 1974.

Pan Am incorporated in 1927 and became one of the strongest airplane companies. They had financial problems, and are no longer flying.

United Airlines incorporated in 1931 and became one of the world's largest airline corporations. The stewardesses they hired in the beginning were to allay the passengers' fear of flying, which was very prevalent in the early days.

PLATE 120 (left to right)

Row 1:

Figural of plane, two engine propellers, nice, not advertising, chrome, 4¼" h $135.00
Grumman American, blue letters in center, ceramic, 4" d .... $ 20.00
Delta Air Lines, gold edge, by Mayer China, 3¾" d .... $ 30.00
United, *Fly the friendly skies of United,* silver colored metal, blue anodized center, 4⅜" d .... $ 20.00
BOAC, *British Air,* blue anodized metal, 5" d... $ 30.00
General Dynamics Convair 440, Metropolitan, chrome figural, 6" h $155.00

Row 2:

BOAC, British Air, blue ceramic, Copeland Spode, 5¾" d..................................... $50.00
TWA, *Bombay to San Francisco,* brass shoe, 3⅜" l.. $25.00
Air France, picture of world and all cities Air France flies to, glass, 7" sq $25.00
Pan Am, milk glass, 4⅜" d $30.00
Lufthansa, cobalt glass, name in gold on rise, 4½" sq....................................... $40.00

PLATE 119

PLATE 120

ASHTRAYS FOR CRUISE SHIPS

The United States Lines has at least sixteen passenger ships, including *The President Arthur,* that were seized by the government from Germany in early 1917. Nine of her ships are named after past American presidents.

The *Finntrader* ashtray, in Plate 121, is very nice to have because it is from her maiden voyage in 1950. This ashtray, as well as most others, was made in the home country of the ship, in this case Finland.

Cunard Line, the largest line of passenger ships with at least fifty-five, is British. The *Queen Mary* and *Queen Elizabeth I* and *II* are among the better known. *Queen Mary's* maiden voyage was in May 1936, Among the supplies taken on for this voyage were 25,000 packages of cigarettes.

Queen Elizabeth I was not completed until the outbreak of World War II. She had a dramatic and secret maiden voyage, and was fitted-out as a troop transport when that voyage was over. For a long time she was the world's largest ship. *Queen Elizabeth II* was completed in 1969, nine years after the retirement of *Queen Elizabeth I* and *Queen Mary.* The silver *Queen Elizabeth* ashtray, in the bottom row in Plate 122, was made from blue butterfly wings.

PLATE 121 (left to right)

Row 1:

Swedish American Line, logo of three small crowns around sides, hi-rise, gold trim, 4¾" sides $15.00

American President Lines, crystal glass, decal with eagle and name, triangle, 3⅜" side . . . . $ 7.00

Finntrader, Finnish, from maiden voyage in 1950, gray ceramic, gold ship & pictures, 5¾" d $20.00

Holland American Line, cream ceramic with green, cream & black ship in center, by Gouda, 4" d $15.00

Maersk Line, *Far East Service,* blue ceramic, logo in front in black, 3⅞" sq $15.00

Row 2:

United States Lines, clear glass with blue logo eagle & name in center, 5" l $12.00

Americana, *Florida,* cruise ship, cream ceramic, picture of globe in center, 5¼" d . . . . $ 6.00

Swedish American Line, logo of three small crowns in center, bottom frosted, 2⅞" sq $11.00

Princess Cruises, glass with blue picture of girl's head & letters, 3¾" d . . . . $ 7.00

PLATE 122 (left to right)

Row 1:

Europa Sud-Centro America, pale gold color metal, letters & picture etched in center, 4½" d . . . . $ 8.00

R.M.S. *Queen Mary,* brass, enameled flags in center, 3¼" sq $35.00

Cunard Line, black plastic , five rests, script name in relief in center, 5⅞" d $25.00

French Line, Cie Gle Transatlantique, green milk glass, logo in right corner, 3¼" x 2⅝" $26.00

Cunard *White Star,* brown plastic, five rests, name in relief in center, 4" d $23.00

R.M.S. *Queen Mary,* ceramic with blue outline ship in center, 4⅛" d $13.00

Row 2:

Matson Lines, *Lurine, Monterey, Mariposa,* blue center with King of Sea picture, triangle, 3¼" sides $13.00

R.M.S. *Queen Elizabeth,* silver metal with center picture of ship made from butterfly wings, 3" d $15.00

Queen Elizabeth II, white ceramic, picture in center of red, blue & black ship, 6" l $15.00

Queen Mary, Long Beach, Ca., glass ship's wheel with picture of ship in the center, 4⅜" d $12.00

Matson Lines, *S.S. Lurine,* clear glass, white center, red flag, triangle, 3¼" sides $12.00

PLATE 121

PLATE 122

ASHTRAYS FOR AUTOMOTIVE INDUSTRIES

Henry Ford began experimenting with gasoline engines in 1892. Soon, in 1908, he produced the first Model T, and the rest is automobile history. By 1919, Ford had incorporated and became the second largest manufacturer of cars and trucks in the world.

In 1899, R.E. Olds helped found the Olds Motor Works and is considered by many to be the founder of the automobile industry. General Motors Company was started in 1908 by William Durant. It was incorporated in 1916, and today it is the largest producer of automobiles and trucks. In 1926, General Motors purchased the Oakland Motor Co. and in 1932, renamed it Pontiac. Note the ashtray below with the name Oakland on it, in Plate 123.

Daimler-Benz incorporated in 1926. In their conservative method, they have become known for quality, and today they are the largest commercial truck manufacturer.

One car company was started by a Japanese businessman who came to America and visited automobile production plants. When he returned to Japan, he established an auto division in his father's loom industry. It was from this beginning that Toyota emerged.

PLATE 123 (left to right)

Row 1:

Toyota for Precedent, *Annual Dealer Meeting,* cream ceramic, 6¾" d, 1970 . . . . $10.00

Oakland, *Product of General Motors,* copper, eagle & letters emblem in center, 3½" w $25.00

Universal Battery, *World's Finest Battery,* figural in center, silver coating over metal, 3¾" h, very old $50.00

General Motors, *Who Serves Progress, Serves America,* silver color over metal, 4" d, 1933 . . . . $88.00

Porsche, white ceramic with shirt in relief showing their logo, 6¼" d $15.00

Row 2:

Buick Motor Division, *Metal Fabrication Plant,* aluminum, about 5" sq $12.00

Oldsmobile, local ad in center, glass with white center & blue letters, 3" d $10.00

Champion Spark Plug, white figural in center of black ceramic ashtray, 5⅛" d $25.00

Buick, *Buick's the Buy,* local ad in center, glass, 3¾" sq. $10.00

General Motors, Fisher Body, chrome, *Of Excellence,* five rests, 4⅞" d $15.00

PLATE 124 (left to right)

Row 1:

AAA, *Fiftieth Anniversary,* cream ceramic, picture of 1902 car in center, 3⅝" sq, 1952 . . . . $12.00

Cadillac, *Motor Car Division,* stainless steel, letters & crown logo embossed in center, 6⅝" d. $35.00

Ford, silver tin, Ford emblem in center, 3½" d . . . . $ 8.00

Chicago Motor Club, *Honor Member,* figural logo in center, brass, 5¾" d, late 1930s $45.00

Nash, crystal glass, blue decal with white letters, local ad, triangle, 3¼" side $20.00

Mercedes Benz, dk green ceramic, old German, probably local ad, 6¼" d, late 1940s. $28.00

Ford, cream ceramic, blue logo name in center, gold edge, 3⅝" d. $11.00

Row 2:

Chrysler Belvidere Assembly, blue painted metal, silver logo emblem raised in center, 5" d $18.00

Ford, local ad, cream ceramic, colored logo in center, triangle, 4¼" sides . . . . $ 9.00

Ford, cream ceramic, blue logo name in center, gold edge, 6¾" d. $14.00

Chevrolet, silver tin, *50th anniv, 1911–1961,* 4¼" sq $12.00

Ford, *Open House Pressed Steel Plant,* figural car shape in center, 5¼" d, 1950 . . . . $55.00

PLATE 123

PLATE 124

ASHTRAYS FOR FUEL COMPANIES

Mobil, incorporated in 1931 as Socony-Vacuum Corp., became the second largest oil company after several mergers. In 1966, Socony Mobil Oil Co. changed its name to Mobil Oil Corp., using "Mobil" as its tradename. They retired the flying red horse in favor of a streamlined "Mobil" with a bright red "O."

Citgo incorporated in 1910 as Cities Service Co., and was one of the largest oil companies at that time. In 1983, they changed their name to Citgo. The ashtray pictured below, in Plate 125, was made before 1983.

Phillips 66 incorporated in 1917, and was one of the first companies to sell natural gas. The story about their name comes from a road test for their gasoline. One of the testers said they were "going like 60." The other tester said, "60 nothing, we're doing 66." This test took place near Highway 66 in Tulsa, Oklahoma. Consequently, they named their product "Phillips 66."

PLATE 125 (left to right)

Row 1:

Exxon, cream ceramic, *Image Program 1975,* picture of tiger, 6¾" d $20.00

Sinclair, figural of "Dino," the dinosaur logo, chrome, 7⅜" l, 1960s $50.00

Marathon Gasoline, *Sign of Great New Gasolines,* picture of man playing golf, metal, 4¾" x 3¾" $15.00

Quaker State, cream ceramic, green letters, red logo, 6¾" d $25.00

Row 2:

Texaco, *Gasoline & Alcohol Don't Mix,* glass, white decal, red letters & picture, 3¾" sq $15.00

Cities Service, local ad, green porcelain enamel, triangular, before 1983 . . . . $20.00

Phillips 66, *U.P. Oil Company,* black glass, gold letters, 4⅝" d $15.00

Mobil, blue porcelain enamel, flying horse logo in red, 3¼" l, prior to 1966 . . . . $70.00

Standard Oil, glass with white decal, red & black letters, picture of logo crown, 3" sq $20.00

Gulf, clear glass with orange center and blue name, 3½" sq $15.00

ASHTRAYS FOR RAILROADS

Railroads were built first in England, followed in the United States in 1827, with the first Baltimore & Ohio Railroad. The Chesapeake & Ohio began in Louisiana in 1836, and by 1852, the B&O reached the Ohio River at Wheeling, West Virginia. With few exceptions, the early railroads were mostly local in route. As travel grew, dining cars were added. Early railroad paraphernalia such as dishes, and so forth, are very collectible today, and sometimes ashtrays can by found along with them.

PLATE 126 (left to right)

Row 1:

CSX, glass, *Transportation,* blue letters, 4¼" sq . . . . $ 10.00

U.P.R.R. Co., Upper Peninsula Railroad Co., *Safety First,* brown plastic, 3¼" sq . . . . $ 20.00

Pennsylvania Railroad Family Club, cream ceramic, picture in black, 7⅛" sq . . . . $ 20.00

Chesapeake and Ohio, cream ceramic, picture of George Washington in black, match pack holder, 7⅜" l . . $135.00

Western Pacific, black plastic base with white letters, chrome "no-fume" top, 3⅝" h . . . . $ 32.00

South Shore Line, clear glass, red decal bottom, yellow letters, 4¼" sq . . . . $ 10.00

Row 2:

Union Pacific Railroad, *Sun Valley, Idaho, Utah Parks, Co.,* blue glass, red letters, 4¼" d $18.00

Erie, crystal glass, *100th Anniversary, 1851–1951,* yellow & black letters, 3½" sq $15.00

Canadian National, crystal glass, octagon, CN logo in center, 5⅜" l $10.00

Santa Fe, *Super Chief, Turquoise Room,* blue glass with white & black decor, 4¾" l $20.00

Union Pacific Railroad, blue glass with red, white & blue shield logo in bottom, 4¼" d $20.00

PLATE 125

PLATE 126

ASHTRAYS FOR RAILROADS

In 1865, George Pullman added the first improved sleeping car, which he named for himself. Before too long, railroads entered an elegant period for passenger travel with elegant appointments and food. The figural of the Pennsylvania R.R. is the only good R.R. figural I've ever seen, and that one only once.

PLATE 127 (left to right)

Row 1:

Clinchfield R.R., *Between the Central West & South East,* cream ceramic, 5½" d, old $28.00
Pennsylvania R.R., Merry Xmas to Engineering Dept., 3¾" d, 1967 .... $18.00
Union Pacific R.R., black glass with rests in center, letters & shield logo on rise in gold, 6" l. $20.00
Pullman, *More than 80 yrs the greatest name in passenger transportation,* black tin, 4" d, about 1945 ... $20.00
Pennsylvania R.R., gray figural of train engine, cream ceramic ashtray, 5½" l. $80.00

Row 2:

Penn Central R.R., silver tin, letters emblem in center, 3½" d .... $ 5.00
Northern Pacific R.R., *Yellowstone Park Line,* clear glass, red & black logo in center, 3½" sq $15.00
Atlantic Coast Line R.R., clear glass, lavender decal bottom, white letters, 3½" sq $12.00
Frisco, *5,000 miles in 9 states,* 3½" sq. $13.00
Detroit, Toledo, Ironton, Ann Arbor R.R., cream ceramic, black letters in center, red & blue lines, 7⅝" d. . $10.00
B & O, clear glass, blue name in center, 3½" sq $30.00
Santa Fe R.R., clear glass with white letters on cross in bottom, 3½" sq $25.00
Gulf, Mobile, & Ohio R.R., cardboard, silver color, wine letters in edging, 3¾" x 2⅞" .... $ 8.00
Penn Central, glass, green logo in center, 4½" d. $11.00

ASHTRAYS FOR TRUCK & BUS COMPANIES

In 1900, the Mack brothers built the first successful bus in America. They converted it to a truck in 1908, continuing to build other heavy duty trucks and buses. In 1911, they built the leading gasoline truck in U.S.

There is a legend that during WWI, a British officer, needing a truck to free an artillery piece mired in mud, yelled to bring that bulldog over. Mack truck management liked the term, and by 1932, were putting bulldog emblems on their trucks. In the 1960s, a square-shouldered, grimly determined bulldog was adopted as their logo.

Oshkosh Truck incorporated in 1919, specializing in truck and transport equipment. Their trucks had four-wheel drive which set them apart. In 1939, they introduced a W series truck for the military.

United Parcel Service is much older than I realized, incorporated in 1907. They are the world's largest package delivery company in terms of sales. In 1927, they began air delivery, and added overnight express in 1980. In 1987, they were the most profitable U.S. package delivery company.

PLATE 128 (left to right)

Row 1:

Mack Truck, gold Mack figural is 4" l, ashtray chrome, 7" d, 1970 .... $38.00
Yellow Cab, silver color metal, letters & picture of old phone incised, *dial 5-8844,* 4¾" d, old $50.00
Mack Buses & Trucks, pictures in center of old style buses & trucks, 6¾" d $35.00
Mack Truck, silver, small Mack figural is 2½" l, chrome ashtray is 5⅝" d, 1950 .... $25.00
UPS, amber glass, name & package in off white, 3½" sq. $10.00
Mack Truck, silver Mack figural is 4" l, chrome ashtray is 7" d. $28.00

Row 2:

Ringsby United Transcontinental, amber glass, orange center with black letters, 6" sq. $10.00
UPS, *delivery service 1907–1977,* pictures of trucks used over 70 yrs., glass, 7½" d. $12.00
Oshkosh Truck, copper-plated ashtray, figural of truck on back rim, ashtray 8" x 6⅜" $75.00
Mack Truck, stainless steel ashtray with Mack outline in relief center, 5¾" d. $20.00
Greyhound, salesman's sample, blue & gray letters and dog in center with two rests, 5¾" w $20.00
Mack Truck, nickel coated metal with bulldog & name embossed in center, 6" sq $40.00

PLATE 127

PLATE 128

ASHTRAYS FOR TIRE MANUFACTURERS

Long before cars came on the market, hard rubber tires were made for carriages and bicycles. Scottish and English inventors led the way in the mid 1800s. Although Charles Goodyear developed vulcanization in 1844, a very important step, he was not successful in developing a tire-producing company.

Kelly Springfield, incorporated in 1894, was the first company to develop and manufacture solid rubber tires for carriages and the early autos. John Dunlop, a Scottish veterinarian, developed pneumatic tires for his son's tricycle in 1888. These eventually appeared on cars in 1895 both in Europe and the United States.

With the growth of passenger cars prior to World War I, many tire companies appeared on the market. Among these were B.F. Goodrich in 1870, Michelin in 1889, Goodyear in 1898, Kelly Springfield as Consolidated Rubber Tire Co. in 1894, and Firestone in 1900, just to name a few. Holyoke, Hood Arrow, Miller, Mohawk, Vogue, and Pennsylvania are a few of the many companies that no longer exist and produce tires under their own names.

Tire ashtrays are a great collectible because they have been on the antique market for some time. There seems to be a growing demand for them now.

PLATE 129 (left to right)

Row 1:

Firestone, *H.D., high speed,* amber glass insert, embossed *Century of Progress Chicago 1934,*
two extended rests, 5⅝" d $90.00

Firestone, red & black plastic insert with three extended rests, 6" d $18.00

Firestone, *Heavy Duty, 6.00–18, gum dipped,* green, clear insert with embossed *Century of Progress
Chicago 1934,* 4" d $80.00

Firestone, *Gum Dipped Balloon, 32 x 6, H.D.,* amber glass insert with two rests & embossed "f," 6" d $65.00

Firestone, *Champion, Safety-Lock Cord,* gum dipped, clear glass insert with embossed "f" & pledge, 6" d . . $80.00

Row 2:

Firestone, *Steel Belted Radial 721,* glass insert with red & white logo name, 6" d $25.00

Firestone, *Tractor, All Traction Field & Road, Shock Fortified, Gum Dipped,* glass insert, 6⅜" d $25.00

Firestone, *Steel Radial 500,* clear glass insert with white decal *The Spirit of 76,* 5¾" d $30.00

PLATE 130 (left to right)

Row 1:

Goodrich Silvertown, *Golden Ply 600–16 4 ply,* amber glass insert, 6⅛" d $85.00

Goodrich Silvertown, *Safest Tire Ever Built,* gray & blue Akro Agate insert with embossed name, 6½" d . . $50.00

Seiberling, *Patrician De Luxe 4 ply,* green glass insert with cream decal on bottom with local ad, 3½" d . . $45.00

Seiberling, *Sealed-Aire, 760–15,* clear glass insert, 5⅞" d $35.00

Row 2:

Goodrich Silvertown, *Lifesaver Radial HR 70–15,* clear glass insert, 6" d $25.00

Goodrich Silvertown, commemorative with box, red, white & blue glass insert, *1776–1976,* 6¼" d $35.00

Seiberling, *All-Tread,* solid, clear glass insert, 6⅝" d $45.00

Seiberling, *Safe Aire 760–15,* clear glass insert, 6" d $35.00

PLATE 129

PLATE 130

ASHTRAYS FOR TIRE MANUFACTURERS

Michelin launched pneumatic tires for bicycles and carriages only, in 1894, and later made the first radial tire. Not until the turn of the century did Goodrich make the first pneumatic tires for cars. In 1910, they made the first cord tire. During World War II, they were known for their important synthetic rubber work. General Tire Co. made the first oversized tires, known as the General Jumbo, in 1920.

As with other companies, many tire companies merged or were bought out. Bridgestone, a Japanese firm incorporated in 1931, bought Firestone and Seiberling. B.F. Goodrich Co. merged with Uniroyal in 1986, and they were both bought by Michelin in the early 1990s. Pirelli in Italy bought Armstrong. The five big tire companies today are Michelin, Bridgestone, Goodyear (the only wholly American owned company), Sumietome, and Pirelli.

The Michelin Man and the Goodyear blimp are two well-known advertising logos. The Michelin man is old, appearing in the early 1900s. I have tried to show these, as well as some pictures of the colorful logos related to the tire companies.

Jeff McVey has written *The Tire Ashtray Collector's Guide,* listing all their features as well as their prices. This has been a helpful cross-check for my survey of market prices.

PLATE 131 (left to right)

Row 1:
Goodyear, *American Eagle Radial, Flexten,* clear insert, white decal with name & eagle, 5¾" d . . . . $ 20.00
General, *Steelex Radial,* glass insert, black letters *"goes a long way to make friends,"* 6½" d . . . . $ 20.00
Bridgestone, *D-Lug, Tubeless,* clear glass insert with logo name in center, 8¾" d, 3" h . . . . $ 30.00
Goodyear, *Aquatred,* clear glass insert with blue decal, 5¾" d, fairly new . . . . $ 20.00
Goodyear, *Hi-Miler Cross-Rib, nylon,* clear glass insert with logo name in blue letters, 6¼" d . . . . $ 40.00

Row 2:
General, *Streamline Jumbo,* green glass insert with *"goes a long way to make friends"* in bottom, 5" . . . . $ 65.00
Goodyear, *Balloon All Weather 6.00-21,* green glass insert with six nut disc wheel, 5½" d . . . . $ 80.00
Goodyear, *Custom Power Cushion Polyglass, Belted,* clear glass insert, 3⅝" d . . . . $ 25.00
Goodyear, *Air Wheel made with Supertwist Cord, all weather, 6.50–16,* green glass insert, 5⅝" d . . . . $ 50.00
General, *Heavy Duty Cushion, 40–12,* green glass insert with match holder, two snuffs, one rest,
   name in bottom, 4⅝" d $125.00

PLATE 132 (left to right)

Row 1:
Mohawk, *Akron, O.,* glass insert with yellow bottom & local ad from Urbana, IL, 5⅜" d, 1930s . . . . $ 45.00
Kelly Springfield, *Voyager, Aramid Belted Radial,* clear insert with green decal, 6" d . . . . $ 20.00
Rare, Pennsylvania Rubber Co., *Vacuum Cup Cord,* all blue glass, match holder back,
   Non Skid in center, 4" d $200.00
Vogue Tyre, *Custom Built, Steel Belted,* white tire, black plastic insert with logo of lions in center, 6" d . . $ 35.00
Cooper Tire & Rubber Company, clear glass, yellow letters, 3½" sq . . . . $ 20.00
Armstrong Rhino-Flex, *Miracle SD,* name on tire in gold, glass insert with picture of rhino & name, 6" d . . $ 35.00
Pennsylvania Tires, pink glass insert, 5¼" d . . . . $ 50.00

Row 2:
Hood Arrow, *Heavy Duty 6 Ply, 600-20,* 6⅜" d . . . . $ 65.00
Miller, *Miller Delux, Long Safe Mileage, Geared to the Road,* clear insert with name in bottom, 7" d . . . . $ 80.00
Holyoke Cord Tires, *New England Tire & Rubber Co., Holyoke, Mass,* embossed, copper plated, 5½" d . . . $ 90.00
Michelin, cream colored figural of Michelin Man on back of raised rim, brown plastic ashtray, 5" h $115.00
Kelly Springfield, *Commercial Heavy Tread, 10.0x20,* clear glass insert, 6" d . . . . $ 45.00
Pennsylvania, *Jeannette, Pa, Low Pressure,* glass insert with pressed pattern bottom, 5½" d, old . . . . $ 50.00

PLATE 131

PLATE 132

MISCELLANEOUS ASHTRAYS

There are ashtrays that represent unions and their functions, but not many. This would make a very interesting group to collect, and this is one category that might still be found at garage sales.

The Say It With Flowers and Yellow Pages ashtrays are two of my favorites, and I have never seen them again. They are pictured in Plates 133 and 134, respectively. This type of ashtray is hard to find, but every now and then, if you keep looking, you get lucky.

I do not have any information on the Serving You In Europe ashtray. If you have any information about it, I would appreciate hearing from you.

Another interesting group seems to be appearing at flea markets, that of public servants. In Plate 133, there are ashtrays involving the FBI, Highway Patrol, Sheriffs, and Fire Fighters. I hope to find more.

PLATE 133 (left to right)
Row 1:
FBI – Dept. of Justice, white ceramic, blue, red & gold seal in center, 7" d $10.00
Funeral home, local ad, clear glass with picture of funeral home in center, 3¾" sq . . . . $ 5.00
Thank You Volunteer Fire Department, *Chaska,* amber glass, black letters, 6" d . . . . $ 9.00
New Jersey Turnpike Toll Booth, white ceramic, blue inside, picture of toll booth, 3½" d $10.00
Collectors' Extravaganza, glass, white & blue center, *Walt Johnson's 69–81,* triangle-3" sides. . . . . $ 4.00
Wells Fargo Protective Services, cream ceramic, red shield center, name & address in center, 7" d . . . . $ 9.00

Row 2:
Say It With Flowers In Haeger Container, lt green ceramic Haeger, crown logo center, 5½" d $10.00
Elect Sheriff, *Norris Froelich,* aqua ceramic, shape of sheriff badge, 5½" across . . . . $ 8.00
State Highway Patrol, *Ohio,* cream ceramic, black in center, picture of tire with wings, 5⅜" d $13.00
S.& H. Green Stamps, clear glass, green letters in center, 6" l . . . . $ 8.00
Sani-Tray, ashtray has filter papers inside for easier to empty, red paint metal, 3" h, rare & old $45.00

PLATE 134 (left to right)
Row 1:
Hazel-Atlas Glass Co., *77th Conv, Chicago. Ill.,* clear glass, 4½" sq $12.00
Brewery Workers Credit Union, black plastic round with extension, gold picture & name, 4¾" d . . . . $ 8.00
R.R. Engineers Assoc. A.E.F., cream ceramic, 1966, picture of train, 8⅝" d $13.00
Yellow Pages, *Find It Fast In The,* yellow ceramic shape of book & telephone, 4⅞" l $35.00
Power & Light Dept., *City of Independence, Mo.,* symbols and letters in center, 4" sq. . . . . $ 7.00

Row 2:
Reddy Kilowatt, clear glass, white head of Reddy logo with light bulb nose, 3½" sq. $30.00
Serving You In Europe, *EES Service,* white ceramic with blue letters, by Johann Haviland, 4¼" d . . . . $ 8.00
Nitrolime, Cal-Nitro, fertilizers, Delft, Holland, hand painted, 7¼" d $14.00
Glass Bottle Blowers Ass'n A.F.L., *Beer Best In One-Way Bottles,* clear glass, 6⅜" d . . . . $ 8.00
UAW-CIO Local, *Kenosha, Wis. 1961,* amber irid glass, 4⅛" sq $10.00

PLATE 133

PLATE 134

NOVELTY ASHTRAYS

This section deals with ashtrays that have another function: they are funny, or different, such as a shoe, or they are a souvenir or remembrance, etc. The subject matter seems to be unlimited, and they are great for building small collections. These ashtrays abound on the market, making them fun to shop for, and to collect.

ASHTRAYS FEATURING ANIMALS, BIRDS & INSECTS

All kinds of animals, made from many materials, are easy to find. Some are very unusual or amusing. Note the dog face with the pipe figural in Plate 135. There are many dog faces, but ones with a pipe take some searching to find. This scarcity is also true with the ladybug, while there are all kinds of crabs. In Plate 136, the bear figural and the pelican figural are well done for this type of ashtray. The nice green swan is by Hull and also comes in white. It is much more frequently seen in green, though.

PLATE 135 (left to right)   **All ashtrays are brass unless noted.**
Row 1:
Small camel, solid, two rests, 5¼" l $26.00

Small fly, solid, wings lift to expose cavity for matches, 4" l $20.00

Whale, iron, two rests, 5¼" l $10.00

Large fly, brass coated, wings lift to expose tray for ashes, two rests, 7" l $20.00

Bi-metal bird, brass & copper, green glass eyes, 4" h . . . . $ 8.00

Turtle, solid, two rests, 4" l . . . . $ 9.00

Large camel, solid, one rest, 7" l $30.00

Row 2:
Brass frog, solid, top lifts, two rests, 5½" l $14.00

Bear rug, solid, local ad on bottom, different, 6" l $13.00

Ladybug, solid, body lifts to expose tray for ashes, two rests, 3" w $15.00

Bulldog/pipe, solid, pipe can be used as match holder, nice, 5¼" w $52.00

Copper frog, brass coating, one rest, 4½" l . . . . $ 9.00

Small crab, solid, body lifts and cavity is for ashes, one rest, 3¼" w . . . . $ 8.00

Large crab, solid, body top lifts to expose removable tray for ashes & two rests, 7½" w $14.00

PLATE 136 (left to right)
Row 1:
Skunk, *For Little Butts and Big Stinkers,* real fur on tail, 4½" h $10.00

Turtle, top body comes off to expose tray for matches, by Wade, 3¾" l $15.00

Dog, two rests, 4½" h $10.00

Bear, fishing, fish is opalized, 5½" h $16.00

Green swan, by Hull, also in white, 4⅜" h $11.00

Green bird, one rest, nicely done, Germany, 3¼" l $17.00

Fox, two rests, 3⅞" h $11.00

Row 2:
Orange frog, ash dump, 4⅝" h $12.00

White Bird, two rests, nicely done, 4¾" l $14.00

Pelican, luster ashtray, nice, 4⅝" l $17.00

Snakes, *Remember when You Didn't Have A Pot To Hiss In?,* 5½" w $10.00

Kangaroo, one rest, 4" h . . . . $ 9.00

Goose, two rests, 4¾" l $10.00

Tan frog, one rest, 3¼" h . . . . $ 7.00

Green frog, ash dump, butterfly on nose, 4⅝" h $14.00

PLATE 135

PLATE 136

BLACK HUMOR ASHTRAYS

There are many ashtrays in this category. Some are great, and bring back many fond memories of an era gone by. Others are crude and should make some people feel ashamed for parts of their history. Some ashtrays are well made, and others not so. Most are old.

Some of these ashtrays were made of chalkware and are very old. They are usually not in very good condition. I have been looking for the Chattanooga Shoe Shine Boy for four years. I have found only two, and the other one is in much worse condition than the one pictured in Plate 137. Chalkware just does not hold up very well in an ashtray that has been used.

PLATE 137 (left to right)
Row 1:
Boys with laundry, two boys peek between three items, *Come Up & See Me Sometime,* 4½" w, 1930s $45.00
Boy with laundry, boy peeking between bloomers & pants, match striker on side, 2½" h, 1930s $35.00
Chattanooga Shoe Shine Boy, chalkware, 5¼" h $78.00
Boy with laundry, boy peeks between bloomers & pants labeled matches & cigs, match strike, 3" w, 1930s. . $38.00
Boy with laundry, boy with three item of laundry, labeled ashes, cigarettes, & matches, 3⅝" w, 1930s. $40.00

Row 2:
Baby on pot, with snufferette on head, ceramic, *For Old Butts And Ashes,* 3½" h $55.00
Black face, on bowl of pipe ashtray, 2⅛" h. $15.00
Boy, pushing large jug of ashes, 3⅜" h. $38.00
Boy with watermelon, chalkware, souvenir from Nashville, 3¾" h $55.00
Boy, pushing barrel of ashes, 4" w $42.00
Boy, sitting with small jug of ashes, 3" w. $23.00
Baby on pot, Occupied Japan, ceramic, this also comes with just Japan on bottom, 3¼" h $60.00

PLATE 138 (left to right)
Row 1:
Man with drums, four snufferettes, 4" h $60.00
Face with painted bee on nose, smoker, orange & yellow hat, 2⅞" h $35.00
Boy with goose figural, chalkware, *The Early Bird Catches The Worm,* 5" h $57.00
Face with bee figural on nose, smoker, one eye closed, collar, 3" h $35.00
Man with saxophone, souvenir from Atlanta, four snufferettes, 3½" h $50.00

Row 2:
Souvenir of Michigan, *The Early Bird Catches The Worm,* shows boy at fence, 5¼" d. $20.00
Boy playing dice, *Come Seven,* 2½" h $43.00
Baby on ash pot, ceramic with wooden seat, labeled matches, cigarettes, ashes, 3" h $18.00
Picture in center, *Mammy,* shows boy at fence, 5¼" d $20.00

PLATE 137

PLATE 138

BUCKET AND PAIL ASHTRAYS

These ashtrays can be found just about everywhere on the collectibles market, such as shows, malls, and flea markets. As you can see, they come in just about every color and size. The most numerous are the crystal, amber, and olive glass pails and coal scuttles. These seem to be about the same price, but every now and then, you can find a crystal one with an inflated price between $10.00 and $15.00. Most of the glass ones have a pressed on pattern called "old oaken bucket," which is designed to look like just what the name implies. The metal, plastic, and pottery ashtrays are more difficult to find. Some of them tend to sell for a higher price.

PLATE 139 (left to right)
Row 1:
Black glass coal scuttle, two rests, 2¾" h $10.00
Crystal coal scuttle, two rests, 2¼" h .... $ 6.00
Gray metal coal scuttle, one rest, 2⅞" h .... $ 8.00
Red coal scuttle, enamel over iron, one rest, 2⅝" h $11.00
Crystal pail, 2½" h .... $ 5.00
Copper coal scuttle, one rest, 2½" h $10.00

Row 2:
White pottery coal scuttle, one rest, 1¾" h .... $ 8.00
Amber coal scuttle, 2¼" h .... $ 6.00
Olive pail, 2½" h .... $ 5.00
Crystal coal scuttle, two rests, 2¾" h .... $ 8.00
Amber pail, 2½" h .... $ 5.00
Olive coal scuttle, 2¼" h .... $ 6.00
Black plastic coal scuttle, 1¾" h .... $ 5.00

ELEPHANT ASHTRAYS

Elephants are one of the most popular animals used for ashtrays. They are found in the glass, china, and metal sections as well. I have gathered them all here to make a visual impact. There are certainly all kinds.

PLATE 140 (left to right)
Row 1:
Green and tan pottery, Indian, four rests, 5⅜" h $27.00
Beige, Czechoslovakia, one rest, 3½" h $30.00
Large metal, cigarette box on top, turn tail & it dispenses, not original ashtray insert, 5½" h $150.00
Green Glass, two rests, 2⅝" h $10.00
Small Brass, five rests, some painting, 3¼" h $14.00
Lots Of moriage, Japan, nicely done, two cigarette pack carriers, ashtray on top lifts out for cleaning, 5" h .. $42.00

Row 2:
Yellow luster, Japan, nicely done, 4" h $23.00
Walking bridge, two rests, luster, 2⅜" h $15.00
Black glass, four rests, 2¼" h $22.00
Green marble, metal elephant on back rim, 6" d $50.00
Two elephants, Deco lines, one rest, luster, 3" h $25.00
Orange, with six snufferettes, Deco lines, four rests, 3" h $15.00
Yellow & black, Gold Castle, Japan, bottom is ashtray, top holds cigarettes, 5" h ... $38.00

PLATE 139

PLATE 140

ASHTRAYS FOR THE CARD TABLE

Cards were a favorite game in the 1920s and 1930s. There are many ashtrays available that were made to be used on the card table, either one for each person, or one for two people. Clowns were a favorite theme at this time, and for some reason, they were frequently used on these ashtrays.

Note the metal ashtray in Plate 141. It was probably designed for bridge, and has a place for a pencil in each suit marker, helping one to remember the suit bid. There is also a dial to remind one who had the bid.

PLATE 141 (left to right)

Row 1:

Three of clown set, heart is missing, each has four snufferettes, two rests, a clown, all are 2⅞" h, each . . . $20.00
Small clown set (4), all have two rests, each is 1⅞" h, set price $45.00
Metal with markers, for suit that is trump & dial for who has bid, patent pending, 4⅞" d, 1930 . . . . $18.00
Black plastic, ashtray is glass, clear plastic over designs, 8" l $13.00

Row 2:

Card suit shape set, set of four vary from 4" to 4⅞" l, set price $20.00
Crystal glass, typical of glass ones, hobnails, spade shape, 4⅜" l $10.00
Metal set, card suit symbol standing up in center, 3" d, set $15.00
Die, it comes in many sizes, 1½" h . . . . $ 5.00

ASHTRAYS RELATING TO HEALTH PROBLEMS

I noticed that there were ashtrays on the market that showed some concern with the health problems related to smoking. Of course, skeletons are somewhat easy to find, but the others need more searching. Some of them are really funny, such as the battery-operated machine with ashtray that coughs, and then says, "no smoking." See this in Plate 142. Scotland's Loch Ness Monster is also funny.

Two of the ashtrays, shown in Plate 142, were designed to filter the smoke. One of these has a patent pending from 1979.

PLATE 142 (left to right)

Row 1:

Smoke filtered, battery-operated fan draws smoke down through charcoal filters, 4½" sq, 1979 . . . . $20.00
Scotland, Loch Ness Monster coughs, plastic, 5¾" w $10.00
Raised skeleton, *Ashes To Ashes,* pottery, 7" d $15.00
Skeleton face, three rests, 6⅞" l . . . . $ 9.00
Skeleton nodder, *Keep On Smoking,* 5½" l $17.00
Smoke filtered, battery-operated fan draws smoke down through charcoal filters, 5" d $20.00

Row 2:

"No Smoking" voice, battery operated, coughs and speaks when lift matches, black plastic, 7" l $12.00
Pottery warning, *The Surgeon General Has Determined That Cigarette Smoking Is Dangerous* . . . . $ 5.00
Non-smoking room, regular ashtray turned over, and decal put on bottom, 5¼" l . . . . $ 6.00
Doctor, picture of doctor's bag, 5½" d . . . . $ 5.00
Metal with warning, *The Surgeon General Has Determined That Cigarette Smoking Is Dangerous*
    To Your Health, 8½" w . . . . $ 9.00
General Hospital, *Waiting Room,* ABC television program, 5" d . . . . $ 6.00

PLATE 141

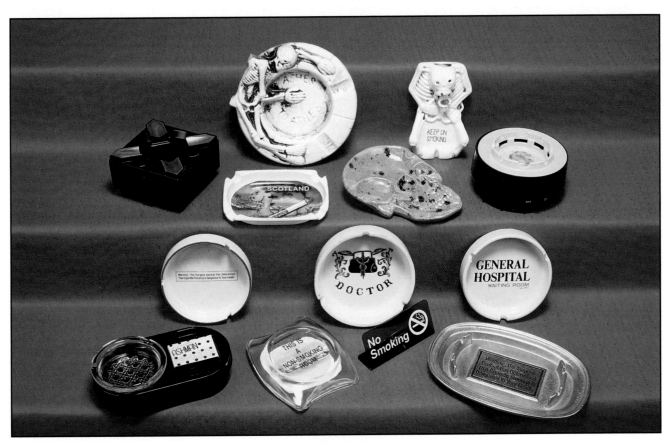

PLATE 142

HANDS AND SHOES ASHTRAYS

These are two more groupings in my collection, and these ashtrays are easy to find in malls and flea markets. Hands come in all sizes and types of decor, as do shoes. It's fun to try to find something different and makes looking worthwhile.

If you buy Dutch shoes, remember that many are also made in this country in Holland, Michigan. Just be sure you know that they are from the right Holland. The Delft from the country Holland is much more collectible. All those pictured in Plate 144 are from Holland.

The unusual metal shoe with a raised toe, in Plate 144, is very nicely done. There are even two birds with a nest painted on the inside. The small metal Dutch shoe is also unusual, and nice. The sides of the shoe have Dutch scenes in relief. Dutch shoe ashtrays are very seldom found in metal.

PLATE 143 (left to right)
Row 1:
Hand with small flowers, white, 5½" l $14.00
Hand, black, one rest, 4⅛" l $10.00
Two hands raised up, matchbox holder at top, Japan, very different, 5" h $28.00
Two hands, black, cupped together, one rest, 3¾" l $11.00
Hand with added-on roses, Lefton like, white, one rest, 5⅜" l $12.00

Row 2:
Hand with thumb & finger raised up, also different, white, one rest, 4½" l $17.00
2 hands, white, cupped together, 3⅝" l $10.00
Brass hand, India, inscribed patterns, 7" l $15.00
Hand with cigarette holder, pink, Lefton like, red finger nails, different, 6¾" l $35.00
Small hand, white, one red rest, 2⅞" l .... $ 7.00
2 green hands, cupped together, unusual color, one added-on rose, 3¾" l $15.00

PLATE 144 (left to right)
Row 1:
Cobalt glass boot, one rest, 3¾" h $12.00
Pottery shoe, bottom shows heel, painted flowers, 5¼" l .... $ 9.00
Brass oriental man's shoe, some color work, 4¼" l $10.00
Green glass cowboy boot, one moveable rest, 2¼" h $14.00
Small Dutch shoe, Delft from Holland, one rest, 3⅛" l .... $ 8.00
Brass man's oxford, even with shoe lace, 5⅛" l $14.00
Black metal shoe, different, very nice, inlaid decoration, 6" l $20.00
Lavender glass boot, one rest, 3¾" h $10.00

Row 2:
Medium Dutch shoe, Delft from Holland, different rest, 5" l (including rest) $12.00
Bulgaria brown shoe, pottery, marked on bottom, 5" l $15.00
Small Dutch metal shoe, different, nice, Dutch decoration in relief, 3⅝" l $15.00
Long brass shoe, India, inscribed patterns, 6½" l $15.00
Oriental slipper, pointed toe, some color inlaid, 3½" l .... $ 8.00
Oriental slipper with raised toe, different & very nice, enamel birds & flowers, 4" l $25.00
Brass high shoe, one rest, 4⅞" l $23.00
Large Dutch shoe, Delft from Holland, two rests, 5¼" l $16.00

PLATE 143

PLATE 144

HAT ASHTRAYS

Hats are another group in of my collection in this section. They certainly seem to come in all styles and colors. I have yet to find hobo and clown hats, as well as those belonging to fire fighters, police officers, nurses, and other professions. Some hats have cigarette rests on the brim, but most have one on the crown.

PLATE 145 (left to right)
Row 1:
Black top hat, glass, two rests, 2⅛" h . . . . $ 9.00
Nashville, souvenir, 4⅝" l . . . . $ 7.00
Blue Mexican, tall hat, flowers, two rests, 1¾" h $11.00
Straw hat with yellow bow, three rests, California, 5¼" w $12.00
Mexican, *South Of The Border,* 4¼" w $10.00
Delft from Holland, upside down hat, ad for Palace Hotel, Amsterdam, 2" h $20.00
Tan luster cowboy hat, green cord around rim, 4¾" l . . . . $ 9.00
Cobalt glass, easily found, two rests, 2½" h $13.00

Row 2:
Mexican, flowers and black decor, 5" w . . . . $ 9.00
Green glass, ridges, comes in other colors, two rests, 1⅝" h $20.00
Large crystal, Val St. Lambert, Belgium Crystal, frosted, two rests, 2⅝" h $30.00
Blue hat with pipe, souvenir of Canada, 3¼" l . . . . $ 9.00
Glass straw hat, hobnails, low hat by Westmoreland, bow at side, four rests, 1¼" h $20.00
Dark amber glass, two rests, 2½" h $10.00
Short crystal, two rests, nice, ⅜" h $18.00
Tan hat with brown cord, weave of material shown, McNees Original, 4¾" l . . . . $ 9.00

PLATE 146 (left to right)
Row 1:
Black hat with brown pipe, red ribbon around rim, 5¼" l $11.00
Gray cowboy hat, metal, souvenir from Las Vegas, 4¼" l $10.00
Carnival glass, cord around crown in relief, 6¼" l $30.00
Plain crystal glass, heavy, nice, two rests, 3⅛" h $34.00
Royal blue high crown, three small feet on bottom, 5½" l $18.00
Military officer's hat, glass by Heisey, insignia on crown in front, one rest, 4" l $35.00
Copper cowboy hat, yellow painted band around crown, 5¾" l . . . . $ 8.00

Row 2:
Blue delphite, glass, cord around crown in relief, 6⅛" l $28.00
Wide brown cowboy hat, El Paso, Texas, 5" l $12.00
Rare Daisy Button tri-cornered, 2" h $40.00
Tan Stetson, smoker's candle, air-freshening candle in crown, one rest, 5½" l . . . . $ 9.00
Confederate hat, gray & black pottery, two rests, 6⅝" l $12.00
Tan cowboy hat, cast iron, painted, 5" l $11.00
Straw low-hat, Westmoreland, Golden Sunset color, hobnails, four rests, 4⅜" l $25.00
Yellow cowboy hat, Catalina Pottery, 6½" l $40.00

PLATE 145

PLATE 146

ASHTRAYS RELATING TO MUSIC, THEATER, OR COMICS

When I first saw the mass of novelty ashtrays that I had collected over the years, I feared I would never be able to organize it. However, it soon became apparent that I had many ashtrays that belonged to the field of entertainment. Some were of cartoon characters, some music personalities, and so on. One even came from a popular theater in New York City, the ashtray with One Shubert Alley marked on it, in Plate 147. Here are some other ashtrays from that group. Plate 148 shows ashtrays with personalities on them, mostly cartoon characters.

PLATE 147 (left to right)
Row 1:
Lawrence Welk, champagne music, 5⅝" d $17.00
Girl flapper figural, song titles on ashtray from flapper era, 2⅝" h $15.00
Tweety Bird, 4⅜" d . . . . $ 6.00
Green piano, with musical instruments, 7" l $13.00
Liberace's piano, nicely done, 4½" l $18.00
Nashville, *Music City, U.S.A.,* 4½" d . . . . $ 9.00
Ashtray from set, see set on Row 2.
Grand Old Opry, *50 Years, 1925–1975,* wide gold rim, 5⅜" d $13.00
One Shubert Alley, *Broadway, New York,* address for famous theater, 4⅛" d . . . . $ 8.00

Row 2:
Capitol Records, *Don Carroll – In My Arms,* 5⅛" d . . . . $ 8.00
Elvis Presley, octagon, 4½" w, 1978 . . . . $16.00
Ziggy, watering thankful flower, 5" w, 1982 . . . . $ 7.00
Garfield on piano, 7½" l $15.00
Set with picture & music titles, *After the Ball is Over, The Band Played On, A Bicycle Built for Two,*
    Frankie and Johnnie, holder is 4" l $12.00
Universal Studios, 5⅜" d . . . . $ 6.00

PLATE 148 (left to right)
Row 1:
Moon Mullins nodder, Germany, luster, 4⅝" h $120.00
Betty & Barney, Hanna Barbera Productions, 8⅛" l, 1961 . . . . $ 65.00
Micky Mouse, old style, 3½" h, 1930 . . . . $100.00
Donald Duck, 7¼" sq . . . . $ 40.00
Smokey The Bear "Snuffit," a snufferette in his hat, plastic, 2" h . . . . $ 15.00
Minnie Mouse, old style, 3⅝" h, 1930 . . . . $100.00
Fred & Wilma, Hanna Barbera Productions, 8⅛" l, 1961 . . . . $ 67.00
Brother Juniper, cartoon playing golf, *Hand me my prayer book,* 3⅞" h, 1958 . . . . $ 30.00

Row 2:
Little Orphan Annie, with Sandy, 3⅛" h $130.00
Dogpatch U.S.A., picture of Mammy & Pappy Yokem in center, 4¾" d, 1975 . . . . $ 18.00
Andy Gump, old, silver-colored metal, 4" sq . . . . $ 40.00
Smokey The Bear, figural, *Smokey – Prevent Forest Fires,* 4" h . . . . $ 95.00
Round green tin, *Smokey – Prevent Forest Fires,* 4" d . . . . $ 9.00
Dogpatch U.S.A., picture of Little Abner in center, 4⅜" d, 1975 . . . . $ 20.00
Three Little Pigs, with musical instruments, 3¼" h . . . . $ 80.00

PLATE 147

PLATE 148

NODDER ASHTRAYS

Nodders, or nodding figures, are metal or porcelain figures whose head, hands, or feet move or nod on a pivot, spring, or wire, hence the name. Although they originated in China, they became popular in France in the eighteenth century. Germany also made many very good ones, particularly those of comic characters. Some recent nodders are made of papier-mâché or plastic.

The nodders pictured of ladies in bed are often seen with parts missing, such as the fan or legs, but at a price that would be right for one complete. So be sure that all parts are there. I bought the bathtub ashtray, without legs, hoping to find the missing part. I have been looking two years, but no luck so far.

The black boy with cigar, in Oriental dress, is a favorite among collectors, despite its high price.

PLATE 149 (left to right)
Row 1:
Lady pulling up skirt, yellow dress & orange shoes, ¾" h.. $ 85.00
Lady on bed, blue pants, lower bed near pillow area, 5⅜" h.. $ 55.00
Lady in bathtub, missing legs, rare, 5½" l.. $ 20.00
Oriental man, nods at ankles, bisque, 3⅜" h, old .... $ 50.00
Lady on bed, black pants, different style bed near pillow area, 5⅜" h.. $ 60.00
Lady on lounge chair, pink clothes & red shoes, ashtray on side, 5¾" h .... $ 80.00
Lady on bed, pink pants, lower bed near pillow area, 5⅜" h .... $ 50.00

Row 2:
Black boy with cigar in mouth, Austria, metal, nods head, 4⅞" h $160.00
Nodding man, *Yes, Dear, Yes Dear,* head nods, 3¼" h .... $ 25.00
Couple kissing, *Welcome,* whole couple rocks, 4⅝" h .... $ 55.00
Oriental man sitting, Austria, head nods, 3¾" h, old .... $ 60.00
Professor, Austria, head nods, 4¾" h, old .... $ 70.00

ASHTRAYS WITH A NEW ORLEANS THEME

There are many black iron ashtrays with figurals leaning against street signs marked "Bourbon Street," a street in the French Quarter in New Orleans, Louisiana. Most are drunks, some are prostitutes, and others seem to be a take-off on this theme. The tall figural ashtray, seen in Plate 150, is chalkware, and still in quite good condition. Some of these ashtrays still have the bottle opener on the post.

PLATE 150 (left to right)
Row 1:
Prostitute leaning against lamp post with street sign, difficult to find, 5" h $35.00
Drunk with no parking sign, drunk sitting, 3½" h.. $27.00
Pottery drunk, lying down or standing up, four rests, *All Lit Up,* 8½" l.. $12.00
Drunk with Bourbon St. sign, unusual shape of ashtray, six rests, probably older, 4¾" h.. $25.00
Confederate soldier, may have been put on base by someone, iron soldier, 4⅛" h $14.00

Row 2:
Drunk with Bourbon St. sign, good condition for this ashtray, 4¾" h $29.00
Bourbon Street, *New Orleans, Birthplace of Jazz,* 5" d.. $10.00
Tall figural drunk, chalkware, 12" h.. $11.00
Hitchhiker, older style ashtray, difficult to find, 4" h.. $38.00
Drunk with lamp post, nice condition, 5" h $30.00

PLATE 149

PLATE 150

SMOKERS

"Smokers" is the name given by collectors to ashtrays that have holes in them that allows smoke to come out when the cigarette is on its rest. Most of them are made in Japan, and the ashtray should be judged on workmanship, which varies greatly.

See the Occupied Japan clown head, in Plate 151. It is the fourth from the left, and is just like the second from the left, which is not Occupied Japan. The only difference is that the Occupied Japan one is much shinier, and, of course, sells for more.

The Oriental boy, in Plate 151, is one of my favorites. The work on it is excellent. The conductor is also great, and seems to be very popular.

There are several other different distorted face smokers that can be found at antique shows. They are getting very popular.

PLATE 151 (left to right)
Row 1:
Distorted face with top hat, *Wanna See Smoke Come Our My Ears?,* well done, 5½" h, ... $45.00
Clown with bee on nose, smoke comes out nose, 3¼" h. $30.00
Man with bee on head, smoke comes out ears, 3¼" h. $15.00
Clown with bee on nose (shiny), Occupied Japan, nice, smoke comes out nose, 3⅜" h. $50.00
Hobo with fur hair, smoke comes out nose, 3¼" h $20.00
Distorted face, *Sweet Adeline,* smoke out ears & mouth, well done, 5¼" h. $43.00

Row 2:
Delft house, smoke comes out chimney, Delft, Holland, 3⅝" h $15.00
Oriental boy, smoke comes out nose & ears, lovely, by Will George, 4" h $75.00
Man with cigar, smoke comes out mouth, by Ucaguo-Japan, 5" h $30.00
Metal house, smoke comes out chimney, 3⅛" h . . . . $ 8.00
Conductor, smoke comes out ears & score roll, great, 10¾" h. $80.00
Man's head with cigarette, smoke comes out mouth, 4⅝" h $25.00
Indian face, smoke comes out nose, Lenwile, Japan, 3⅛" h $45.00
Indian with teepee, smoke comes out top of teepee, 4¼" h $25.00

PLATE 152 (left to right)
Row 1:
Barbecue, smoke comes out chimney, all metal, two match pack holders and holder for cigarettes, 6⅛" h . . $13.00
Bag with padlock, smoke comes out top of bag, 5⅜" h . . . . $ 7.00
Musical barbecue, smoke out chimney, chalkware, places for cigarettes, matches & ashes,
    Smoke Gets In Your Eyes plays when cigarette placed on grill, 5" h $30.00
Ship, smoke comes out funnel, 7" l $20.00
Four eyes, smoke comes out ears & mouth, 6¼" h. $15.00

Row 2:
Man in pot, smoke comes out behind man's shoulders & mouth, wood is rest, ceramic, 4¾" h $15.00
Dog face, smoke comes out nose, 4⅛" l. $20.00
Cat face, smoke comes out nose, 3⅝" h $18.00
Small dog face, smoke comes out nose, 1½" h $12.00
Pig face, smoke comes out nose, 4⅝" l $20.00
Tower, smoke comes out in tower, from Berardos, Portugal, 5¾" h. $30.00

PLATE 151

PLATE 152

HISTORICAL ASHTRAYS

I told a story once about the history of our country, using ashtrays as props. I will repeat parts of it here. In 1602, Pilgrim settlers started to arrive in the colonies by ship. Here they met the natives, the Indians, who were friendly (1). Cities were eventually settled, and a form of government began to emerge — democracy. But first many battles (2), and a great war had to be fought.

After freedom was won, our Declaration of Independence was signed (3). George Washington became the first president (4), and he and his wife, Martha (5), built Mt. Vernon in Virginia (7).

Soon the pioneers started their travels westward, and this time the Indians they met along the way were not so friendly (6). But the settlers continued in their covered wagons, and built their towns (8). Some of these soon blossomed into cities, and some into states, which were in time added to the original thirteen.

Freedom was great, and we continued to ring the Liberty Bell in Philadelphia, Pennsylvania, until it cracked in 1835 (9).

PLATE 153 (left to right)
Row 1:
Figural Indian (1), glass insert ashtray, composition, 5" h. $20.00
Wedgwood (2), from Revolutionary War, 4¼" d, 1940s–1950s. $14.00
Signing of Declaration of Independence (3), no mark, 5½" sq $16.00
George Washington (4), by Dwight Morris, USA, 3⅞" d. $10.00
Martha Washington (5), by Dwight Morris, USA, 3⅞" d. $10.00

Row 2:
Indian face (6), Japan, 3¾" w. . . . . $ 6.00
Mt. Vernon, VA (7), by Harker, hexagon, 6" w. $15.00
Covered Wagon (8), by Francoma. . . . . $ 9.00
Cracked Liberty Bell (9), figural, shaped insert holder for glass ashtray, 5½" h. $25.00

Another famous American soon became president, Abraham Lincoln (1). He faced many difficult times when our nation was split in two over the controversy of slavery. The Confederate Nation was formed (2). But the North won the Civil War. President Lincoln gave his famous Gettysburg Address in 1863 (3).

The government strengthened, and maintained mostly a two-party system. The slogan " we do have a choice, under our flag" was as good then as it is now (4). Many fine men were elected president, to serve the country (5). The House of Representatives and the Senate, as well as the Presidency, all had good men who were also smokers (6, 7, 8). These ashtrays were used in the various offices in the Capitol in Washington, DC (9).

America grew and grew. Education was very necessary, and public schools were formed for all children. The first kindergarten was established in Watertown, Wisconsin, in 1856 (10). However, kindergarten was not widely introduced into the public school system until after 1873.

PLATE 154 (left to right)
Row 1:
Abraham Lincoln's birthplace (1), pictures of KY, his home & Lincoln Memorial, 6" d. $10.00
Confederate States Of America (2), Civil War states & their flag shown, 4¾" d. . . . . $ 8.00
Lincoln's Gettysburg Address (3), end of speech printed, 4½" w $12.00
Political slogan (4), from 1952 convention, but good anytime, 6" d $15.00
Picture of Presidents (5), through Lyndon Johnson, 7½" d $13.00

Row 2:
House of Representatives (6), ashtray from there, glass by Fostoria, 4" l. $23.00
House of Representatives (7), ashtray from there, pewter, 5⅜" l $20.00
Senate (8), ashtray from there, by Fostoria, each rest designed to hold both cigarette & cigar, 8" d. $30.00
The Capitol (9), figural of front of Capitol, pot metal, 3¼" w, 2½" h. $18.00
First kindergarten (10), Watertown, WI, by House of Moore, 5½" d. $10.00

PLATE 153

PLATE 154

HISTORICAL ASHTRAYS

America continued to grow and prosper, in ways never imagined by our forefathers. In 1884, France gave America the Statue of Liberty, which was to stand in the New York harbor, and be a symbol of protection and welcome for all who entered here (1). The Industrial Revolution began, and soon after, labor unions were formed and collective bargaining began in 1888 (2). We seemed to be on the way to a more prosperous future. This was about the time of Henry Ford and the automobile. Ford's first car was introduced in 1896 (3).

Education, industrialization, and religion were all important during these years. Many colleges were founded. In 1903, the Lutheran religion began a system of secondary education (4). Other organizations were formed with aims to help the total growth of the individual. In 1910, the Boy Scouts of America was formed to promote service (5). Boys Town, in Nebraska, was founded in 1917 (6, 7).

American progress was abruptly stopped with the advent of World War I. Enemies plagued Europe, and the United States joined "the war to end all wars." (8). Eventually, with the end of the war, Americans turned their thoughts and minds to their own country and its freedom. The Sesquicentennial of the United States, was celebrated in Philadelphia. One hundred and fifty years of independence was a great achievement, and everyone celebrated, and smoked (9). God Bless America (10).

PLATE 155 (left to right)
Row 1:
Statue of Liberty (1), copper, statue in center in relief, 3¾" d . . . . $ 7.00
National Brotherhood Operative Potters (2), *60 years collective bargaining, 1888–1948, A.F.L,* 5" d $15.00
Ford's first car (3), 1896, pictured, 5¼" d . . . . $ 7.00
Growing In The Lord (4), *75 years of Lutheran Secondary Education,* 5⅜" d, 1978. . . . . $12.00
Boy Scouts – National Jamboree (5), *1910–1960, 50 years,* rests for both cigars & cigarettes, 8" d $15.00

Row 2:
Boy's Town, Nebraska (6), scenes from there in relief in center, pot metal, silver coat, 5½" l . . . . $ 5.00
Boy's Town (7), pottery, picture in center of boy carrying younger child, 4½" l $15.00
WWI tank (8), figural, three rests, bronze finish, made USA, 2⅛" h $30.00
Sesquicentennial (9), lead, gold flash worn off, Liberty Bell in relief, 5¼" l $30.00
God Bless America (10), pot metal with copper finish, flag & eagle in relief, 5⅛" l . . . . $ 8.00

After the war, Americans looked at their country with pride. Business and education came into the limelight. A football stadium was dedicated in 1926 at the University of Missouri (1). Americans expanded the National Parks, starting Mt. Rushmore in 1927 (2). However, attention soon turned to the new war in Europe, and America helped the allies. Remember Pearl Harbor, in 1941 (3)? Our Navy was great in responding, and this is a sample of "trench art," put together by a Navy man (4). There is even an ashtray from Holland, liberated May 4, 1945 (5).

After the war, everyone's attention turned to home. The Theodore Roosevelt National Park was established in 1947 (6), commemorating a great president. Some of the early established colleges were celebrating their centennial (7). I'll finish this page with a lighter note, an ashtray celebrating Groundhog's Day (8). This is based on a custom that the people from Great Britain and Germany brought to America.

PLATE 156 (left to right)
Row 1:
University of Missouri (1), Memorial Stadium, dedication 1926, 5" sq $10.00
Mt. Rushmore (2), 6" l . . . . $ 8.00
Remember Pearl Harbor (3), glass heavy, 3¾" d $40.00
USN trench art (4), 5" h $48.00

Row 2:
Liberated Holland (5), May 4, 1945, 4½" side $10.00
Theodore Roosevelt National Park (6), 5¼" d . . . . $ 5.00
University of Pennsylvania Centennial (7), 5" l, 1955 . . . . $10.00
Groundhog's Day (8), *World Headquarters of,* 3⅜" sq . . . . $ 8.00

PLATE 155

PLATE 156

HISTORICAL ASHTRAYS

The 1950s can be remembered for many things, but one of them certainly is the entrance of Elvis Presley (1). Elvis became America's King of Rock and Roll (2) and died in 1977.

In 1959, two events happened that were of great importance: Hawaii became the fiftieth state (3), and the St. Lawrence Seaway opened (4). The Hiawatha Bridge, across the Mississippi River between Wisconsin and Minnesota, was dedicated by President Eisenhower, in 1960 (5).

One of the most exciting events at this time started in 1957, when Russia launched Sputnik 1. The Space Age began. It wasn't too long before the Kennedy Space Center opened in Florida (6). Another ashtray commemorates the Engle-Truly flight (7). Many ashtrays about space can be found on the market, including these two (8, 9). The last ashtray that I will show in this group celebrates the first lunar landing by Neil Armstrong, one of the most celebrated of all space flights (10).

PLATE 157 (left to right)

Row 1:

Elvis (1), small hand held, rest pops out when opened, 1⅝" sq $25.00
Evis Presley (2), *King of Rock & Roll, 1935–1977,* 4⅝" l $30.00
Hawaii – 50th State (3), copper coating, 5" d . . . . $ 9.00
Opening of St. Lawrence Seaway (4), 5¼" d . . . . $ 7.00
Dedication of Hiawatha Bridge by President Eisenhower (5), 1960, by Red Wing, 8" d $45.00

Row 2:

Space Shuttle (6), Kennedy Space Center, 5¼" d $10.00
Columbia Space Flight (7), by Engle-Truly, 5¼" sq . . . . $ 9.00
3rd Century America (8), Kennedy Space Center, 5¼" d $10.00
Columbia Space Flight (9), by Young & Crippen, made USA , 5" d . . . . $ 9.00
First Lunar Landing (10), Neil Armstrong, Air & Space Museum, 1969, 5½" d $25.00

In 1976, Americans celebrated their bicentennial (1). The people felt that this was 200 years of progress and were very happy. Philadelphia, as well as Washington DC, had many celebrations and produced many ashtrays (2, 3, 4). In 1976, many, many Americans were still smoking.

Weather-related events kept happening, and I was lucky to find an ashtray commemorating the volcanic eruption of Mt. St. Helens (5). There are probably other ashtrays in this category, and they would be interesting to find.

Being an American was great during the twentieth century! The American Freedom Train traveled across our country in the 1970s, and their foundation produced this ashtray in 1975 (6). Business also thought it was great to be an American and encouraged everyone to "Be American, Buy American" (7). This was to help keep jobs here in the United States and our citizens working. With that thought, I will conclude this historical section with an ashtray of our national bird, the eagle (8).

PLATE 158 (left to right)

Row 1:

1776 Bicentennial 1976 (1), *200 years of progress,* 5⅜" d . . . . $ 7.00
American Revolution Bicentennial (2), brass hexagon, 7½" w $10.00
The 200th Anniversary (3), *1776–1976,* 4½" d . . . . $ 7.00
1776–1976 (4), eagle and dates, 6" w . . . . $ 8.00

Row 2:

Mt. St. Helens Volcano (5), copper coating, 5" d . . . . $ 7.00
American Freedom Train (6), 4¾" w $10.00
Be American, Buy American (7), made by International Brotherhood of Operative Potters, 5¼" d $12.00
Eagle & Stars (8), 8" d . . . . $ 9.00

PLATE 157

PLATE 158

ROYALTY AND CENTENNIAL ASHTRAYS

I tied these two groups of ashtrays together because everyone loves a parade, and both royalty and centennials have parades. British royalty ashtrays are sometimes difficult to find, but here are a few. The yellow ashtray in Plate 159, seems much older than the others, but it isn't; perhaps it is the color that makes it seem so. The rest of the ashtrays in this plate are all from centennials, both for our states and for Canada.

PLATE 159 (left to right)
 Row 1:
 Texas Centennial, 1936, 5¼" d $10.00
 Queen Elizabeth, *Coronation,* 1953, by Wedgwood, 4⅜" d. $25.00
 Texas Centennial, 1936, symbols of Texas in relief as well as a map, 4" d . . . . $ 8.00
 Minnesota Centennial, 1958, local ad, 5¾" d. $10.00
 King George & Queen Elizabeth, visit to Canada & US in 1939, 4" sq. $25.00
 Canadian Confederation, centennial, 1967, 4" d $10.00
 Canadian Confederation, centennial, 1967, 3½" sq. . . . . $ 8.00
 Prince Charles & Lady Diana Spencer, *Marriage, July 29, 1981,* 4¾" d $20.00

 Row 2:
 King Edward VII, *Coronation, May 12, 1937,* 4½" sq. $15.00
 Queen Elizabeth, *Coronation, June 2, 1953,* 3½" sq. $13.00
 Alaska Purchase, Centennial, 1967, 5½" w $10.00
 Principaute de Monaco, Heads of State, 4" sq $13.00
 Nevada Centennial, 1964, pictures from their history, 3½" sq . . . . $ 8.00
 King George & Queen Elizabeth, *Coronation, May 12, 1937,* 5" d $25.00

ASHTRAYS FROM THE AMERICAN POLITICAL SCENE

Political ashtrays are easy to find. American presidents would be an interesting category to collect. So would ashtrays from the American political scene, and past election campaigns. For more ashtrays with past president's pictures, see page 166.

PLATE 160 (left to right)
 Row 1:
 Lyndon Johnson, his white cowboy hat, 6½" l. $25.00
 Everett-McKinley-Dirksen, from Illinois, GOP, octagon, 3⅞" w. $15.00
 Ohio Republican, campaign ashtray, 1965, 6¾" d. $12.00
 Nixon For President, octagon, 3⅞" w $20.00
 Everyone For Elephants, Republican, 1972, 5½" sq. $10.00

 Row 2:
 Inaugural Ball, Governor Knowles of Wisconsin, 1965, 5¼" d. . . . . $ 9.00
 1980 Democrat, 4½" d . . . . $ 7.00
 President & Mrs. John F. Kennedy, 5⅞" d $20.00
 1980 Undecided, 4½" d . . . . $ 7.00
 Jimmy Carter, 39th President, 5⅜" d. . . . . $ 8.00

PLATE 159

PLATE 160

ASHTRAYS FROM WORLD FAIRS

There are many ashtrays from the 1933, 1939, and 1964 World's Fairs and surprisingly, not that many from the later fairs. The fairs before 1933 are quite hard to find.

The black-rimmed ashtray, in Plate 161, was from the 1933 fair. People were able to buy this as a souvenir and have their name written on it.

In Plate 161, the blue-rimmed one from 1939, is very nice. The date is in shadow printing in the center, and it also says San Francisco Bay. I have seen this in a large plate that was in better condition in the center. Evidently, the ashtray has been used.

Most souvenir ashtrays from the more recent World Fairs were flat and made of ceramic or metal. Only a few were glass. Occasionally, something new comes along that is really exciting. The Unisphere figural in Plate 162 is one of these, and it is from the 1964 New York World's Fair. Also seen in Plate 162 is a small square wooden ashtray, the only wooden piece that I have.

PLATE 161 (left to right)
Row 1:

1933 – Century of Progress, Armour building, metal painted blue & gold, 4⅛" sq $16.00

1933 – Century of Progress, Administration, Science, Travel & Transport buildings, brass, 5" sq $15.00

1933 – Century of Progress, Fort Dearborn, Sky Ride, brass, 3⅝" sq. $15.00

1939 – Golden Gate International Expo, scene from different countries attending, Homer Laughlin, 6¼" d . . $25.00

1939 – Golden Gate International Expo, blue ceramic, 2 rests, 4¾" d . . . . $12.00·

1933 – Century of Progress, Hall of Science, brass, 4¾" w $15.00

1933 – Century of Progress, Plymouth, Dodge, De Sota, Chrysler building, 3" sq. $14.00

1939 – New York World's Fair, fair symbols in relief in center, brass, 4½" w $20.00

Row 2:

1933 – Century of Progress, crossed stakes campfire, blue liner, fair symbol 1933 on rest, 4¼" h $38.00

1939 – New York World's Fair, food building, glass, 4" l $12.00

1933 – Century of Progress, Luddy, black rimmed enamel over metal, personalized, 5½" d $18.00

1933 – Century of Progress, scenes between six rests, pot metal, 5¼" d $12.00

1933 – Century of Progress, Sky Ride in relief in center, copper, 5⅜" l $15.00

1939 – New York World's Fair, aviation building, 3⅜" l $12.00

1933 – Century of Progress, hanging pot, symbol of 1933 on front base, 4⅜" h $30.00

PLATE 162 (left to right)
Row 1:

1984 – New Orleans World's Fair, pelican, solid brass, 7¼" w $14.00

1982 – Knoxville World's Fair, fair scenes, copper, 3⅛" d . . . . $ 8.00

1982 – Knoxville World's Fair, symbol of fair, 5½" sq $14.00

1968 – San Antonio World's Fair, brass, 4½" d $15.00

1964 – New York World's Fair, symbols in relief in center, wood, 2½" sq. $12.00

1964 – New York World's Fair, solid brass, waterfowl scenes at sides, 6½" l $20.00

Row 2:

1984 – Louisiana World's Fair, fair symbol center, 4" d. $12.00

1964 – New York World's Fair, Chinese Pavilion, patterned glass, scenes from China, 3⅛" sq $10.00

1964 – New York World's Fair, Unisphere in background, 4" d. . . . . $ 8.00

1964 – New York World's Fair, Unisphere figural, one rest, 4⅝" h $45.00

1964 – New York World's Fair, Unisphere in relief, silver metal, 5" l $12.00

1962 – Seattle World's Fair, Space Needle, mold is used often for souvenirs, 4" d. $10.00

1964 – New York World's Fair, picture of Unisphere in center, metal, black paint, 3¾" sq $12.00

1982 – Knoxville World's Fair, fair scenes, 4" d $10.00

PLATE 161

PLATE 162

INDIAN AND WESTERN AMERICANA ASHTRAYS

Indian and Western artifacts are very collectible today. There are many ashtrays that would fit into this category, and soon they should be quite collectible. Since these ashtrays are already being collected in the Western Americana area, the prices should increase because there is more demand. Another example of two groups of collectors is with Depression ashtrays. They sell well because they are purchased by both Depression era collectors as well as ashtray collectors.

Within this large area, there are many smaller groupings, such as mining, saloon & gambling items, and cowboy paraphernalia. These smaller areas also make very exciting ashtray collectible areas.

There are a series of ashtrays with animal's and men's faces, but the Indian face seen in Plate 163 is rather unusual. It is well done by Ardalt of Japan.

PLATE 163 (left to right)
Row 1:
Indian tepee, smoke comes out of tepee, 4" h $25.00
Indian face, smoke comes out nose, 4¼" l $45.00
Large Indian face, pottery, McMaster, Canada, 7⅜" l $30.00
Donkey & Pot Of Ashes, *Elcie's Old Butts & Ashes,* Occupied Japan, 4¼" l $25.00
Indian, with heart-shaped ashtray, Occupied Japan, 4" h $24.00

Row 2:
American Indian with pipe, pic in center, match holder at back, hexagon, Selb, Bavaria, 6¾" l, early 1900s . . $110.00
Cherokee Indian reservation, *North Carolina,* picture in center, Occupied Japan, 5" d $15.00
Mexican Indian & cactus, figural, two rests, 5½" w . . . . $ 9.00
Indian with Indian symbols, *Running Water,* 6¼" d $11.00
Indian figural, with pipe, some paint, pressed wood, 4¾" h $25.00

PLATE 164 (left to right)
Row 1:
Cowboy hat, copper, yellow band around crown, 5¾" l . . . . $ 8.00
Cowboy boot, green glass, one rest, 3¾" l $11.00
Wooden cowboy, figural, pressed wood, some paint, 6" h $23.00
Cowboy hat, white pottery, brown cord around crown, 4" l . . . . $ 5.00
Indian style ashtray, wooden, designs around rise & on rim, copper dish at top, three rests, 5½" d . . . . $ 6.00

Row 2:
Cowboy on horse, copper flash, two rests, 5" w $10.00
Derringer, *.41 Caliber – 1850, Famous Antique Firearms,* two rests, 3½" sides $12.00
Arrowhead, copper coating, Indian inscribed in center, 5⅝" l $15.00
Copper ashtray, solid, bird at corner, Indian markings, 4⅛" l . . . . $ 9.00
Colt .44, Model 1860, picture of gun, six rests, 5" w $10.00
Copper cook pot, one brass rest, three brass legs, 2¾" h with handle $12.00
Donkey, bronze & copper coating, 4" l $13.00
Colt Peacemaker .44, figural gun handle, five rests between bullets, 7" w $14.00
Mexican hat, amber glass, three rests, 2½" h . . . . $ 7.00

PLATE 163

PLATE 164

MILITARY ASHTRAYS

Militaria is a collectible category today, so I have tried to find ashtrays that would fit into this grouping. A good source might be former servicemen and women who sometimes brought home souvenir ashtrays from their company, or boat, or plane. Service academies also have their own ashtrays.

There is another type of ashtray that should not be overlooked — "trench art" from both World Wars. This is a soldier's attempt to make a useful object from objects available to him, such as metal casings from bullets and mortar shells. One theory is that this activity was started to pass time while the soldiers waited in the trenches, hence the name. There is a sample of this in Plate 166.

PLATE 165 (left to right)
  Row 1:
U.S. Naval Academy, picture of seal in center, 5⅜" d $12.00
U.S. Military Academy, picture of the West Point seal in center, 5⅜" d $13.00
USS *Fechteler,* 3" d . . . . $ 6.00
USS *Yorktown,* *Patriots Point, Charleston, S.C.,* picture of ship in center, 5¼" d $11.00
The Citadel, *Military College of South Carolina,* 3½" sq . . . . $ 9.00
U.S.S. *Alabama,* ship in relief in center, 4½" d . . . . $ 8.00
U.S. Naval Training Center, *United States Navy, Great Lakes, Ill,* 5½" sq. $12.00

  Row 2:
Old Ironsides, *"This Material Was Taken From The US Frigate Constitution,"* bronze, 6¼" w $28.00
West Point, picture of the seal in center, by Wedgwood, 4⅜" d $20.00
U.S. Naval War College, picture of the seal at top, 6⅛" d $12.00
World War I tank, pot metal, bronze finish, made in USA, 2⅛" h. $30.00
United States Military Academy, seal of West Point in relief in center, aluminum, 4" d . . . . $ 9.00
One Star General, solid brass, probably from World War I, matchbox holder, 4" h $30.00

PLATE 166 (left to right)
  Row 1:
562nd AAA BN, *Ausburg, Germany,* 1945, copper & brass, 4" d . . . . $ 8.00
U.S. Coast Guard Auxiliary, 4¼" square . . . . $ 8.00
Air Force Museum, *Wright-Patterson Air Force Base, Ohio,* picture of "Flying Tiger," 5⅜" d $12.00
Trench art, USN emblem, nice work, .45 cal bullets were used in both world wars, 5" h $48.00
Judge Advocate General's Corps, *1974 Jag Nat. Guard Conference,* 5⅜" d $10.00
United States Marine Corps, *193rd Anniversary,* 3⅞" d, 1968 . . . . $11.00
Air Force Academy, impressed designs, academy emblem, steel, 3⅜" sq $12.00

  Row 2:
Remember Pearl Harbor, *1941,* paperweight type, two rests, 3¾" d $40.00
United States Army Air Defense Command, milk glass, 5¼" d $10.00
Thunderbirds, three rests, 6⅜" w $14.00
32nd Infantry Division, rests on inner ring, 6¼" d $13.00
United States Naval Gun Factory, *150 Anniversary 1799–1949,* solid brass with silver color plate, 5" w . . . $20.00
U.S. Army Corps Of Engineering, *200th Anniversary, 1775–1975,* 5¼" d $12.00
U.S. Navy, *We Serve With Pride,* 3⅝" sq $10.00

PLATE 165

PLATE 166

FIGURAL ASHTRAYS

This page pictures some novelty figurals. There are many of these, some very well done. See Hobo in Plate 167. It is great, right to his hobo pack, both in careful workmanship and his facial expression. Also note the bellhop. This has Nippon on the bottom as well as a Japan mark and probably was made towards the end of the Nippon era in the early 1920s. There is a place for cigarettes and matches, as well as the ashtray.

In Plate 168, note the two squashed men. The one with glasses is Benjamin Franklin. They remind me of the Toby mugs with their old people and their appearance. Also, with the same feel, is the triangular ashtray with three Old Englishmen's faces.

PLATE 167 (left to right)

Row 1:

Bellhop, luster, place for cigarettes & matches, three rests, 5⅝" h $75.00
Boss at desk, chalkware, *Old Bosses Never Die, They Just Sit On Their Assets,* 5⅜" w $30.00
Hobo, by Pedwin, very well done, 6¾" l x 6⅞" h $45.00
Hillbilly, one of the nicer ones, two rests, triangular, 5¼" sides $16.00
The Bull Shooter, chalkware, 5⅛" h, 1950's $25.00

Row 2:

Drum major, luster, one rest, 3¼" h... $22.00
Cat, six cigarette holders, well done, Germany, 4¾" h....................................... $38.00
Pig, arms make two cigarette holders, 3⅝" h $30.00
Man in car, sticker on back: *The Foreign Sports Car,* 6¼" l $20.00
Skier, 4⅝" w... $12.00
Pon My Soul, a food store in Illinois used this for Xmas in 1937, toes hold matches, striker on side, 4½" l.. $40.00
Man with top hat, four cigarette holders, one rest, 4⅝" h................................. $28.00
Who Left This Behind, luster, place for matches & cigarettes, match striker on side, 4" h $13.00

PLATE 168 (left to right)

Row 1:

Pot-bellied stove, one rest on top, lid lifts off for ashes, 4½" h.............................. $10.00
Man with brown pants, chalkware, *Only Man In Washington Who Knows What He's Doing,* 4⅜" h $30.00
Hobo, composition, two pipe holders & place for ashes, 7" h $16.00
Fire hydrant & dog, *I Thought I Knew All The Dogs In Town,* 5" l $14.00
Toilet, flowers, *Rest Your Weary Ash Here,* one rest, 5⅛" h $17.00

Row 2:

Man with blue pants, *Everything I Like Is Either Improper, Illegal or Fattening,* 4⅛" h................. $15.00
Three Old English Men, in relief, triangular, 5" sides.................................... $16.00
Benjamin Franklin, squashed, three rests on top, 4⅜" w, about 1952 .... $18.00
Pixie, nice, 7⅛" w $10.00
Winking man, squashed, three rests on top, 4⅜" w...................................... $14.00
Watch, luster, one rest, 4⅝" l $13.00
Car, *36 Payments and It's Mine,* 2½" h $12.00

PLATE 167

PLATE 168

NO DEARTH OF IDEAS

I think the title describes this grouping very well. As I said for a section in glass, "Would you believe?" There are always some ashtrays that amaze me.

In Plate 169, there is a solar paddle wheel inside a glass globe. If put in the sun, or under light, it will spin.

The rotary ashtray in Plate 169 is a unique combination of cigarette holder and ashtray. It is nicely bound in leather. It has twenty hair-spring loaded cylinders to hold cigarettes and push them up through the hole when the tray is rotated. It is great to also have the original box that it came in.

The book with the title *Smoke and Ashes* was written by A. Flame, according to the cover. It is pictured in Plate 170. Inside is a place for cigarettes, matches, and ashes.

Keeler, a brass Manufacturing Company, gave an unique solid brass ashtray, like the one in Plate 170, to their employees, customers, and suppliers each Christmas for many years. They are dated on the back and have become very collectible.

PLATE 169 (left to right)

Row 1:

Butt bucket, *Put Your G.D. Ashes Here,* yellow metal, 3½" h . . . . $ 6.00

Old Red Eye, green pottery, one rest, *Embalmers Beverage Corporation,* 3" h . . . . $ 9.00

Green marbles, rests between marbles, 3¼" d $16.00

Toilet (wall mount), pottery, 5" h $13.00

Blue marbles, rests between marbles, 3¼" d $17.00

Wood & Brass with music box, plays the song from Moulin Rouge, 4" d, 1950s $17.00

Happy Days, green spittoon, plastic, 4¼" h . . . . $ 9.00

Row 2:

Solar paddle wheel in glass globe, sun gives energy to move blades, 4" h $40.00

Dust pan, tin, 5" l . . . . $ 5.00

Old cannon, white Akro Agate, metal moveable cannon, two rests, 5" w $18.00

Hand held tire, rubber, metal cover, rest on lid when open, 2½" d, 1975 . . . . $11.00

African face, pottery, 5⅞" l, 1956 . . . . $15.00

Cigarette box with two lids, Rotray, move tray top around & cigarette pops up through hole, three rests,
  with two tops, 3¼" h $50.00

PLATE 170 (left to right)

Row 1:

Ship's compass, figural compass & wheel, solid brass, 6" h, 1930s $60.00

Smoke & Ashes **book,** opened book provides a place for cigarettes, matches, ashes, 7½" l, 1928 . . . . $20.00

Sink, solid brass, two pieces, two rests, note faucet, 4⅛" l $28.00

Telephone, brass coating, made in Italy, 5½" h $15.00

Row 2:

Sardine can, brass, 5¼" l $14.00

Man in armor, very heavy, figural, 9¾" h $22.00

Match holder, three boxes held together by boys, brass, 2" h $10.00

Lamp, two rests, pulls down to show cigarette holder, 8⅛" h $25.00

Face, solid brass, two rests, by Keeler Mfg. Co., 6⅛" l, 1967 . . . . $28.00

PLATE 169

PLATE 170

ODDS & END ASHTRAYS

One of the more difficult challenges in writing this book has been to arrange the ashtrays in some sort of order. For a long time, I put everything I did not have another place for into novelty. Gradually, I began to see some patterns developing, and some collections emerged. Yet, I still was left with many odds and ends that did not fit into any of my categories.

The Braille ABC ashtrays are not easy to find except in Ohio and Pennsylvania. Unfortunately, adults do sometimes lose their vision and want to learn Braille. What more relaxing time to practice than when they were sitting and smoking. These ashtrays came in several colors but in only two styles, either with a cane or a seeing-eye dog in the center.

PLATE 171 (left to right)
Row 1:
Amber canoe, one rest in each end, Daisy Button pattern, 6½" l $17.00
Sailboat, blue plastic sail, one rest, 6" l $14.00
Wheelbarrow, nicely done, one rest, 5" l $15.00
Brown car, pottery, two rests, 4" h $18.00
Donkey pulling cart, one rest, 4½" l $10.00
Pale yellow apple, glass, one rest, 4¼" l .... $ 8.00
Crystal canoe, one rest in each end, Daisy Button pattern, 6½" l $10.00

Row 2:
Green boat, one rest in wide end, Daisy Button pattern, 5¼" l $10.00
Cobalt car, glass, one rest, 3½" l $20.00
Green apple, glass, heavy, one rest, 4¾" l $12.00
Crystal fish, glass, one rest, 5" l .... $ 8.00
Cobalt fish, glass, three rests, 6½" l $20.00
Glass & stainless steel fish, cover is to keep smoke from disturbing neighbor at dining table, 4½" l $15.00
Amber car, glass, one rest, 3½" l $20.00
Crystal boat, one rest in wide end, Daisy Button pattern, 5¼" l .... $ 9.00

PLATE 172 (left to right)
Row 1:
Amish couple, iron, painted, Wilton Prod. Wrightsville, PA, 4" sq $19.00
Cigarette box with lid, lid is ashtray, four rests, 4½" l $10.00
Blue pin-up, metal, ad for Northernair Cafe, 4⅛" sq $12.00
Cigarette box on legs with lid, ashtray is between legs, 4" w $12.00
Red hand-held, rest pops up when opened, 2½" d $10.00
White box, two rests, clock face on other side, 3¾" w .... $ 7.00
Blue pin-up, metal, ad for Otto's, 4⅛" sq $12.00
Coaster & ashtray, black iron, has *The Homestead In Winter* tile, 6" w $11.00

Row 2:
Humor, pewter-like metal, turn over to see man (Ahh!) pinching lady (Ohh!), 5¾" l $27.00
Olive braille ashtray, cane in center, 6¼" d $35.00
Pin-up, china with opalized center, old, 4⅜" w $16.00
Hand-held with handle, rest pops out when opened, 2⅞" l $11.00
Yellow Pin-up, metal, souvenir of Riverview Park, 4¾" l $15.00
Life raft, two rests on inside raft, 6⅝" l $13.00
Bathtub, *Cool your Hot Butt In My Old Tub,* two rests, 7½" l, 1954 .... $12.00
Square hand-held, rests pops out when opened, 1⅝" sq .... $ 9.00
Calendar, red metal tray, map of world, dates change as map of world is rotated, 3⅛" h .... $ 9.00
Pink braille ashtray, seeing-eye dog in center, 6¼" d $35.00
Bedpan, gold edging, *For Old Butts And Ashes,* one snufferette, 5" l .... $ 8.00

PLATE 171

PLATE 172

SOUVENIR ASHTRAYS FROM STATES

Souvenir ashtrays, both domestic and foreign, are easy to find. Many people love to collect souvenirs. They collect spoons, cups and saucers, plates, and so forth. Others can't stand them. There are some interesting ashtrays, and I've shown some of them here. See Section II for other ashtrays under the entertainment, hotels and motels, and restaurant headings.

There are different ways to organize souvenirs. You can do it by country, state, city, place of interest, parks, manufacturer, event, and so on. These pictured here are a grouping of ashtrays collected by the different states.

PLATE 173 (left to right)

Row 1:

Arkansas, Hot Springs National Park, two rests, 5¾" d .... $ 8.00
Arkansas, ceramic tub, Hot Springs, 4⅛" l $10.00
California, San Francisco cable car, scene in relief, 9½" w $10.00
California, four ashtrays in holder, scenes of San Francisco including Golden Gate Bridge, 3½" sq $10.00
California, picture of Hearst Castle in center, 4⅝" d .... $ 7.00

Row 2:

Arizona, cactus base, glass tray over picture of desert near Phoenix, 4¾" d $10.00
Arizona, glass, London Bridge in Lake Havasu City, 3½" d.. $ 6.00
California, state shape, cities on reverse side, 10" l $15.00
Alaska, ceramic, Mt. McKinley, 8" d... $15.00
California, San Francisco cable car figural, copper finish, 1½'" h $15.00
California, Marineland of the Pacific, 4½" d... $ 8.00

PLATE 174 (left to right)

Row 1:

Louisiana, *Bourbon Street, New Orleans, Birthplace of Jazz,* 5¼" d $10.00
Florida, state shape, one rest, 4" w .... $ 8.00
District Of Columbia, scenes of Washington, DC, 5" d... $12.00
Louisiana, *New Orleans, Pirates Alley,* 6" w.. $10.00
Kentucky, picture of cabin birthplace of Abraham Lincoln, 4¾" d .... $ 9.00
Georgia, scenes of President Carter's hometown, Plains, GA, 4" w................................. $ 9.00
Colorado, scenes of Denver, 5½" d $10.00

Row 2:

Colorado, scenes of Berthoud Pass, silver color metal, Occupied Japan, 4½" d....................... $12.00
District of Columbia, the Capitol building in relief, pressed wood with glass insert, 4" w $15.00
Illinois, dolphin figural, Brookfield Zoo, Chicago, 6" l $14.00
Illinois, state shape, outline of Lincoln, 9½" l.. $15.00
Florida, figural of dolphin, 6" w.. $15.00
Hawaii, signs from language, ceramic, 4½" w .... $ 9.00
District of Columbia, the Capitol, silver color metal, ornate rim, 5" d $10.00

PLATE 173

PLATE 174

SOUVENIR ASHTRAYS FROM STATES

Souvenirs come in all sizes, shapes, and materials. They are made by many different kinds of manufacturers, including some very well known ones. See the Mackinaw Island ashtray in Plate 175. This is Staffordshire Ware made in England. The ashtray from North Carolina in Plate 175 was made in Occupied Japan.

Frankoma Pottery of Oklahoma made many ashtrays in the shape of states. See Texas in Plate 176. Because of the quality of Frankoma, grouped together, they make a very nice collection.

Many of the metal ashtrays shown were made in Japan, and some were made in Occupied Japan. However, occupied or not, many of these metal ashtrays were cheaply made and are not in very good condition today.

PLATE 175 (left to right)

Row 1:

New York, scenes from Niagara Falls, 7⅝" w $13.00
New York, scenes of Albany, copper coating, opens up for matches & striker, very unusual, 6" l $35.00
New York, New York City, *smiles,* 4½" d $12.00
Minnesota, scenes painted on thin metal, 5¾" d $13.00
New Mexico, brass, oxen & prairie wagon etched in center, 4¼" sq $13.00
Minnesota, Rochester, Mayo Clinic, 4¾" d $10.00
Nebraska, scenes of the Corn Husker State, copper coating, 4½" w $13.00
Michigan, Mackinaw Island, Staffordshire, 7⅜" d $25.00

Row 2:

Montana, *Old Faithful & shining mountains,* 6" d $14.00
New York, NYC, Rockefeller Center figural, brass coating, 3⅝" h $25.00
Nevada, Fabulous Las Vegas, plastic, 5¾" w $18.00
Nebraska, scenes of, coaster ashtray, 4¼" w . . . . $ 8.00
Missouri, Kansas City, Union Station, 5" w $10.00
Massachusetts, Boston beans, 4¾" w . . . . $ 7.00
Nevada, Las Vegas, Golden Nugget, working roulette wheel, 5⅜" d $15.00

PLATE 176 (left to right)

Row 1:

Wisconsin, black painted metal with flowers, Minocqua, 5¼" d . . . . $ 8.00
Virginia, Williamsburg, scene in relief in silver color metal, ornate rim with scenes, 5" d $15.00
Tennessee, Opryland, Nashville, 3¾" d . . . . $ 9.00
Wyoming, Yellowstone National Park, aluminum with glass over center picture, 5½" d $12.00
Virginia, Jamestown, Birthplace of America, three boats in relief, 4⅛" d $18.00
North Carolina, scenes from Great Smoky Mountain National Park, Occupied Japan, 4⅜" d $11.00
Wisconsin, scenes from state with Indian in relief in center, Occupied Japan, 4¾" w $14.00
Wyoming, scenes from, 5¼" d $13.00

Row 2:

Rhode Island, the Ocean State, state house, 4¾" d $12.00
South Dakota, Flintstone's Bedrock City, Custer, octagon, 4½" w $10.00
Ohio, seal of state, 4¼" l $12.00
Texas, state shape, by Frankoma, 6" w $17.00
Wisconsin, State capitol in Madison, 5½" d $13.00
South Dakota, scenes from, 4½" d $13.00
Tennessee, scenes from Lookout Mountain, 5" w . . . . $ 7.00

PLATE 175

PLATE 176

FOREIGN SOUVENIR ASHTRAYS

Many of the foreign souvenirs that I have seen in the antique malls or fairs were from hotels or places unknown to me. I have tried to picture only those places that everybody knows. The souvenir from Rio de Janeiro, Brazil, in Plate 178, was partially made from butterfly wings, which were used for the color blue. This was popular in the 1920s and 1930s. Souvenirs that have three-dimensional buildings are very collectible now, and their prices are rising.

PLATE 177 (left to right)
Row 1:
Innsbruck, Austria, picture in center, one rest, by KPM, 4" w .... $ 5.00
London, England, scene in center, pottery, 4" d .... $ 7.00
Mannheim Wasserturm, Germany, picture in center of water tower and fountains, 4½" w .... $ 6.00
Munich, Germany, picture in center, gold rim, 3" sq .... $ 6.00
Ireland, scenes from the country in center, 6¼" d .... $ 7.00
Bad Windsheim, Germany, town's coat of arms, 4½" sq .... $ 5.00
Piccadilly Circus, London, scene in center, 3" sq .... $ 7.00
Heidelberg, Germany, black etching in center, old, 3⅜" l $10.00
Shakespeare's birthplace, Stratford on Avon, England, picture, pottery, 4" d .... $ 8.00
New Zealand, stones in resin around rim, picture of bird in center, 3¼" sq .... $ 5.00

Row 2:
Jerusalem, solid brass with some enameling, cut-out camels around upper rim, 3⅝" d $10.00
Bruxelles, Belgium, figural of famous boy statue, cathedral in relief, pot metal, 3⅛" h $14.00
Durban, South Africa, ricksha boy, brass with enameling, 4⅜" l .... $ 8.00
Parthenon in Athens, Greece, patterns in relief including building, some painting, 3½" sq $17.00
Rhein River, Germany, shown path of river & cities on way, glass with painting, six rests, 6⅞" d $10.00
Madrid, Spain, scenes in relief, thin metal, painting & enameling, 2¾" sq .... $ 6.00
Monaco, coat of arms in center, by Limoges, 4½" w $10.00
Acapulco, Mexico, silver in center, Mexican coins, 4¼" d, newest coin is from 1974 .... $12.00
Piratis Resti, Bahamas, resort, stainless steel, enameled center, 3½" d .... $ 5.00

PLATE 178 (left to right)
Row 1:
Leaning Tower of Pisa, Italy, pot metal, silver color finish, 4¼" h $15.00
Tijuana, B.C., Mexico, scene in center, other scenes on rim, 4⅛" d .... $ 7.00
Peru, thin copper with colored stone decor, 5⅛" d .... $ 5.00
Rothenburg, Germany, old castle, 3" sq .... $ 5.00
Vancouver, Canada, figural Canadian Mounted Police on horse, pot metal, 3¾" h $28.00
Notre Dame of Paris, France, picture in center, by Limoges, 3" sq .... $ 6.00
Puerto Rico, scene in center, cobalt blue ceramic, 4½" d .... $ 8.00
Nice, France, coat of arms picture in center, by Limoges, 3⅛" sq .... $ 7.00
Nassau, The Bahamas, figural traffic policeman in lead, 4" h $18.00
Scotland, shield in center, silver plate, 4" d $10.00

Row 2:
Switzerland, plunger type, gold color metal, 3½" d $13.00
Niagara Falls, Canada, pot metal, bronze plate, 5" w $10.00
Paris, France, pot metal, figurals of La Tour Eiffel and Arc de Triomphe, 3" h $25.00
Reims, France, solid brass, cathedral, 5" l, 1945 .... $12.00
Rio de Janeiro, picture in center of Rio with butterfly wings for blue, wood ashtray, 6½" l $13.00
Lausanne, Switzerland, La Residence, 5" w .... $ 6.00
San Pietro, Rome, pottery, picture in center, 4" d .... $ 8.00
Paris, France, picture of La Tour Eiffel and figural Arc de Triomphe, copper finish, 2" h $18.00
Known buildings in Italy, cathedrals, Tower of Pisa, Colosseum, bridges, lead, 4⅜" sq, old $14.00
San Pietro, Rome, figural of cathedral and Pope, pot metal, 2⅛" h $20.00

PLATE 177

PLATE 178

SPORTS ASHTRAYS
(BASEBALL & BOWLING)

Most people have an interest in at least one sport. I have included many sports here, hoping to find something for everyone. These ashtrays are quite easy to find now, so if you want to start a collection, now is the time. Baseball and golfing seem to be the two areas that have a lot of collectors.

Baseball developed from the old English sport of rounders and the game of cricket. Cricket was played by youngsters in colonial times. It was not until 1869 that the Cincinnati Red Stockings formed the first professional baseball team. Then it was just a question of time for this sport to develop. The National League was organized in 1876 and the American League in 1900.

Bowling is one of the oldest and most popular indoor sports. It has been played for thousands of years. The Egyptians played it, as well as the English, Germans, and Dutch.

PLATE 179 (left to right)
Row 1:
Yankees, 1950s, 4" w $10.00
Red Sox, 1950s, 4" w $10.00
Cardinal games, glove shape, also ad for Griesedieck Bros.'s Beer, 5" w $35.00
Nationals, 1950s, 4" w $10.00
Baseball Hall of Fame, Cooperstown, N.Y., glove shape, one rest, 5" l $18.00
Chicago White Sox, 1950s, 4" w $10.00
Indians, 1950s, 4" w $10.00

Row 2:
Cincinnati Reds, 4½" d $15.00
Boston Red Sox, 3½" d $10.00
Cubs, ceramic, bats & ball in relief in center, 4⅛" d $20.00
Athletics, 1950s, 4" w $10.00
Tigers, 1950s, 4" w $10.00

PLATE 180 (left to right)
Row 1:
Gutter Gus, chalkware, old, 6½" h $35.00
Bowling ball & pins center, figure in center, ceramic by Lefton, 5¼" d $12.00
Bowlers ashtray, ceramic, 4½" h $10.00
Old Bowlers Never Die, *Their Balls End Up In The Gutter,* chalkware, 4¼" h, 1953 . . . . $35.00

Row 2:
Black bowling pin shape, plastic with black glass ashtray, 8⅜" l . . . . $ 9.00
Bowling pin, also ad for Winston-Salem cigarettes, 9⅛" h $20.00
Pink tin, wooden bowling pin on back rim, 3½" d . . . . $ 7.00
Alibi Al-Rail Splitter, chalkware, probably not very old, 9⅝" w $50.00

PLATE 179

PLATE 180

SPORTS ASHTRAYS
(FOOTBALL, GOLF, HORSE RACING & HUNTING)

Football is an American sport that began in the 1880s. It was similar to soccer in the beginning, but stricter rules turned it into a different sport. The first college football game was played, Rutgers against the now-Princeton, in 1869. The first game between two professional teams took place in 1895. Today, collecting football memorabilia has become almost as popular as baseball collecting.

Golf is another very old sport. It probably began in Scotland in 1100, developing from a Roman game. It spread to England, Ireland, Canada, and the United States. In 1888, the first permanent golf club in the United States was organized in Yonkers, NY. As well as being an immensely popular spectator sport, it is a very popular form of recreation.

PLATE 181 (left to right)
Row 1:
Pheasants & rifle, by Lefton, 3¾" h $20.00
Pittsburgh Steelers, helmet in center, 5¼" d $13.00
Green Bay Packers, helmet in center, 5½" sq $15.00
Detroit Lions, football field shape, ceramic, 1960, 8½" w $55.00
Wisconsin Badgers, mascot in center, 5½" sq $15.00
Arkansas Razorbacks, mascot in center, 5¼" d $15.00
Fishing, rod & basket figural in center, 5¼" d $14.00

Row 2:
Iowa Hawkeyes, ceramic, mascot in center, 8" w $20.00
World Boxing Association, Las Vegas, 1965, 5¾" d $12.00
Curling Club, Poynette WI, 3½" sq $10.00
Ducks & rifles, different ducks in relief in center, 10" l $11.00
Drake University, mascot in center, 4¼" d $10.00
Green Bay Packers Hall of Fame, 3½" sq . . . . $ 9.00
Green Bay Packers, helmet in center, 5¼" d $13.00
University of Louisiana Fighting Cardinals, mascot in center, 5¼" d $15.00

PLATE 182 (left to right)
Row 1:
Jockey on horse, copper ashtray on wood block, 4" w $28.00
Matchbox cover, enamel with picture of Passage & rider, nice, 2⅛" l $30.00
1971 Polam Golf, Tuckaway Country Club, Milwaukee, WI, 6⅞" d . . . . $ 8.00
Vantage Golf, PGA Tour, flag stick, three rests, 6½" w $11.00
Golfer figural, knickered golfer, pewter, 3" h, 1977 . . . . $75.00
Head of golf club, two rests, 4¼" h $20.00

Row 2:
National Open – 1964, Congressional Country Club, Washington, DC, plastic, 4¼" d . . . . $ 8.00
Assault, ceramic, picture of horse's head, 4" sq $12.00
Intaglio, horse jumping scene, very nice, five rests, 4¼" w $20.00
Golf hat, with club & ball, one rest, 3" h . . . . $ 9.00
Jockey & horses, gold color metal, Chicago, 5" w $13.00
Kentucky Derby 1990, picture of Churchill Downs in center, ceramic, 4¼" d $10.00

PLATE 181

PLATE 182

SPORTS ASHTRAYS
(RACING, TENNIS & OLYMPICS)

Everyone knows about the Indianapolis Motor Speedway. There are many other raceways across our country, where various types of cars and motorcycles race. This is a big spectator sport and a huge business. The helmet ashtrays, in Plate 183, are from this sport. A lot of the raceways had their own ashtrays.

I thought that tennis ashtrays would by easy to find, but I have only four. Perhaps I need to look harder. Tennis actually developed from a handball game played in ancient Greece. In the 1400s, France developed a game similar to present-day tennis.

Although the first recorded Olympic race was in 776 B.C., many believe that games were held hundreds of years earlier. Eventually, the games became corrupt, and were abolished in 394 A.D. Interest was renewed after the excavation of an ancient Olympic stadium in 1878, and the games were renewed in 1896. Women first competed in 1900. The 1972 Munich Olympics had a terrible incident when terrorists attacked and killed some members of the Israeli team. Possibly because of this happening, the prices for these Olympic ashtrays seem to be high.

PLATE 183 (left to right)
> **Row 1:**
> **Rider,** '86 Americade Motorcycle Touring Club, black & red decoration, two rests, 4½" h $18.00
> **Penske Racing,** '84 Indy 500 Winner, Mears-Unser, helmet shape, two rests, 4⅜" h $32.00
> **Indianapolis Motor Speedway,** "500," no date, 8" w $38.00
> **Harley-Davidson,** *Motor Cycles, made in U.S.A.,* stainless steel, 4½" sq $25.00
> **Honda,** motorcycle racing, Jeb's Helmets, two rests, 4½" h $18.00
> **Ford Motorsport,** shades of blue for decor, two rests, 4½" h. $20.00
>
> **Row 2:**
> **Tennis player figural,** silver color, one rest, 3½" h $15.00
> **Let,** cartoon picture in center, 5¾" d. . . . . $ 6.00
> **Dropshot,** cartoon picture in center, 5¾" d . . . . $ 6.00
> **Virginia Slims,** *World Championship Series,* no date, 5½" d $10.00
> **U.S. Lawn Tennis Association,** *1965 annual meeting,* ceramic, 6⅝" l . . . . $ 8.00

PLATE 184 (left to right)
> **Row 1:**
> **Olympics Munich–1972,** by Goebel, very nice, etched scenes of Munich around rim, 5" d $65.00
> **Olympics Canada–1976,** metal, made in Canada, maple leaf in center, 3⅜" d $18.00
> **Olympics Berlin–1936,** brass, athletic figures in relief in round top, 4⅝" d. $70.00
> **Olympics Munich–1972,** sterling, enamel shield of Munich and Olympic rings in center, 3¼" d $50.00
> **Olympics Montreal–1976,** milk glass, made in France, triangular shape, 5¼" across $20.00
>
> **Row 2:**
> **Olympics Mexico–1968,** sterling, 19th, Mexican commemorative silver coin in center, 5¼" d $45.00
> **Olympics Lake Placid–1980,** heavy glass, picture of mascot's raccoon head, 7¼" d. $32.00
> **Olympics Seoul, Japan–1983,** metal, 24th, mascot in center, 5¼" d $18.00

PLATE 183

PLATE 184

MISCELLANEOUS & LATE ARRIVAL ASHTRAYS

As I continued to record prices of ashtrays for the latest price information, I kept seeing ashtrays that appealed to me, and I ended up buying them. Since the book is now almost complete, I will group all these new or miscellanies ashtrays together.

See the red clip-on ashtray in Plate 184. It is great for a heavy smoker because it can be clipped onto any vertical edge or post. Made in West Germany.

In Plate 185, there is a great ash dump made by Schafer & Vater. This is a German firm, established by two men, in 1890. They continued until after World War II, making many different kinds of items. They used many color washes, and much of their work was of bisque or jasper. They had a wonderful sense of whimsy and that can be seen in the ashtray pictured here.

PLATE 185 (left to right)

Row 1:

Who Burned The Hole In The Tablecloth?, blue pottery, ad on back for food store, 5⅝" d . . . . $ 13.00
No mark, very similar to Royal Bayreuth, pic of two women & goats, 3⅛" sq, old . . . . $ 35.00
Schafer & Vater ash dump, Germany, jasper, gnome-like face, 2½" h, very old $165.00
Japan, Imari type pattern around inside of rise, marked Maebata, 7½" w . . . . $ 35.00
Handle with nine holes for cigarettes, flowers in center, 4½" sq . . . . $ 30.00
Reversible, pottery, other side is green flower scene, two rests, 3¾" sq . . . . $ 10.00
Old souvenir, *Hotel Custer, Galesburg, Ill,* match holder, Germany, 5" w, old style . . . . $ 15.00
Shelley, England, floral decor, 5¼" d, old . . . . $ 75.00

Row 2:

Japanese scenes & characters on rim, blue & white pottery, not for export, match pack holder, 4⅞" d . . . $ 15.00
RS Germany, three wide extended rests, windmill decor on rise all around, marked, 4½" w, old . . . . $ 40.00
Figural Man with set, Staffordshire type, four ashtrays, cigarette holder, Japan, 5" h . . . . $ 20.00
Man and woman with ashtray, some luster, Japan, 3⅛" h . . . . $ 12.00
Cigarette box, enamel & cut out work in bronze, silver lined (see page 89 for rest of set) . . . . $ 45.00
Bohemian, two layers of glass, white cut to ruby, gold decor, painted flowers, lovely, 3⅞" d,
   from around turn of century . . . . $ 75.00

PLATE 186 (left to right)

Row 1:

Akro Agate with match holder, matches pull off the holder, bottom is ashtray, 5¾" h, old $60.00
Aluminum round, upright ball with depression as rest, 5¼" d $10.00
China clown, two rests, one in each hand, stands or lays on back, 9" l $15.00
Copper slide-on, to add to a plate or saucer, two rests, set of four, 2½" w $12.00
100th Kentucky Derby, *1875–1974, Churchill Downs, Louisville, KY,* 6¾" d $11.00
Old brass with match holder, glass insert, two wide rests, 2¾" h, probably 1910–1920 . . . . $18.00
Cigarette holder, Akro Agate bottom, metal painted cigarette holder opens when lift top, 6¾" h $35.00

Row 2:

White ash dumper, by Porcellana Bianca, Italy, six rests, 4¼" w, recent $15.00
Chrome slide-on, shown added to saucer, set of four, 2½" w $12.00
Clamp-on, red painted metal with spring clamp, ADRO mark, 4⅝" l . . . . $ 9.00
Seaman smoker, cigarette smoke comes out pipe, lots of gold, 6" h $22.00
Aluminum with rods, rods are cigarette rests, by Wendel August Forge, hammered, sailboat scene, 6½" d . . $30.00
Christmas, by Berggren, "Merry Christmas," 4¼" sq . . . . $ 5.00
25th Anniversary, by Lefton, holder with four ashtrays, 2" h . . . . $ 8.00

PLATE 185

PLATE 186

MISCELLANEOUS & LATE ARRIVAL ASHTRAYS

The horse ashtray, in Plate 187, is fairly easy to find, but glass does not always have the horse on the back of it. The horse is plastic, and fits into the holes in the rim at the back.

The ashtray for the "2 Stiffs Motel" in Plate 188 is very interesting. At one time, it was not too unusual to find motels also selling gasoline from a small filling station. This was before the era of the large motel complex.

The green steel McDonald's ashtray and the Avis Rent-A-Car ashtray are both very nice, and I was glad to add them to my collection.

PLATE 187 (left to right)

Row 1:

Yellow beer stein, verse about reasons for drinking, 7¾" l . . . . $ 6.00

Cup, saucer, ashtray, *Your Daily Double – A Sip N' A Smoke – Refreshing Pause,* 4½" h . . . . $ 7.00

Hanging basket ashtray, white pottery ashtray with three rests, three holes to hang, 4" h . . . . $ 5.00

Nevasmok, patent pending, chrome top with two rests, cigarette drops down hole and goes out
   because of no oxygen, 3½" h. $15.00

White beer stein, political about voting, 7½" h. . . . . $ 6.00

Cartoon, *There's Always One At Every Bar,* picture of horse's rear, 4" d . . . . $ 5.00

Row 2:

Kitchen ashes, picture of ear of corn, two rests, 5" w . . . . $ 4.00

Ash-Coasta, card table ashtray, two rests, 5⅝" l, set of 4. . . . . $12.00

Toilet & two pots, *Cigarettes, Ashes, Matches,* wood lid lifts up, 2⅜" h . . . . $ 7.00

Eagle, brown pottery, 6¾" w . . . . $ 6.00

Bean bag ashtray, gold color ashtray, two rests, popular in the '50s – '60s, 1⅝" h . . . . $ 5.00

Ash-Coasta, card table ashtray, two rests, 5" w, set of four, see above

Horse on horseshoe, plastic horse on glass horseshoe, 3⅛" h . . . . $ 9.00

PLATE 188 (left to right)

Row 1:

Ford, *Chicago Stamping, 1956–1981,* aluminum, 5¾" d $10.00

Chicago Typographical Union 16, *Centennial, 1852–1952,* safety designed cigarette rest, plastic, 5" d $18.00

Mikasa, 1968, calendar around rim, china, three rests, 7⅜" d $13.00

National Association Of Cost Accountants, 1944, *Peoria Chapter,* 3¾" w $23.00

Police Department – Waterloo, Iowa, 1960, *Chief Krieg,* metal, 7¾" l $10.00

Row 2:

McDonald's, baked-on paint, steel, two rests, 5⅞" w. $20.00

2 Stiffs Motel, *selling Standard Oil Gas, Lovelock, Nevada,* 3¼" sq $16.00

Fire Dept, pottery, three rests, 7" w. . . . . $ 5.00

Ship funnel with four small funnels, usually colors identify shipping line, not identified yet,
   largest is 4⅜" l $20.00

Camel shot glass, great for cigarettes, 2⅛" h . . . . $ 8.00

Avis Rent-A-Car, *Red Cab Taxi,* cobalt glass, 3¾" sq. $18.00

PLATE 187

PLATE 188

ASHTRAYS FROM THE PAST

The ashtrays pictured in this book come from Victorian times through the turn of the century with the Arts and Craft Movement, to Art Nouveau, Art Deco, the Depression years, and, finally, ending with the 1940s, 1950s, and 1960s. There are also some more recent ones. If I had known the dates that all the ashtrays were manufactured, I could have grouped all of them by date. However, some I do know, and I have pictured some of them here, grouped in their own time periods.

VICTORIAN ASHTRAYS

Whether something is made by hand, or manufactured by machine, the style is influenced by everything happening at that time, the social climate, political happenings, art, architecture, and so forth. This was a time of lavish decoration, in dress, art, and architecture. The Victorian period for cigarette ashtrays refers to the 1880s to the end of the century. This is when ashtrays were beginning to be made.

These ashtrays were also very ornate. Most of the rests were large enough to handle cigars, because cigarettes were just coming into use in the home by men. Smoking sets were large, often with cigar cutters. Women did not smoke, as it was definitely frowned on as improper. See Plate 189 and 190 for ashtrays that were used during that time.

PLATE 189 (left to right)

Row 1:

Girl by well smoking set, terra cotta, places for cigars, matches, and ashes, gold touches, 5⅛" h $100.00

Wooden smoking set, great, three brass lined cups for cigars, matches & ashes, also cigar cutter,
     match striker, gold decoration, 7⅜" h $270.00

Owl, black pottery, bat faces under rests at corners, 5⅛" h $125.00

Row 2:

Sailor boy smoking set, terra cotta, place for cigars, matches and ashes, 7⅝" h $150.00

Three pot smoking set, metal with removable cups, cigarette rest on cup at left, 4¾" h $65.00

PLATE 190 (left to right)

Row 1:

Brass ashtray with red decoration, cameo-type embossing around ashtray, matchbox holder, 5⅝" h $18.00

Elk, notice width of rests, Bavarian, 5" w $45.00

Pottery smoking set, towards end of Victorian era, 7½" w $55.00

Row 2:

Kalk, crossed arrows mark, Victorian style, lovely, Germany, 7⅜" l, around turn of century $95.00

Heavy square, metal with bronze coating that is mostly worn off, very old type matchbox holder, ornate
     decoration, transition to Art Nouveau, 6¼" w $20.00

PLATE 189

PLATE 190

ASHTRAYS FROM THE TURN OF THE CENTURY

At the beginning of the twentieth century, it seemed that ornate Victorian decoration went out. During the transition, there seemed to be a time when ashtrays were less ornate, mostly metal, large, and often with cigar rests. You can definitely see the change that occurred. The ornate Victorian ashtray or smoking set finally went out of style. Most of the ashtrays, in Plate 191, show samples of ashtrays around the turn of the century. I have seen the raised two pot ashtray with three pots, but this one was made for two only.

PLATE 191 (left to right)
Row 1:
Black metal with matchbox holder, ad for Roberts Brass Co. in Milwaukee, 4½" h $25.00
Cigarette dispenser with ashtray, leather jar & metal top, push handle & cigarette feeds into holder
    at side, owl design in leather on other side, holds 20 cigarettes to dispense, different, 3¾" h, very old . . . $50.00
Two wood pots, painted metal, boys playing & smoking, 7" h $27.00
Pivot opening, faux tortoise shell sides, silver color top with four rests, 4⅛" h, near 1920s. $30.00
Brass with glass insert, matchbox holder, wide rests, 4⅜" h, about 1915. . . . . $14.00

Row 2:
Plunger type, tan leather on sides, plunger opens tray to drop ashes, two bar rest, 3⅛" h $17.00
Green iron, glass insert with picture of girl of that time period, 5¾" w. $20.00
Bronze coated with cigarette container, lift lid & cigs pop up, three snufferettes, leather jar, 4⅝" h $35.00
Pink copper, solid, very heavy, color chemical application, 4⅞" w. $12.00
Brass, two rests at top, two snufferettes, counter in base to keep track of cigarettes or cigar smoked,
    great, never seen another like it, 3⅞" h $45.00

ASHTRAYS FROM THE ARTS AND CRAFTS MOVEMENT

The Arts and Crafts Movement originated in England as a rebellion against mechanized mass production. They believed in a purification of design, only using what is necessary. This allowed their good design and workmanship to show. This movement influenced most areas of artistic design. The furniture was very plain, square, and often of heavy oak. This style became known as "mission." The Arts and Crafts Movement was popular from the end of the 1890s to the early 1920s

Metal work was very popular and done by some well-known crafts people. As with all old metals, do not scrub or polish them, or you could remove the dark, rich patina that is typical of this age. If the patina is missing, the price is lowered. Keep articles dusted with a clean, soft cloth.

I have some ashtrays by Heintz and Roycroft, who were both metallists, and Van Briggle, a potter of the Arts and Crafts Movement. They are pictured in Plate 192.

PLATE 192 (left to right)
Row 1:
Copper, flowers in relief around rim, Art Nouveau influence, 5¾" d $25.00
Silver Crest, marked, sterling decorated bronze, matchbox holder, 4⅞" l, 1919–1929. . . . . $60.00
Silver Crest, marked, decorated bronze, matchbox holder, 7⅝" w, 1919–1929. . . . . $42.00
Brass, solid, children playing with long pipe, 6" w $40.00
Heintz, marked, sterling on bronze, 6¾" w, patented August, 1912. . . . . $48.00

Row 2:
Heintz, marked, sterling on bronze, matchbox holder, 3⅓" h, patented August, 1912 . . . . $45.00
Van Briggle, pottery, one of his earlier pieces, 6" l. $38.00
Copper with cork in center, useful for pipes, solid, 6¼" w $15.00
Roycroft, marked, 4¾" w $85.00
Hammered copper, rests lift up to dump, patented Jan.,1917, 2¼" h. $30.00

PLATE 191

PLATE 192

ART NOUVEAU ASHTRAYS

Art Nouveau, in the artistic sense, was "beginning anew." This even related to society, which was to begin anew. The Art Nouveau movement was really a protest against old morals, values, laws, and institutions. Old styles were no longer to be copied, but original art, which expressed the times, was to be created. However, there was some lingering influence of classical antiquity. It was not until Art Deco came into its own, around the 1920s, that this fascination with classical antiquity was completely overthrown.

Art Nouveau started in Europe around the end of the nineteenth century. Some say that it lasted until 1905, some say until 1910. It influenced all areas of artistic endeavors, including furniture. There are many examples around of its lovely lines and its grace. Ladies with long flowing hair and long flowing dresses were typical of this style.

The silver ashtray in Plate 193 is a lovely example of Art Nouveau. The silver, the design of the girl with luxurious tresses, and the overblown flower, all contribute to this lovely work.

The ashtray and match holder with the bulbous flower, as seen in Plate 194, is silver plate. This is a perfect example of how silver plate will tarnish black with age. Sterling will tarnish a golden color, very different from silver plate.

PLATE 193 (left to right)
Row 1:
Ashtray with matchbox holder, copper over iron, lovely work, design in relief, 6½" h . . . . $ 65.00
Girl in dress, lead, a coating probably wore off, soft lead broke off at top & bottom, 5½" l . . . . $ 38.00
Nude smoking, solid bronze rim Nouveau feeling but subject Deco, very nice design, 5⅝" w . . . . $ 65.00
Ashtray with matchbox holder, bronze, ornate matchbox holder with Cupids, 4⅛" h . . . . $ 52.00

Row 2:
Three girl bowl, copper over iron, three rests, 4⅛" w . . . . $ 60.00
Silver plate, girl with flowing tresses and raised flower in hand, 1 rest, lovely, 8" w $135.00
Arc De Triomphe, Paris, really a souvenir, but a good example of Nouveau, metal, 4" sq . . . . $ 25.00

PLATE 194 (left to right)
Row 1:
Man smoking pipe, probably brass plating worn off, 5¼" l $27.00
Nude on center post, saber grip, ashtray is brass, rest is bronze with brass coating, 6" h $55.00
Girl applying make-up, copper over metal, nice detail in center, 6⅜" l $50.00

Row 2:
Bulbous flower on matchbox holder, quadruple silver plate, 3⅞" h, June 1904 . . . . $70.00
Angel playing string instrument, brass coating, frogs in relief, very different, several rests, 9" l $58.00
Matchbox holder at back, nice typical Nouveau design, bronze coating, very heavy, 3⅞" h $35.00

PLATE 193

PLATE 194

ART DECO ASHTRAYS WITH ANIMALS

The Art Deco movement liked to use lush materials when possible. They also extended this usage to ashtrays. Marble, silver, stone, exotic woods, alabaster, and other interesting materials were often used. One theme they seemed to like, in the twenties and thirties, was the use of a large piece of marble or Akro Agate with an animal figural on the back rim. And here again, they used exotic animals: greyhound dogs, bears, elephants, lions, bulls, etc. In Plates 195 and 196, you will see some examples of this.

Note the similarity between the metal base and ashtray with panther, in Plate 195, and the green ashtray with cat, in Plate 196. The green cat ashtray appears to have had a lot of use.

The bronze dog, in Plate 196, is a good example of cubism. This movement started in France in the early 1900s. It sought to break down objects into basic shapes of cubes, cones, spheres, and cylinders. Other Art Deco animal ashtrays can be found with this same influence. They are usually well done and costly.

PLATE 195 (left to right)
  Row 1:
  Bronze seal, marble, two rests, 7" w $45.00
  Greyhound, chrome, baked-on red paint, 6½" l $35.00
  Romulous & Remus, black glass & silver color metal, 5½" w $18.00
  Bull desk set, on marble, bull was brass coated, two rests, 7" l $33.00

  Row 2:
  Dog on green Akro Agate, three rests, two snufferettes, 5¼" w $35.00
  Lion, pewter-like metal, perhaps made at the end of Art Nouveau movement, 6" w $22.00
  Bronze dog, on Akro Agate, three rests, 6⅛" l $32.00
  Carved animal, all from one piece of marble, two rests, 6" l $30.00
  Panther, a typical mount with impressed design, metal, 2⅞" h $40.00

PLATE 196 (left to right)
  Row 1:
  Bull fight, bronzed coating, marble, two rests, lovely, 3⅝" h $65.00
  Dog, black finish over pot metal, two rests, 4¾" h $28.00
  Lion, pewter color, on green Akro Agate, three rests, 7½" w $45.00
  Greyhound, was brass coated, ashtray brass coating with mottled gray, 6¾" d $38.00

  Row 2:
  Bear on rock, bronze coating, two rests, 3⅞" h $20.00
  Dog, on green Akro Agate, three rests, two snufferettes, 5¼" w $35.00
  Cat with duck, painted lead, 6¾" w, old $30.00
  Dog, solid bronze, red paint inside ashtray, stylized, cubism influence, five rests, 3⅛" h $48.00
  Horse, on pale green Akro Agate, bronze coating, two rests, 4¾" h $20.00

PLATE 195

PLATE 196

ART DECO ASHTRAYS
(BLACK GLASS AND CHINA)

Black is often considered a sophisticated color. Many ashtrays with good Art Deco lines are black. Here are a few of them.

PLATE 197 (left to right)
Row 1:
Panther, pottery, some gold on ashtray, 3" h $17.00
Unusual black shape, three rests, patent applied for in 1929, 4½" l $12.00
Horse's head, pottery, six rests, 7" l $24.00
Chase, glass & Chase brass, top slides, four rests, 3⅜" l $29.00
Beagle dog, pottery, four rests, 7" w $10.00

Row 2:
Black with gold round, glass, matchbox holder, 4¾" d $10.00
Mosaic Tile Co., one wide rest, matchbox holder, 3¾" l $25.00
Federation of Eagles, ceramic, two cigarette rests which tip cigarette into ashtray center when cigarette
    burns down & heats bi-metal spring, 7⅛" w $16.00
Match holder, glass, surface is match striker, 3½" l $15.00
Black slashed ball, one rest, 3⅜" h $15.00

ART DECO ASHTRAYS
(CHROME ANIMALS WITH RESTS)

The ashtrays in Plate 198 all belong to a group that was manufactured in the 1950s. They are easy to find and usually come in two sizes, large with 5⅝" diameter base and small with a 4⅜" diameter base. The small bird ashtray is an exception. Its base is only 3⅝" diameter. They all have body parts, such as tails, trunks, and beaks, which become rests to hold cigarettes. Many of them were manufactured by Hamilton.

The elephant ashtrays come with the elephant standing on two or four legs, both in the large and small sizes. All the other ones that I have seen are the same, regardless of size, and usually come in only one style.

PLATE 198 (left to right)
Row 1:
Large bird, two rests, 5⅝" d $14.00
Small fish, two rests, 4⅜" d $14.00
Large elephants, standing on two legs each, two rests & one snufferette, 5⅝" d $28.00
Small elephants, standing on all legs, two rests, 4⅜" d $14.00
Large monkeys, two rests & one snufferette, 5⅝" d $17.00
Small hippopotamuses, two rests, 4⅜" d $15.00
Large stylized fish, rests between tail & body, 5⅝" d $17.00

Row 2:
Large cactus with Mexican, two rests & one snufferette, 5⅝" d $17.00
Small pelicans, two rests, 4⅜" d $12.00
Large cats, rests in tails, 7⅜" l $22.00
Small birds, one rest only, not as easy to find this size, 3⅝" d $10.00
Small alligators, two rests, 4⅜" d $12.00
Large squirrels, two rests & one acorn snufferette, bushy tails, 5⅝" d $17.00

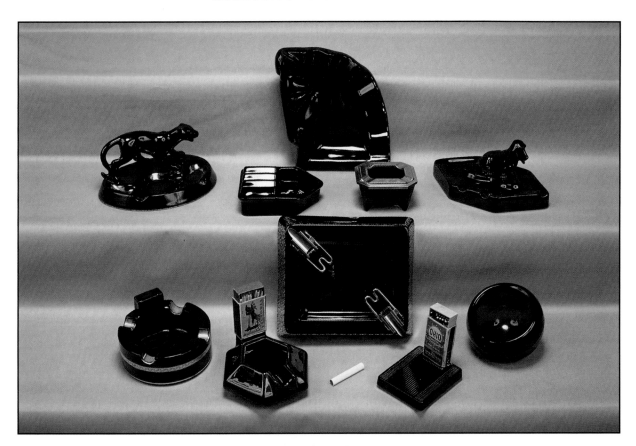

PLATE 197

PLATE 198

CHROME ART DECO ASHTRAYS

Chrome and Art Deco just seem to go together. Chromium is a chemical element, hard and brittle. It is gray and becomes bright and shiny when polished. It resists corrosion, which makes it very popular for household items. It is widely used to plate other metals, to give them the durable qualities of chrome. Alloys that contain more than ten percent of chromium are called stainless steel.

Although chromium was discovered in 1797, it really became popular in the American home in the 1930s. Many of the chrome Art Deco pieces during this time frame were high style. Some nice ones were manufactured by Chase Brass and Copper Company in Connecticut.

The chrome ashtray in Plate 199 has a round circle of pins in the center, similar to a flower holder. Evidently, these pins are a place to put your cigarette. The ashtray is called Park-A-Lite, and has a patent pending.

PLATE 199 (left to right)   **All ashtrays are chrome.**

Row 1:

Vernay's ball, opening reveals rest, from Calcutta, brass base, 3¼" h $22.00

Chase, chrome ashtray with brass whale (rest) in center, 4¼" d $16.00

Large round, matchbox holder & match pack holder with three rests, 6¾" d $15.00

Chrome with red pin center, pins in center to hold cigarettes, Park-A-Lite, patent pending, 4⅛" sq $10.00

Chase ball with lid, cobalt blue base & handle, rest is chrome, opens to reveal rest in center, 3¾" h $65.00

Row 2:

Faux turtle shell, plastic sides, chrome top, four rests, 4" w $20.00

Faux marble with chrome trim, chrome box opens with rest inside of lid, glass liner, 1¼" sq $35.00

Large triangle with glass insert, probably from the late 1940s or 1950s, 8½" w $13.00

Chase round, extended rests, chrome, 5½" w $35.00

PLATE 200 (left to right)   **All ashtrays are chrome.**

Row 1:

Sweeper, felt pad inside, when knob is turned on top, it moves ashes under & cleans ashtray,
    two rests on top, 6" l $33.00

Sailboat, often seen without sail, two rests at back, 6⅛" h $16.00

Rectangle, two rests, rubber pad on bottom, 3¾" w $14.00

Chase round, six plastic rests, 6" w $20.00

Row 2:

High cup, fingers in center are 3 rests, 3⅝" h $18.00

Large square, twelve rests, 6⅝" sq $10.00

Holder for cobalt blue glass cup, chrome holder, 2 rests, 5" l $20.00

Ring around cup with stars, chrome with some brass, rest on tray which pivots to dump, 3⅜" h $50.00

PLATE 199

PLATE 200

ASHTRAYS WITH ART DECO NUDES

The Art Deco movement began in Europe in the early twenties, and examples were shown at the Paris International Exposition in 1925. To some extent, it continued into the early 1950s, changing as times changed. However, most people believe that the movement really ended in the late 1930s or early 1940s.

The wonderful pieces seen at the Paris Exhibition were well made. Streamlined curves, geometric designs, aerodynamic shapes, slender and elongated nudes, greyhound dogs, chrome and glass, plastics, and exotic woods, are some of the images characterized by the Art Deco movement. The ashtrays in Plates 201 and 202 will show these characteristics.

As with all art styles, from jewelry to furniture, Art Deco emerged to represent changing attitudes toward life. Remember that in Victorian times, the cigarette was frowned on, particularly for women. By the late twenties, the cigarette became a mark of sophistication. Women even began to smoke in public. Ashtrays became indispensable. Both the floor model and the table-top version were found in many rooms in the home. A lot of the ashtrays were made of metal, but china and glass soon came into their own. For ashtrays of the 1940s, 1950s, and 1960s, see pages 64–70.

PLATE 201 (left to right)
Row 1:
Black plastic with chrome nude, similar to 1950 Packard hood ornament, 5⅝" h . . . . $ 47.00
Brass nude, sea animals impressed at side, two rests, France, 7⅜" l . . . . $ 50.00
Shell base with bronze nude, lovely work, probably transition from Nouveau to Deco, 7¼" h $190.00

Row 2:
Egyptian woman, pewter-like metal, 3¾" h . . . . $ 38.00
Marble with bronze nude, solid bronze, very nice, 6" h $150.00
Girl applying make-up, copper over metal, Nouveau influence, nice detail, 6⅜" l . . . . $ 50.00

PLATE 202 (left to right)
Row 1:
Nude with skirt, marble base with two rests, nude has lovely lines, 9" h $130.00
Girl with cocktail, solid brass, smoking & drinking, 2 rests, 5" w, 1930s . . . . $ 65.00
Bronze nude, solid, small amount drapery, 7" l . . . . $ 75.00
Cobalt base with chrome nude, a reproduction, good lines, 9⅜" h . . . . $ 42.00

Row 2:
Cobalt pottery ashtray with white nude, angular lines, 5¼" w . . . . $ 20.00
Frankart, nude is white metal with black finish, 8¾" h, 1920s $200.00
Chrome base with bronze nude, 2⅜" h . . . . $ 30.00

PLATE 201

PLATE 202

ODDS & ENDS ART DECO ASHTRAYS

There are a lot of ashtrays left over in the Art Deco movement that I have not assigned to any group. Some of them are much too nice to leave out altogether, so I have grouped them here in Odds & Ends.

The next group which belongs to a time period after Art Deco would be Depression glass. However, that was covered under Glass in Section I. After that would come the 1940s, 1950s, and 1960s with their big ashtrays, bright colors, and sometimes wild lines. These were also covered in the glass category of Section I.

Even though I finish this section with these time periods, the collector does not have to stop collecting with the 1940s, 1950s, and 1960s. Unusual ashtrays were made through the 1970s. Since not many ashtrays are being made anymore, the ones on the market can still be collected and should be. Remember, even if they do make ashtrays today, they don't make than like they used to!

PLATE 203 (left to right)

Row 1:

Clown, similar to Noritake but not, luster & opalized tray, nice, 3½" h $100.00

Pair, bright colors, made by Marutomoware of Japan, other one shown on this row, 4⅛" d . . . . $ 22.00

Clown with banjo, two rests, 3⅝" l . . . . $ 12.00

Chinese boy with box, great Art Deco figural, two rests, cigarette holder, 5⅝" h . . . . $ 45.00

Yellow clown, girl lying on diamond, good for cards, 4⅜" l . . . . $ 20.00

One of pair, by Marutomoware, see above

Clown, colored ruff, two rests in hands, 4¾" l . . . . $ 16.00

Row 2:

Blue glass on legs, by Imperial, 2¼" h $18.00

Blue extended rests, pottery, two rests, 5¼" w . . . . $ 9.00

Noritake swans, green mark, some moriage, hexagon, 6⅝" across $90.00

Blue glass with extended rests, 5⅛" l . . . . $ 6.00

Black & white pottery, Grecian picture in center, 3¾" d $13.00

Crystal square, straight lines cut into glass, heavy, 3⅝" sq. $50.00

PLATE 204 (left to right)

Row 1:

Copper ball, brass decoration, three rests, unusual, 5" h $40.00

Wine Snuf-a-rette, eight snuffs, 3⅝" w, patented in 1937 . . . . $12.00

Rookwood, wooden ball holding rests & two snufferettes, ball lifts up to drop ashes into tray, 6" d, 1950 . . . $75.00

Green Snuf-a-rette, three snuffs, 4⅞" w, late 1930s $12.00

Green marble, ball holds cigarettes, one rest, 4" h $25.00

Row 2:

Ashtray on small legs, two men meeting & tipping hats, metal/pale gold finish, nice, 7" l $38.00

Yellow Snuf-a-rette, five snuffs, 4" w, late 1930s $10.00

Girl spreading skirt, bronze over steel, some finish worn off, nice, 4" h $55.00

Painted brass, solid, Egyptian figure, 3½" l . . . . $ 8.00

Bronze coating, probably beginning Deco movement, 6½" w $16.00

Never-Spill, pink, 3¼" w . . . . $ 9.00

PLATE 203

PLATE 204

ASHTRAYS WITHOUT A COUNTRY

ASHTRAYS FROM CZECHOSLOVAKIA

Czechoslovakia existed as a country in central Europe from 1918 to 1992. It was made up of Czechs living in Bohemia and Moravia in the west and the Slovaks living in the east. During World War II, Czechoslovakia was under German occupation, and after the war, it was under Communist rule. In 1989, a non-Communist government for Czechoslovakia was formed, but the Czechs and the Slovaks could not agree on how to run the country. In January 1993, Czechoslovakia ceased to exist, and the Czech Republic and Slovakia were created as new countries. The high quality Czechoslovakian porcelain and glass that is now being collected was made before World War II. The marks on the porcelain refer to the country of Czechoslovakia. Any new product made since 1992 is marked Czech Republic or Slovakia. Ashtrays shown here are old ones made prior to 1945.

Bohemian glass is still made in Bohemia, the largest province in the old Czechoslovakia as well as the new Czech Republic. Some glass is still found with older paper labels saying "made in Czechoslovakia," but glass ashtrays made after 1993 say "made in the Czech Republic."

PLATE 205 (left to right)

Row 1:

Dark red cut to crystal, unusual color called "port," probably old Czech, 4½" d $80.00

Cigarette holders, raised cigarette holders, picture of cigarettes in center, old Czech mark, 5⅛" l $35.00

Green glass oval, one snufferette at end, two rests at other end, 3½" l $14.00

Orange round, orange, black & purple on outside, old Erphila, Czechoslovakia mark, 5" d $25.00

Cigarette holders on pedestal, wine ashtray, old TK-Thung, Czechoslovakia mark, 5" sq $38.00

Bohemian cut glass, two layers, white cut to amber, gold decoration, probably old, 4" d $58.00

Row 2:

Green oval, ceramic, border of flowers at bottom, old round Czechoslovakia mark, 6" l $28.00

Yellow square, classical picture in center, old Czech Victorian China mark, 3⅛" sq $10.00

Cobalt & gold, glass with lots of gold & enameled flowers, old Czech paper label, 3¼" d $40.00

Pink fish, pattern on bottom, one rest in tail, old Czech paper label, 4" l $18.00

Heart with birds, opalized center, luster rise, old round Czech mark, 4¼" l, probably 1920s $30.00

ASHTRAYS FROM GERMANY — EAST & WEST

Most German porcelain in this book is marked either Germany or Austria, but since World War II, there have been some other marks. Western Germany, East Germany, and Germany - U. S. Zone were used to denote a division of Germany that no longer exists. The ashtrays pictured in Plate 206 were made in one of these areas.

PLATE 206 (left to right)

Row 1:

Western Germany, Bavarian chalet scene in relief, 4⅝" sq . . . . $ 7.00

Western Germany, Heidelburg, black etching, KPM, 4¾" w . . . . $ 8.00

Western Germany, seagull, blue center in tray, 6" w $30.00

Western Germany, Frankfurt, black etching, KPM, 4¾" w . . . . $ 8.00

U.S. Zone, wine border, classical scene in center, 5½" d $10.00

Row 2:

U.S. Zone, flowers, bumps on three rests, Jaeger & Co, PMR, 4¾" w $15.00

U.S. Zone, gold decor in center, four rests, 3" d . . . . $ 6.00

Western Germany, three birds, all white, 5¼" w $30.00

U.S. Zone, classical scene, gold edging & rests, Schumann, 3¼" w . . . . $ 7.00

East Germany, Chateau Frontenac in Quebec, Canada, 4⅜" w $10.00

PLATE 205

PLATE 206

ASHTRAYS FROM OCCUPIED JAPAN

Japan made many, many ashtrays during the American occupation, from 1945 to 1952. Items with the Occupied Japan mark have become popular with collectors. However, these words, Occupied Japan, must be marked in some way on the ashtray, not just Made in Japan, even if you know it was made during the occupation. Not all merchandise made then was marked that way, partially because of the natural Japanese resentment of the occupation.

Prices on these ashtrays vary a great deal, depending mostly on the quality of work. The work also varies, some very good, and some not very good. Bisque pieces usually command higher prices. All of the ashtrays pictured here are marked Occupied Japan. They are more ashtrays from Occupied Japan in other parts of the book.

PLATE 207 (left to right)
Row 1:
North Carolina souvenir, scenes from Great Smoky Mountain National Park, 4⅜" d.................. $11.00
Copper horse & rider, copper coating, flowers in relief around rim, 4½" w $12.00
Indian, with heart-shaped ashtray, 4" h $24.00
Western roping scene, copper coating, western objects in relief on rim, 4⅛" d, 1950 .... $15.00
Colorado souvenir, scenes of Berthoud Pass, silver color metal, 4½" d $12.00

Row 2:
Silkworm, shows different stages of silkworm & silk thread, unusual, 4¾" w...................... $25.00
Indian face, silver color coating, one rest, 4⅛" w $10.00
Ashtray & lighter, thin silver coating, marks on back match, ashtray is 6" w $23.00
Elephant, bronze coating, one rest, 4¾" w $10.00
Wisconsin souvenir, scenes from state with Indian in relief in the center, 4¾" w................ $14.00
Cherokee Indian Reservation, *North Carolina,* picture in center, 5" d $15.00

PLATE 208 (left to right)
Row 1:
Green flower cup, with revolving section in center that drops ashes into cup, nice, 3" h........ $16.00
Frog on lily pad, blue collar, smokes pipe, nice, 3" h $33.00
Swan, Lefton like, add-on flowers, 3¾" l $12.00
Green fan, rests on rim, Ardalt of Japan, hand painted, 7¼" w.................................. $10.00
Blue Jasper, Wedgwood-like, nicer than most of this type, 4" w................................. $12.00
Frog on lily pad, orange collar, smokes pipe, nice, 3" h $33.00
Cigarette holders in center, gold & green at edge tray, sixteen holders, Ucagco, 7" w $25.00

Row 2:
Bird with blue ashtray, two rests, 4¼" w... $15.00
Green round, classical scene in center, by Andrea, hand painted, nice work, 5⅞" d............... $18.00
Frog on lily pad, larger leaf than in other ashtrays shown, two rests, 5" l.................... $38.00
Elephant, three removable ashtrays, brown luster, 6" w $30.00
Green triangle, old European scene in center, gold decoration, moriage on rise, 5" sides $15.00
Chicken & rooster, *It's business I'm after,* 2¾" h.. $15.00
Bird with green ashtray, two rests, 4¼" w.. $15.00

PLATE 207

PLATE 208

NON-ILLUSTRATED PRICE GUIDE

ADVERTISING
All glass is crystal unless a color is given.

Abbey Rents, older version than in book, black & cream ceramic, picture of old health aids in center, 5" l $18.00

Agri-Radial, tire shape, *co-op,* clear glass insert, 6¼" d $32.00

Allen Bradley, pink anodized metal, *A-B Quality* logo in relief in center, 6⅝" l .... $ 7.00

Allison, *Air Power, May 1947,* aluminum, 4½" d... $ 8.00

Asbach-Uralt Weine, cream china, name in center, made by Thomas, 5¼" sq, before 1945..................... $ 6.00

B & O, glass, letters and railroad building dome in blue in center, 3½" sq................................... $15.00

Balle Flensburg, German fish food, *zum grog,* brown & white ceramic, fish shape, 6" l $25.00

Bally's, glass, ridges under rim, red center, logo & name clear, *LV, Reno, AC,* 4½" d........................ $ 4.00

Barbary Coast, smoke glass, orange center, black letters, *Las Vegas,* 3⅝" sq .... $ 4.00

Barney's, black amethyst glass, white name & picture on rise, *Casino $50,000 Jackpot,* 3½" d................ $ 5.00

Barton Distilling Co., amber iridescent glass, red picture of museum of whiskey history, 4⅜" d .... $ 9.00

Beck's Bier, green glass, name in gold repeated on rise, 4¼" d .... $ 6.00

Ben-Hur Coffee, A1 Flour, blue ceramic, *San Diego 1935,* by Metlox, old, 4½" d $25.00

Benjamin Moore Paints, glass with orange letters for name & local store, 3½" sq.............................. $ 7.00

Bertani, Italian wine, milk glass triangle, 4½" side.. $ 5.00

Best Western, yellow center with red crown & name, amber glass, 3½" sq...................................... $ 5.00

Best Western Motels, yellow center with red crown & name, phone reservation, amber glass, 3½" sq............ $ 6.00

Big Boy, newer model, glass, thin rim, three rests, logo & name in red in center, 3¾" d..................... $10.00

Billie Baxter, Clear Bottles, amber iridescent glass, matchbox & match pack holder center, rays to rise, 5¾" d $30.00

Blue Cross Plan-Capital Hospital Service, milk glass triangle, *25 Anniversary 1938–1963,* 5" sides....... $10.00

Bradford House, *Nashua, Iowa,* milk glass, name on rise in brown, triangle with 4½" sides.................. $ 4.00

Brigsteel, white enamelware shape of tub, black name, 5" l .... $ 6.00

Budweiser, red logo on white glass center, *Budweiser King of Beers,* almost 4" sq.......................... $11.00

Budweiser, glass, red letters around rim, 5" d .... $ 5.00

Budweiser, glass, red logo & name in center, almost 4" sq... $13.00

Budweiser can top, white plastic round, converts beer can into ashtray, red name on rise, 2" h............. $ 4.00

Buick, blue aluminum, logo in silver in center, 4½" l... $14.00

Buick & Pontiac, local ad in black print, orange plastic, rests in center, 4" sq............................ $ 4.00

Buick & Pontiac, local ad, brown plastic, rests on raised square inside, 5" sq.............................. $ 5.00

Bunkel Brothers Cocoa, metal, *In the morning we drink breakfast cocoa,* blue rise, 8" d.................... $ 9.00

Caesars Palace, glass, blue strip on rise, white Roman symbols on blue, 3⅝" d................................ $ 6.00

California Club, amber glass, black center, gold name, dice, chips, *Phil Long's,* 3½" sq.................... $ 4.00

Canadian Club, orange plastic, hi-rise sloped in, white name on side, 4½" d.................................. $ 5.00

Canadian National R.R., glass, etched CN logo letters in center, octagon, 5½" across........................ $15.00

Capri Cigarettes, frosted glass oval, name in gold letters on rise, one rest each end, 4¾" l................ $ 6.00

Carling Black Label Beer, white plastic, red rise with black & white logo, 3¾" sq........................... $ 7.00

Carlsberg Beer, milk glass, hi-rise with crown & name in red, triangle with 4" sides........................ $ 5.00

Carlyle, The, well-known hotel in New York City, butterflies & flowers center, cream ceramic, 6½" l......... $12.00

Carter Hall Smoking Tobacco, small silver tin, pack tobacco in relief in center, 3½" d...................... $ 6.00

CBS Hytron Electronic Tubes, *1921–1952,* brass, letters on rim, 5¼" d....................................... $10.00

Cereal City Festival, Battle Creek, MI, picture in center of cereal bowl & spoon, glass, 4⅛" sq............. $14.00

Chamber of Commerce, *Waukegan North Chicago-Gurnee, Illinois,* ceramic, 7¼" sq............................. $ 4.00

Champion Spark Plugs, *Aviation, It's Fun to Fly,* glass, red, white & black center, 5" d................... $10.00

Chevrolet, *Golden Anniversary, 1911–1961,* metal embossing, 4¼" sq... $10.00

Club Bingo, amber glass, yellow center, black building, *Downtown Las Vegas,* 3½" sq........................ $ 4.00

Coca-Cola, brown tin, white letters, *In Bottles — Refreshing New Feeling,* 4½" d, 1962..................... $15.00

Coca-Cola, red metal, white letters, *Coco-Cola,* 5¼" d $11.00

Coca-Cola, red metal, black letters, *Things Go Better With Coke,* 4" sq, 1963.............................. $15.00

Coca-Cola, red tin, black letters, *In Bottles -Refreshing New Feeling,* 4½" d, 1962........................ $11.00

Coca-Cola, gray tin, red letters, *da mas Chispa,* 4½" d $21.00
Coca-Cola, smoke glass, red letters, *Have a Coke & a Smile,* 4½" d . . . . $ 8.00
Comfort Inn, logo & name in center in gray & white, glass, 4½" d . . . . $ 4.00
Continental, Hotel, *Chicago,* thin black glass, gold logo & lion center & edge, triangle with 5½" sides . . . . $ 4.00
Coors, white china, red rise, white letters around rise, 4⅛" d, 1985 . . . . $ 5.00
Coors, ceramic, red & gray letters, *America's Fine Light Beer,* yellow, 5⅞" d. . . . . $ 7.00
Coors, ceramic, red & gray letters, verse center, *America's Fine Light Beer,* cream, 5⅞" d $30.00
Coors, red plastic, white name on rise, round bump in center, deep rise, 3¾" d . . . . $ 8.00
Coors, ceramic, center not full circle, red letters at bottom, blue letters top, yellow & cream, 5⅞" d $30.00
Coors Light, gray plastic with red & white letters on side, 3¾" d. . . . . $ 6.00
Coors Light, *The Silver Bullet,* white china, 4¼" d. . . . . $ 5.00
Coors Light The Silver Bullet, blue plastic, high rise, name red & white, 3¾" d. . . . . $ 5.00
Country Kitchen, glass, orange picture in center with boy & large sandwich on roof, 4½" d. . . . . $ 5.00
Country Kitchen, glass, white decal, red boy, sandwich & letters, manufacturer's sample, 3½" sq . . . . $ 7.00
Court of Two Sisters New Orleans, *French Quarter,* smoke glass, black letters, 4½" d. . . . . $ 7.00
Courvoisier, *Cognac, The Brandy of Napoleon,* milk glass, 4½" d. . . . . $ 6.00
Demijohn's Choice Liquors, shape of flat jug, black picture & letters in center, cream & brown china, 6½" l. . . . . $ 5.00
Desert Inn, black amethyst glass, white letters on rim, *Country Club, Las Vegas, NV,* 4" d. . . . . $ 6.00
Diamond Jim's, pale amber iridescent glass, yellow letters in center, 4" sq . . . . $ 5.00
Diplomat Resorts, cream ceramic, gray name on rim, logo in center, *Hollywood, FL,* 3⅜" d. . . . . $ 4.00
Disneyland, amber glass, pressed pattern of Magic Kingdom, ridges under rise, 3½" sq . . . . $ 9.00
Disneyland, white ceramic, picture of old-fashioned policeman in center, 4¼" sq $12.00
Doral, *advertised in TV Guide,* white letters, black plastic 4¼" d, 2" h . . . . $ 6.00
Dr. Pepper, glass with red decal on bottom, 4" sq . . . . $ 9.00
Edgewater Beach (Chicago), white building & blue name in center, glass, thick rim, 4½" d. $19.00
El Morocco (NYC), smoke glass, blue center, gray letters, 4" d. $20.00
El Rancho, black amethyst glass, orange letters on rim, *Hotel Las Vegas,* 4" d. . . . . $ 4.00
El San Juan Hotel, *Puerto Rico,* glass octagon, green logo & name in center, 4½" across . . . . $ 4.00
Embassy Suites, logo name in gold in center, glass thick & heavy, 5¾" d. . . . . $ 6.00
Fairmont, *Hotels,* San Francisco, logo in center, glass with stepped rise, 4⅛" d. . . . . $ 5.00
Falstaff Beer, amber iridescent, red letters on rise, rings on bottom, 3½" d. . . . . $ 6.00
Firestone, tire shaped, *Deluxe Champion, gum dipped,* solid, glass insert with embossed name, 5⅞" d. $45.00
Firestone, tire shaped, *Transsteel Radial XR 4, Protector Ply,* glass insert with red & white logo name, 6½" d. $25.00
Flour-Feed, Grain & Coal, black pottery, flowers & letters embossed on rim, 4½" sq, very old. $20.00
Fortuna, Ky, *Straight Bourbon Whiskey,* writing & trademark in center in blue, 3¾" d. . . . . $ 6.00
Four Queens, black amethyst glass, white letters on rim, *Las Vegas, Nevada,* 4" d. $10.00
Fox Head "400" Beer, gold aluminum, logo & name in center in shiny gold, 4½" l $12.00
Fremont Hotel, black amethyst glass, white name on rise, *Las Vegas,* 3½" d. . . . . $ 7.00
Frontier, smoke glass, thick ridges on tilted rim, *Hotel & Casino, Las Vegas,* 4½" d. $ 6.00
G&W Seven Star, glass , white letters center, *Blended Whiskey,* 4⅛" sq. . . . . $ 6.00
General Electric Lamps, GE logo in center, raised circles on bottom, 7" d. . . . . $ 9.00
General Electric Motors, yellow ceramic with gray plastic motor on back ashtray, nice, 7" l. $45.00
Glenmore, figural of man, bronze chalkware with black center, *Ky's Finest Whiskies,* 5" d. $30.00
Gluek (beer), 1962 convention, black letters, red lion, 5¼" d $15.00
Golden Gate, black amethyst glass, name & dice, cards, slots in white on rise, 3½" d. $ 5.00
Golden Nugget, black amethyst glass, gold name repeating around rise, 3⅝" d. . . . . $ 5.00
Golden Nugget, black amethyst glass, white name & cards on rise, *Gambling Hall,* 3½" d. . . . . $ 5.00
Goodyear, tire shaped, *Vector,* glass insert, 5⅞" d. $19.00
Goodyear, tire shaped, *Custom Power Cushion Polyglas,* glass insert with blue name & local ad, 6" d. $21.00
Goodyear, tire shaped, *G167 Unisteel,* glass insert, blue bottom, white name, 6½" d. $19.00
Goodyear, tire shaped, *Custom Super cushion,* glass insert, 5⅝" d. $25.00
Goodyear, tire shaped, *G800 155SR15 Industrial Brasileira, Sao Paulo,* glass insert 6½" d. $40.00
Goodyear, tractor tire shaped, *Power Torque,* glass insert with blue bottom, white name & ad, 6⅝" d. $30.00
Goodyear, tire shaped, *Deluxe All Weather, 4 Ply,* glass insert, 6" $45.00
Goodyear, tire shaped, *Custom Cross Rib Hi-Miler,* glass insert with tire logo & local ad on white bottom, 6⅜" $40.00
Griswold, black iron fry pan without match holder, 6" l $35.00
Hamm's, glass, white rim blue name, *from the land of sky blue waters,* 5⅝" d. $11.00

Hardee's, gold pressed aluminum, name impressed in center, 3½" d. . . . . $ 8.00
Hardwick, old stove manufacture, black rim, cream center, enamel ware, 5" d, old $25.00
Harrah's, glass, red center, white name, *Reno & Lake Tahoe,* 3½" sq . . . . $ 7.00
Harrah's, lt amber iridescent glass, red letters on rise, *Reno & Lake Tahoe,* 3½" d. . . . . $ 6.00
Harrison Choice Fruits, tan metal, old time picture in center, 8" d. . . . . $ 9.00
Heineken, dk green plastic, name in gold repeating on rise, 6⅝" d, 2" h $10.00
Heineken, green anodized aluminum, name on rim, white letters, 5¾" d. . . . . $ 8.00
Holiday Inn, cream center with brown name & repeated logo sign, glass, 4⅛" sq . . . . $ 6.00
Holiday Inn, green sign in center with name showing clear, glass octagon, *World's Innkeeper,* 4½" across. . . . . $ 9.00
Holiday Inn, name in relief on bottom, cigarette rests raised up in center, glass, 4⅞" x 5¼". . . . . $ 6.00
Holiday Inn, yellow center & green sign with name, glass octagon, *Nation's Innkeeper,* 4½" across . . . . $ 8.00
Holland American Line, cream ceramic, name in gold around rim, 4¼" d. $24.00
Honey Bear Farm, picture bear in center, white ceramic, *Powers Lake, Wis,* 4½" d. . . . . $ 7.00
Horseshoe, black amethyst glass, gold letters on rise, *See $1,000,000, Sombrero Room,* 3½" d . . . . $ 5.00
Hotel Strand, *Atlantic City, N.J.,* glass hexagon, logo & name center in blue, 3¾" across. $ 4.00
Howard Johnson's, *motor lodges,* white stylized building & letters, glass, 3¾" sq. . . . . $ 5.00
Howard Johnson's, stylized building center in turquoise & orange, glass, octagon, 4½" across . . . . $ 4.00
Howard Johnson's, Simple Simon Pieman silhouette in center in blue, *ice cream shops & restaurants,* 4⅛" d $35.00
Hulstkamp, man in relief in center with pipe & glass, *Zeer Oude Genever,* Gouda, 7" d. $25.00
Humphry Dairy, glass, red letters & picture of girl drinking milk, 3½" sq . . . . $ 5.00
Hyatt Lodges, *First In Hospitality,* logo name & US outline in center in black, smoke glass, 4½" d. . . . . $ 4.00
I.W. Harper, Ky. bourbon, glass with raised matchbox holder in center, 2⅞" h, old. $15.00
International House of Pancakes, glass, blue center with black logo & letters, orange sign, 3½" sq . . . . $ 5.00
Jacques French Restaurant, *Chicago,* cream ceramic, green letters in center & on rim, 5⅜" d. . . . . $ 6.00
John Deere, green & white enamel, local ad, 6⅜" l. $13.00
John Deere, local ad for Leipsic Farm Supply, enamel ware, green & white, 6⅝" l. $14.00
Johnnie Walker Red, red plastic, white name on rise, 3¾" d. . . . . $ 4.00
Johnson & Johnson (Band Aids, etc.), cream ceramic, picture of red building in center, NJ, 8½" d. $14.00
Kelly-Springfield, tire shaped, *Mark Imperial Radial,* glass insert, 5¾" d. $16.00
Kirby, *Vacuum Cleaners,* glass with red logo name in center, 3½" sq . . . . $ 6.00
Kohler of Kohler, tan enamelware, rests raised up in center with logo K, rectangle, 6½" x 5". . . . . $ 7.00
Kohler of Kohler, hexagon, nickel-plated steel, name inscribed in raised center, 5" across . . . . $ 8.00
Ladish Employees Credit Union, picture of man in center, amber glass, *Cudahy, Wis,* 3½" sq $10.00
Lake to Lake, *Dairy Products, Wisconsin,* cream ceramic, 7" w. $10.00
Landmark, green glass, gold name rim, *Hotel, Las Vegas, Nevada,* 4⅛" d. . . . . $ 6.00
Lapine Co. Laboratory Supplies, white china mortar with attached pestle, Rosenthal, 3½" h . . . . $ 8.00
Las Vegas, small blue bean-bag, picture of Golden Nugget in center, 3" d. . . . . $ 6.00
Las Vegas Hilton, black amethyst glass, name in white on rise, 4¼" d. . . . . $ 5.00
Liqueur labels, pictures in center of different European labels, china, 8¼" sq . . . . $ 8.00
Lone Star Beer, cream ceramic, star in center, logo on rim in gold, 7½" l $12.00
Lone Star Beer, glass, red logo center, red letters, *From the Big Country,* 5" d . . . . $ 7.00
Loyal Order of Moose, *Muskegon Convention,* glass, yellow picture of moose & name in center, *1965* . . . . $ 6.00
Loyal Order of Moose, *Kokoma Lodge 179,* glass, black name & moose in center, 3¾" sq $12.00
Madeira Aromatic Mixture, tobacco, small silver tin, logo in relief in center, 3½" d. . . . . $ 6.00
Manhattan Square, Anchor Hocking, 4½", 1938–1943 . . . . $18.00
Manufacture's samples, box, nine in different colors & different businesses, 4¼" d. $24.00
Marc's Big Boy, smoke glass, white letters & logo of Big Boy in center, *America's favorite Hamburger,* 4" d $12.00
Marina Casino, black amethyst glass, name & logo on rise in orange, *Las Vegas,* 3½" d . . . . $ 4.00
Marlboro, white name on rise, small red plastic, Ges-Line bottom, 3⅛" d, 1¼" h. . . . . $ 6.00
Martell Cognac, dk blue ceramic, name on rise in gold & white, rectangle is 4" x 4¼". . . . . $ 6.00
Maxim, black amethyst glass, white name, logo on rise, *Hotel/Casino Las Vegas,* 3½" d. . . . . $ 5.00
McDonald's, pressed aluminum, arches and name in center, 3½" d . . . . $ 9.00
McDonald's, silver tin, logo in relief in center, 3½" d. . . . . $ 5.00
Mercury Marine, *Black Max* name & picture raised in center, cast iron, *1977 plant tour,* 5½" d. . . . . $ 8.00
Miller High Life, glass, red & white logo around rise, 3½" d . . . . $ 7.00
Miller Lite, glass, blue name & logo center, *A Fine Pilsner Beer,* 6⅜" d . . . . $ 6.00
Moet & Chandon Champagne, smoke glass with profile of Dom Perignon in center, 4" l. . . . . $ 8.00

Mohawk, tire shaped, *Super chief* glass insert, 6" d $20.00

Molasses Candy, green metal, old-time picture in center, 8" d . . . . $ 9.00

Nob Hill, glass, white center, blue name & picture building, *Casino Las Vegas,* 3½" sq. . . . . $ 5.00

Northern Assurance Co., 100th Anniv. 1836–1936, solid brass, inscribed pics around rim, 5¼" d, old . . $15.00

Old Fitzgerald, Kentucky bourbon, cream ceramic, picture of horse race, rests on inner ring, 8¾" d . . . $18.00

Old Forester, gray metal, name & description impressed center, rectangle is 8⅜" x 7⅛" $13.00

Old Forester, milk glass, blue letters on rim, *Now at 86 & 100 proof!,* 5¼" d . . . . $ 5.00

Old Milwaukee, red plastic, name & logo repeating on rise, 3¾" d . . . . $ 5.00

Old Shay Fort Pitt Beer, aluminum sides, name impressed on rim, 4⅜" sq . . . . $ 6.00

Olympia Beer, white ceramic, name & logo center in blue & yellow, *Premium Lager Beer,* 4" d . . . . $ 5.00

Olympia Beer, black amethyst glass, white letters on rim, 4" d . . . . $ 8.00

Oscar Mayer Federal Credit Union, glass, blue & white decal in center with name, 4¼" sq. . . . . $ 7.00

Pabst, metal with gold flash, name in blue around rim, 5⅝" d. . . . . $ 6.00

Pabst, pressed aluminum, blue, logo in relief in center, 4" d $11.00

Penn Fishing Reels, name on rim raised letters, fish in center, black plastic, 3¼". $25.00

Pennsylvania Patrician, tire shape, clear glass insert, hard rubber, 5½", 1950s $40.00

Phillips 66, *Chinatown, Chicago* local ad, glass, decal center, 4" sq $10.00

Piels Real Draft, pressed aluminum, name in center, *Be Convinced! Try,* 3½" d . . . . $ 5.00

Piper Planes, *Fly Piper,* outline of plane embossed in center, aluminum, 4½" d $12.00

Pizza Hut, glass, stylized logo impressed in bottom, rests on inner ring, 5" d. $ 6.00

Planters Peanuts, Mr. Peanut figural in center, gold metal, ashtray is 5¾" d $45.00

Playboy Club, black glass, picture of girl holding key in center in white, name in white in circle, 4" sq . . $12.00

Playboy Club, glass, logo bunny head molded center, stacking type, 1" rise, 4" d . . . . $ 6.00

Playboy Club, glass, logo bunny head molded center, stacking type, 1½" rise, 4" d . . . . $ 6.00

Playboy Club, white glass, VIP letters in gold, bunny in center of letters, 4" sq. . . . . $ 6.00

Playboy Club, orange glass, picture of girl holding key in center in black, black name circle, 4" sq $20.00

Playboy Club, white glass with black bunny head logo in center, 3¾" sq. . . . . $ 8.00

Polar Ware, *Centennial 1847–1947,* lt blue enamelware, 4⅝" d $50.00

Polled Herefords-Registered, glass with picture of cow in center, 4¼" sq. . . . . $ 6.00

Princess Cruises, glass, blue logo center, octagon, 1½" deep, 3¾" w . . . . $ 7.00

Pschorr Brau Munchen, glass, gray decal center with blue letters, 7" d . . . . $ 5.00

Purina Chow, glass, red & white checkerboard center, 4" sq, 1970s. . . . . $ 6.00

Queen Elizabeth & Place Ville Marie Restaurants, Montreal, lavender center, white letters & logo E in center, 3½" . $ 8.00

Rahr's Beer, *Green Bay, WI,* glass, white logo in bottom, 4¼"sq. $12.00

Ramada Inn, *Luxury for Less,* red letters in center, glass, 4⅛" sq . . . . $ 5.00

Ramada Inn, *Welcome home,* letters in red on rise, glass, 3½" d . . . . $ 7.00

Reichenhaller Burgerbrau, dk green ceramic, letters & shield in center in relief, 6¼" d $12.00

Ritz Carlton, white ceramic, blue letters & logo in center, 3½" d . . . . $ 7.00

Riviera, glass, red on rise with white letters, *Lighthouse, Delmonico, Cafe Noir,* 3½" d. . . . . $ 5.00

Roadway Inn, blue name in center, glass stepped rise, 4½" d. . . . . $ 4.00

Roadway Inns, *Of America,* blue letters in center, glass, 4½" d . . . . $ 4.00

Robinson Clay Product Co., *Akron, Ohio,* green ceramic, top has opening & three rests, 4½" d. $29.00

Round Table Pizza Restaurants, black amethyst with white letters around rise, 3½" d. . . . . $ 5.00

Royal Doulton, blue china, ad for company, bumps on rim for rests, nice, unusual, 2" h, 6" d $55.00

Ruberoid, *Building Products, Asphalt & Asbestos,* ashtray made of Ruberoid, gray, 5" d $13.00

Salem China Co., cream china with green & black ad in center, 5¼" d. $18.00

San Miquel, gold name on rim, amber glass, 5" d . . . . $ 4.00

Sanka, glass, orange center, *97% Caffeine Free Coffee, 100% Real Coffee,* 4¼" d. . . . . $ 5.00

Santa Fe Super Chief, turquoise glass, white letters design in center, 4" x 4¾" $20.00

Sapporo Beer, white china, black name on rise, in center *Japan's Oldest Brand,* 4¼" d. . . . . $ 6.00

Schlitz, white plastic, red logo sign on rise with name in white, 3¾" d, 1⅝" h . . . . $ 6.00

Schlitz, brown bottle, white letters, *Had The Schlitz Squeezed Out Of Me In Florida,* 7¾" l . . . . $ 4.00

Schlitz, pressed aluminum, name & logo in relief in center, 3½" d . . . . $ 6.00

Schlitz & Old Milwaukee, *Bergseth Brothers Dist.,* red metal, 4½" d $11.00

Schoonberger Cabinet, German wine, bottle figural, white china, 3⅝" h $14.00

Sea World, black amethyst glass, name & pictures around rim in gold, 4" d . . . . $ 5.00

Seagram's VO, cobalt ceramic, name in gold on rim and in center, 5" sq $12.00

Seagram's VO Canadian, cobalt ceramic, name in gold on rise, 5⅛" d, 1¾" h $11.00
Seagram's VO Canadian, cobalt ceramic, gold name on rise, triangle with 5½" sides, 1½" h . . . . $ 8.00
Sears, *Sales Excellence '79,* presentation award to best salespersons, 6⅝" d, 1979. . . . . $ 7.00
Seiberling, *Safety-Tire, heat vented saf-flex cord,* glass insert, 5¾" d $26.00
Seiberling, *Special Service,* solid, green glass insert with cream decal and red & black design, 6½" d. $20.00
Sheraton, logo S encircled with wheat in white in center, glass, 3¾" sq . . . . $ 4.00
Skokie Mfg Co., aluminum round with lid that opens in center, name etched in center of bottom, 4¾" d. $18.00
Smirnoff, glass, red name repeated around rise, heavy, 7" d. $10.00
Smirnoff Silver (Vodka), black ceramic, *For the Silver Martini,* triangle with 4¾" sides, 1972. . . . . $ 5.00
St. Pauli Girl, off-white ceramic, blue name on rim, name in three languages, made West Germany, 6⅝" d. . . . . . . $ 8.00
Stardust Hotel, black amethyst glass, name on rise in white, *Las Vegas,* 3½" d . . . . $ 6.00
State Bank Ixonia, glass, red center with white letters, *Drive In Banking,* 3" sq. . . . . $ 5.00
Stock Italian Vermouth, black plastic, white name on rise, triangle with 5" sides . . . . $ 4.00
Stokely's, blue & gold logo center, *Finest Frozen Food,* frosted glass rectangle is 4½" x 3⅜" $10.00
Stork Club, black ceramic, white letters on outside of rise, heavy, by Hall, 5" d. $22.00
Stouffer's Motor Inns, red name in center, glass, 3⅝" sq . . . . $ 5.00
Sundowner, amber glass, rings on bottom, yellow letters on rise, *Best Western, Reno's Largest,* 3½" d. . . . . $ 4.00
Suntoy Whisky, ceramic, tan outside with brown letters, blue on inside, 4" d $12.00
Syracuse Rubber, *Quality Rubber Parts — Since 1946,* hardened rubber compound, 6¼" d $10.00
Tennent's Extra, black amethyst glass, logo center, rise in gold, red & white, 5⅝" d. . . . . $ 9.00
Texier (brandy), white china, blue name & logo on rim, almost round, 6¼" d, 1968 on, Royal Bayreuth. $12.00
Thunderbird & Red Lion Motor Inns, yellow center with logos of two motels in red & green, amber glass, 4⅜" d . . . $ 7.00
Tomco Seed Corn, yellow metal 5" triangle, *A Step Forward With Tomico Seed Corn.* . . . . $ 7.00
Top of the Mart, New Orleans, La., glass, blue picture of hotel in center, letters in red, 4½" d. . . . . $ 5.00
TraveLodge, *For the Best Rest – East or West,* green center with sleepwalking bear, glass, 3½" sq. . . . . $ 6.00
Tripoli Golf Club, green name & picture of windmill in center, *Milwaukee, WI,* 4⅛" d . . . . $ 4.00
Tropicana Hotel, green glass, gold name on rise — *follies bergere, Las Vegas,* 4½" d . . . . $ 5.00
Tuborg, milk glass, red name on rise, *Imported beer,* triangle with 3¾" sides $11.00
Tuborg Beer, red enamel over metal, white name on outside of rise, 5⅞" d . . . . $ 9.00
US Steel-Stainless, name etched in center, pattern etched inside on rise, 4⅜" sq. $10.00
U.S. Pump, green ceramic, figural of yellow ceramic pump, nice, 8" w $40.00
UAW-CIO, *Local 72 Kenosha, Wis.,* amber opal glass, picture of building in center in white, 4⅛" sq . . . . $ 4.00
United States Lines, logo of eagle & name in center in blue, octagon, 3¾" w. . . . . $ 8.00
University of No. Iowa, aluminum, *Cedar Falls,* 4" d, 1" rise . . . . $ 5.00
Usinger, cream ceramic, free form, picture of sausage man in center, *Fred Usinger* on back, 8" . . . . $ 6.00
V&S Hardware Store, glass, black name & local store in center, 3½" sq . . . . $ 4.00
Viceroy, *Viceroy the taste that's right!,* blue & red letters, B&W with leaf bottom, 5⅛" d . . . . $ 6.00
Wagner Ware, green & black enamelware fry pan, name & #1050 on back $21.00
Wan Fu, white china, red center, *Unique White Wine For Oriental Fare,* 4¼" d. . . . . $ 4.00
Warner & Swasey, cream with picture of construction equipment in black, logo in red, 6¾" sq. . . . . $ 8.00
Weller's Cabin Still, Ky. bourbon, off-white ceramic, black letters, 6½" d . . . . $ 8.00
White Horse, blue ceramic horseshoe shape, name & picture of horse on high rise, 6" l, by Wade. $36.00
White Horse Cellar (scotch), yellow horseshoe shape, name & white horse on rise $25.00
White Horse Cellar (scotch), letters & horse in relief center, pewter color metal $14.00
Winston, *advertised in ARGOSY,* white letters, red plastic, 4⅛" d, 2" h . . . . $ 6.00
Winston, impressed name in center might have been red at one time, aluminum, 8½" l, Taiwan. . . . . $ 6.00
Winston Select, collectible ashtray, copper finish on metal mold, raised as scene center, 4⅞" d, 1994. . . . . $ 6.00
Worthington "E," blue "E" in white center, English beer, glass, 6¼" d . . . . $ 7.00
Zero-Max, picture of variable speed motor, cream ceramic, picture in center, 6¾" d. . . . . $ 8.00

GLASS

Akro Agate, orange & white, USA mark, 3" sq . . . . $ 8.00
Alexandrite, blue in fluorescent light, lavender in incandescent and sunlight, plain, two rests, 8¼" l. $15.00
Amberina round, '40s, '50s & '60s, ring with rests near center, 10¼" d. . . . . $ 9.00
Anchor Hocking hexagonal, crystal, 5" . . . . $ 5.00
Astrology signs, pressed pattern on rim, signs in bottom, heavy, 7½" d $10.00
Balls around outside, twelve balls, crystal, heavy, 5⅛" d. $12.00

Black amethyst, two rests, plain, 3½" d . . . . $ 5.00

Black amethyst, three rests, cross-hatched bottom, 3½" d, 1¼" h rise . . . . $ 5.00

Black glass, hard-to-see silver picture of golfer in center, *Sterling,* ring in center with rests, 5" d. . . . . $ 9.00

Cambridge, gold rectangle, two rests, 3⅜" l $15.00

Cambridge in Crown Tuscan, Cambridge's name for this color, four rests, 5" d. $11.00

Cambridge square, in Ebony, 3⅝" d, 1952 to mid-1950s $10.00

Canvasback, crystal, canvasback duck in center, almost sq, 4" $10.00

Carnival, new, hobs under rim, rests in ring in center 5" d. $10.00

Center knob, crystal, one rest in center knob, wavy undersides, 5½" d $10.00

Crystal oval, extended rests at each end, rings in bottom, 5⅜" w . . . . $ 9.00

Depression in amber iridescent, hexagon, plain, six rests, 4½" w . . . . $ 8.00

Depression, Candlewick like, crystal, pressed rose pattern in center, 4" d. . . . . $ 4.00

Depression, checkerboard pattern, crystal, matchbox & match pack holder center, four rests, uneven rays $10.00

Depression, color flashed corners, set of three, blue corners, ruby corners, amber corners, corner rests. $12.00

Depression, crystal oval, matchbox holder at center back rim, 2 large rests at ends of oval, 5½" l $13.00

Depression, crystal oval, pale yellow, matchbox holder at center of back rim, two large rests at ends of oval, 5½" l $13.00

Depression, crystal round with four edge rests, rays in center of uneven length, 5" l. . . . . $ 8.00

Depression, crystal checkerboard rim, four rests, two snuffs, matchbox & match pack holder, rays not all way out. $15.00

Depression, Daisy Button cup, gold, three legs, 2¼" h . . . . $ 8.00

Depression, Green Threading, circles in center, olive green, three rests, 3½" d. . . . . $ 5.00

Depression, milk glass, one rest for cigars, two rests for cigarettes, match pack holder, 7¾" d $16.00

Depression, milk glass, shell shape, 5½" l. . . . . $ 8.00

Depression, milk glass, one oval match pack holder, one cigar rest, two cigarette rests, plain, 7¾" d $16.00

Depression, Queen of Hearts, set of four, red heart at two corners, queen impressed in bottom, 3½" l $20.00

Depression, square with ridges on rise & rim, crystal, rest is plain, 4½" . . . . $ 4.00

Depression, square with ridges on rise & rim, crystal, rest is plain, 3" . . . . $ 3.00

Depression, trapezoid, crystal, one wide rest & one small rests at one end, 4" l $12.00

Duck, large crystal round with duck in relief in center, depressions around rim for rests, 7⅜" d . . . . $ 8.00

Duck, pink Depression glass, 5½" l. $12.00

Duncan Miller, set of three, crystal, with geese etched in center, 3¾" sq $30.00

Duncan Miller in Canterbury, chartreuse, Duncan's name for color, 4½" l, 1937 . . . . $12.00

Eagle, large green round, eagle in relief in center, two rests, 9¼" d $10.00

Enamel rim, gold enamel with dogwood flowers, 4" d. $13.00

Enamel rim, gold enamel with daises, 4" d $13.00

Fish-shaped, small crystal, one rest in tail, 4½" l. . . . . $ 4.00

Fostoria, Coin pattern, amber, four coins in center, frosted coins, 7¾" d. $25.00

Fostoria like, similar to Spool pattern but circle in center, blue, 5½" d $14.00

Fostoria like, similar to Spool pattern but circle in center, gold, 3⅛" d . . . . $ 7.00

Fostoria, Mayfair, pink, 3⅞" sq. $13.00

Fostoria, Mayfair, light blue, 3⅞" sq $13.00

Georges Briard, crystal with white dots, gold painted pattern in center, six rests, 8" l . . . . $ 6.00

Grecian frieze, blue & white frieze around outside of rise, rest is crystal, 3½" d. . . . . $ 6.00

Green fired-on color, almost square, rest at corners, 4" sides . . . . $ 5.00

Green glass nude, dancing with bubbles, named "Moondance," maker unknown, 4¾" l. $27.00

Green oval, Czechoslovakia, one rest at each end of oval, 2⅞" w. . . . . $ 6.00

Hat, crystal glass, one rest in crown, cowboy style, braid around base of crown, 2" h $24.00

Imperial, Candlewick pattern, crystal, 6" d $10.00

Leaf shape, lavender, one rest, 5¼" l . . . . $ 8.00

Lt blue frosted, pear-shaped, graceful lines in bottom, cigarette rest heats bi-metal spring that tips cigarette into ashtray
   when reaches certain temperature, 4⅝" l $12.00

MacBeth-Evans, mold is theirs, crystal, one rose in relief on rim near each rest, about 4" sq $10.00

MacBeth-Evans, #7541-A, crystal, 3¼" sq, 1932 . . . . $ 7.00

National, hobs in center only, wide petal-like rays bottom & rim, rests, amber 5½" d $10.00

National, hobs in center only, wide petal-like rays bottom & rim, rests, milk glass, 3⅓" d . . . . $ 8.00

National, hobs in center only, wide rays bottom & rim, rests, crystal, 3⅓" d . . . . $ 8.00

Octagon, crystal, three rests at each side near center, 5" w. . . . . $ 7.00

Octagon, crystal, fingers stick up in center to form rests, 5½" d, 1¾" h $10.00

Old, center lowered, matchbox holder on back rim, one big rest center on front rim, old glass, 4¼" d $14.00
Owens-Illinois, glass art, patented, Deco lines, round with extended rests both sides, 5⅞" w. $13.00
Pipe holder & ashtray, slag brown, gray, off-white, 6⅝" l, patented June 1923. .... $14.00
Plain round, crystal, old glass, three rests, 1¼" h, 4¾" d .... $ 9.00
Pressed pattern, gold, ridges on rise, pattern on bottom, 6" d .... $ 8.00
Rooster, painted black in center, crystal, round with two extended rests, 5⅛" l $10.00
Round with rounded rays on bottom going to rim, crystal, 5½" d. .... $ 6.00
Safex, crystal, trough in center, two angled rests on sides, circular edges, 4¼" l .... $ 8.00
Sailboats, crystal rectangle with sailboat scene in relief in center, four rests, 2⅞" x 4⅜" $16.00
Scotty dog, crystal, dog impressed in bottom, 2¾" sq. .... $ 9.00
Ship's wheel, crystal, three rests, picture of Indian in center, 6¾" w .... $ 8.00
Silvered shell shape, 5½" l. $10.00
Silvered heavy round, two extended rests each side, 4¾" w. $12.00
Silvered oval, two rests each end, 5" l .... $ 5.00
Small green, cup shape, chrome rim & rest, 2¼" d. .... $ 6.00
Small rectangle, crystal, one rest at one end, Italy mark, 3¼" l .... $ 4.00
Square with four feet, crystal, '40s, '50s &'60s, 4½" sq. .... $ 8.00
Square with divisions, crystal, two rests on opposite corners, diagonal trough in center, 3⅜" .... $ 7.00
Square with extended rests, two rests on opposite sides, 5¾" l .... $ 6.00
Vaseline, small square, Czechoslovakia, one rest at each of two opposing corners, 2⅞" sq $16.00
Vaseline square, heavy, four rests, thick glass, mold lines on outside of rise, 4" sq $15.00
Violin shaped, blue, one rest, 5⅛" l $10.00

HISTORICAL

1964–1965 New York World's Fair, *Unisphere,* brown plastic, extended rests, triangle with 5¾" sides. .... $ 9.00
1964–1965 New York World's Fair, white ceramic, Unisphere in center, different scenes, 4" d .... $ 8.00
1967 Expo, *Montreal, Canada,* red plastic, almost triangle, 5¼" sides .... $ 9.00
1976 Olympics, Montreal, Canada, bronze, oakleaf & rings in center, four rests, 3⅛" d. $18.00
1982 Knoxville World's Fair, Tennessee, cream ceramic, raised center with red symbol, 8" d. $10.00
1984 Louisiana World Exposition, *May 12 – Nov 11, 1984,* brass plated, 5⅛" d $13.00
1986 Expo, *Vancouver, Canada,* picture of fair's logo in center, white ceramic, 4" d. .... $ 8.00
90¢ Postage Stamp, Lincoln's picture in black etching in center, 6" d, 1959 .... $12.00
Alamo, Texas, composition, Alamo in relief in center, covered with glass insert, match pack holder at back, 5⅛" d .... $ 7.00
America's Bicentennial of Freedom, 1776–1976, Philadelphia, Pa., cream ceramic, 5¼" d. $13.00
American Ceramic Society, 1932 in Golden Colo., cream ceramic, place for cigarette pack under ashtray, matchbox holder center of tray, very unusual and nicely done, by Coors USA, 4⅛" h $45.00
Campfire Memories, gold glass pine branch in relief in center, one snufferette, 2¼" sq. .... $ 5.00
Carter-Mondale, election ticket team, pictures in center, white metal, 5½" d $15.00
Corning Glass Works, *Replica of 200" Pyrex Telescope Disc,* glass, 3¼" d $10.00
Democratic National Convention, *'84, San Francisco,* white ceramic, shell shape, 4¼" l $10.00
J.F. Kennedy & family, family picture in center, cream ceramic, 5⅛" d $18.00
Jim Brown's 50th Birthday, *and 75th Anniversary, 1889–1939,* painted metal, 4½" d $12.00
Jimmy Carter, 39th President, clear glass, green letters, 4½" d $12.00
Jimmy Carter – Home of, *Plains, Georgia,* black glass, white letters on rise, 3⅝" d. .... $ 8.00
National Metal Exposition, *1950 Chicago, TM Verson, 32nd Nat,* hammered aluminum, 4⅝" d. .... $ 7.00
Oberammergau, *1950,* white china, flowers center, by Winterling of Bavaria, Germany, 4¼" d. $10.00
Ohio Republican elephant, political ashtray, wine ceramic, elephant in relief in center & around rim, 6⅝" d. $15.00
Pearl Harbor, *Remember, 12/7/41,* gold glass, triangle, 6" sides. $25.00
Scout National Jamboree – 1973, cream ceramic, picture in center, 5⅜" d. $10.00
Scout National Jamboree – 1977, cream ceramic, picture in center, 5⅜" d. .... $ 9.00
Space shuttle, *Kennedy Space Center, Fla,* blue & white decal in center, clear glass, almost triangle with 3½" sides. $10.00
Veterans of Foreign Wars, *Congressional Dinner, Feb. 5, 1952,* clear glass, black center, 5" w. .... $ 5.00

METAL

Bean bag, large, yellow & black plain material, brass tray, 5" d. .... $ 7.00
Black painted metal, red card suit emblems at one end, made by Brown & Bigelow, 4½" l .... $ 6.00
Blue enamel & brass, cup with wooden handle, made in Israel, 3¼" d $13.00

Brass, filigree work around rise set with stones, one rest in copper, 2⅜" d................................. $16.00
Brass cube, solid, top has crisscross pattern of brass with openings for ashes to fall through, 2⅛" h $14.00
Brass frog, small with red stone eyes, handle over mouth with one rest, 3" l .... $ 6.00
Brass Oriental, no mark, rim with Oriental marks in relief, center raised for pipe, 7" l $18.00
Brass shell, no mark, two small feet, two rests at small end, 5" l .... $ 5.00
Brass with etched flowers, made in India, good work, 4" sq. $10.00
Brass with pixie center, Lucky Pixie in relief, 3⅛" d .... $ 7.00
Butter dish shape, silver color metal, top lifts off & makes two ashtrays, three rests at each end, 5¼" l ...... $ 5.00
China picture, brass outer edge, two layer of glass in center with enameled Chinamen carrying sedan chair, nicely done,
   colorful, two rests in brass, inscribed China, old $18.00
Chrome-plated ashtray with elephants standing on one foot, trunks make rests, 4⅜" d $18.00
Cloisonné, China, brass cells, blue with pink & red flowers, blue inside, old. $16.00
Copper Indian Set, three rounds, no mark, Indian signs etched on rims & center, largest is 5¾" d $20.00
Copper with road runner in center, hammered, Gregorian mark, rippled rim, 5¼" d $10.00
Enamel brass pivot top, China, red, grn, blue panels on sides, enamel & figures, 3" sq $14.00
Fish shape, stainless steel, rest in tail, by Napier, 4⅜" l .... $ 6.00
Globe & ashtray, brass finish, globe will also close, 5¾" h $45.00
Green painted metal, clamps on side of table, red diamond painted on handle .... $ 5.00
Hand-held, black metal, one rest pops up when opened, 2½" w .... $ 7.00
Pewter two decks of cards holder & ashtray, unusual, pewter, two rests, square ashtray, 2⅝" h, old...........$22.00
Pewter like, drinking scene in relief, five rests, no mark, 8½" d... $ 9.00
Pewter like with Scotty in relief, Japan, nice, one rest, 2¾" x 2" $10.00
Saf-T-Snuff, solid brass, two snufferettes in center, four rests, 5⅞" d $12.00
Scotty figural at back, pot metal with bronze finish, nicely done, old $18.00
Shoe, brass, inlaid color, round toe, India, 3⅛" l .... $ 8.00
Shoe shape, brass, long, toe raises up, one rest at heel, India, 6¾" l....................................$15.00
Silver plate, swan holder & ashtray with two extra ashtrays, 4¼" l $12.00
Turtle shape, brass, shell lifts back for ashtray, two rests, 4¼" l.......................................$12.00
Wine painted, aluminum, two silver snufferettes & four rests in center, 5⅞" d............................ $ 6.00

PLASTIC, MARBLE, SOAPSTONE & WOOD

Alabaster, lt tan, calendar etched in center, four corner feet, 6" sq .... $ 8.00
Black plastic, ripple edge providing cigarette rests, matchbox holder on back rim, 5" d .... $ 6.00
Black plastic stand with four rests, dragon shape legs, gold metal rests, Oriental ceramic ashtray, 3¾" h.......$14.00
Brown plastic, three indentations on rise for cigarette rests, Bakelite, 3⅛" d .... $ 5.00
Dk brown plastic, matchbox & match pack holder on back rim, 2 wide rests, etched decor on rim, probably '20s, 7"d $12.00
Merry Christmas, large off-white plastic, *Merry Christmas* in center in many languages, 8" sq .... $ 8.00
Mexican, Incan carving figural on back rim, Incan faces for legs, cream alabaster, design in center, 3¼" h.......... $ 5.00
Mexican, Incan design in center, gray alabaster, Incan faces for feet, 2½" sq .... $ 7.00
Pale cream marble, pale gray markings, some stain from putting out cigarettes in center, 7" l $10.00

POTTERY & PORCELAIN

Bavaria, H & Co., Burley & Co., Germany, match holder in center of tray, poinsettias, 3¼" h................$14.00
Bavaria, Arzberg, picture of outfits from Black Forest, 4" sq .... $ 4.00
Black bird shape, Indian markings, black on black, 7½" w $52.00
California Orig, #2210, parallelogram shape, green pottery with black center, rests in center, 8⅝" l........... $ 6.00
Carrigaline Pottery, Ireland, cream color, shamrocks scattered around, 5⅜" d $11.00
Cronin China, Minerva, white, tapestry type flowers in center, 5⅛" d, 1930–1940 ....$13.00
Dachshund shaped, brown ceramic, one rest, 5⅝" l .... $ 6.00
Delft Holland, small blue & white windmill scene, 4⅛" l $14.00
Delft Holland, somewhat round with figural of two shoes, blue & white, Windmill pattern, 4¼" d............$21.00
Delft Holland, windmill scene, three rests in cobalt blue, 4½" d, recent $12.00
Dutch village, luster, moveable windmill, one rest, 2⅞" h, 1934 ....$18.00
Fiesta, by Homer Laughlin, marked, aqua, 5⅜" d $42.00
Frankoma, #456, brown glaze, deep, two rests, 3⅝" l .... $ 8.00
Frankoma, small four leaf clover, brown edge, white glaze, 3⅛" l .... $ 8.00
Haeger, olive & gold, rests in center, somewhat oval, 5¾" l... $ 7.00

Haeger, Royal, red, boomerang shape, rests in center, 13½" l . . . . $ 9.00
Hall, #676, matchbox holder in center, emerald green, 5¼" d, 1930–1970 . . . . $28.00
Hall, dark green, matchbox holder back rim, 3⅝" sq $21.00
Harlequin basketweave, not marked as is usual, aqua, 4½" d $36.00
Henry Ford Museum, cream china, picture of Cadillac in center, 5¼" d . . . . $ 9.00
Hyalyn, set, cigarette cup & ashtray, picture old-fashioned printing of press, ashtray is 5½" sq $12.00
Hyde Park, large green round with center raised up & initial on metal, by Roseville, 8⅜" d $25.00
Japan, white swan with add-on flowers & leaves, 4¼" l $10.00
Japan, by Andrea, leaf shape dish with cigarette holder on back rim, white & gold, 5¼" l $12.00
Japan, double diamond, hand painted, flowers in center with blue lines, 3¼" sq . . . . $ 7.00
Japan, black laquerware, five-piece set with tray, well done enameled trees, water & houses, tray is 8¼" d $20.00
Japan, mandolin shape, white ceramic with gold, one rest, 3⅞" l . . . . $ 6.00
Lefton, bisque, oval dish, add-on blue balls, 3⅝" l $13.00
Lefton, bisque, green highlights, Cupids & flowers, 3⅞" sq $13.00
Lefton, set of four, white with hand-painted scenes of boy & girl courtship, somewhat round, about 4¼" d $18.00
Limoges, France, white with classical couple in center, gold rim, 4" d $10.00
Limoges, France, *Mousquetaire –1724,* 4½" d $11.00
M.A. Hadley, folk art style, picture house, heavy pottery, blue rim, 7⅞" d, recent . . . . $ 8.00
M. Black Tail Deer, cream pottery with rests in center, green & gold pottery around edge, 5⅞" d $12.00
Mouse shape, orange ceramic, hollow in back for ashes, one rest, 6" l . . . . $ 6.00
Nippon, hand painted, K More on front, picture of flower, high rise dish, 4½" l $15.00
Nippon, hand painted, high rise dish, scene of trees, house & water, brown moriage, 4⅝" l $45.00
No mark, opalized bowl type with gold horse on back rim, 4" d . . . . $ 8.00
No mark, opalized bowl type with gold squirrel on back rim, 4" d . . . . $ 8.00
No mark, picture of Dodge car, 1916, white china, 4⅜" x 3¼" . . . . $ 7.00
No mark, white china ball with two side openings with extended rests, flowers on outside, 2¾" h $11.00
No mark, blue & white pottery, high straight rims, snufferette in center, 3¾" d . . . . $ 6.00
No mark, black boomerang shape, heavy pottery, plain, 6⅜" l $10.00
No mark, off-white pottery, picture of beagle dog in center in gray, 5⅛" d $11.00
No mark, cobalt leaf shape with branch type holder at one end, Germany, 5¾" l $20.00
No mark, duck shape, cream ceramic, like Red Wing's duck, match pack holder in tail, 4½" l $12.00
No mark, cup & saucer, cup for cigarettes, saucer is ashtray with three rests, Grecian dancers, lots of gold, 4" h $14.00
No mark, cream ceramic, butterfly picture in center, yellow extended rests, 4¾" w . . . . $ 6.00
Noritake, round wide rust rim with flowers, Noritake-Nippon Toke Kaisha Japan, 5" d, after 1953 . . . . $28.00
Occupied Japan, tri-shaped dish, gray flowers, two rests, Ardalt, 4¾" l . . . . $ 9.00
Occupied Japan, white ceramic, small square with rose center, four gold rests, 3" sides . . . . $ 7.00
Occupied Japan, white ceramic, small round with pink rose in relief in center, 3" d . . . . $ 7.00
Occupied Japan, white ceramic, small square with bamboo & bird in center, 3¼" sides . . . . $ 9.00
Orange slice shape, orange ceramic, two green rests, 4⅛" l . . . . $ 4.00
Pickard, gold covered rectangle with wavy edge, tiny flower pattern, 5" l $33.00
Red Wing, #857, caramel color, rests in center, triangular with one point extended, 7½" l $14.00
Red Wing, early, green Deco shaped bowl, 2" h, c. late 1920s $22.00
Red Wing, wing shape, wine color, not anniversary model, 7¼" l $40.00
Reitta Calif, small round of cream bone china, blue add-on flowers on rim, 3⅜" d . . . . $ 5.00
Romolo Apicella, Italy, folk art type, boy with fish, house & water, 3 yellow rests, 6⅛" d, recent $12.00
Santa Claus, cream ceramic, Christmas scene in center, three rests, 4" d . . . . $ 6.00
Siena, Italy, picture goat in black, brn, & wht, 4¾" sq, recent . . . . $ 9.00
Slice pineapple shape, green ceramic, two rests in center, by Maurice Ceramics, Calif, 8¾" l . . . . $ 6.00
Smoker, blue ceramic house, smoke comes our chimney, plain, long rest in front, 2⅜" h . . . . $ 7.00
Snuf-A-Rette, green, five snuffs across center, 4⅛" w $10.00
Stangl, large plate type, three rests at one end, picture of pheasant in center, lt blue center, 10½" w $45.00
Stella, black terra-cotta, picture in gold in center of ancient Grecian couple, hand made in Greece, 4¾" d . . . . $ 9.00
Syracuse China, Old Ivory, Grecian design, match holder back rim, Grecian pattern rim, 5½" d $15.00
Tettau, Stembach-Germany, picture of mountain goat, 4⅝" d $15.00
Ulmer Keranik, Germany, four-sided square with pictures of different parts of a city, high sides, 3½" sq $20.00
Villeroy & Boch, Dechor Eger pattern, dish shape, blue edge, red & blue flowers in center, 5¼" d $10.00
Vomann USA, Hoodwink, olive green, slashed ball variation with rest near center, 1¾" h $12.00

Wade, Irish porcelain, olive triangle, picture Irish jaunting car in center, 3¾" side $14.00

Wade, Irish, olive cigar & pipe ashtray, cork for knocking ashes from pipe, 6" d. $16.00

Wedgwood, black jasper, white grape vine on rim, white classical decor in center, 4⅜" d $29.00

Wedgwood, black jasper, white grape vine border, nothing in center, 3⅝" d. $25.00

Wedgwood, black jasper, black grape vine border, nothing in center, 3⅝" d, 1959 . . . . $23.00

Wedgwood, blue jasper, white grape vine border, white classical scene in center, 4⅜" d, prior to 1930 . . . . $25.00

Wedgwood, blue jasper, white grape vine border, nothing in center, 3⅝" d. $21.00

Wedgwood, sage green jasper, white grape vine border, white classical scene in center, 4⅜" d $28.00

Wedgwood, embossed Queen's ware, gray with white grape vine border, 3¼" sq, 1957 . . . . $16.00

Wedgwood, embossed Queen's ware, cream with black etching of Headless Horseman, 4¼" d $22.00

Wedgwood, terra cotta jasper, round, grape leaf border, white classical decor in center, 4⅜" d, 1959 . . . . $27.00

West Germany, three bird figural on branch, blue ashtray, nice, 3" h $25.00

Winfield, cream ceramic with yellow & blue marks, one rest, 3⅞" l . . . . $ 6.00

SOUVENIRS

Arizona, yellow & brown ceramic, *The Grand Canyon State,* map & picture in center, 8¾" w . . . . $ 7.00

Carlsbad Caverns National Park in New Mexico, white ceramic coaster & ashtray, *Rock of Ages,* 4¼" l. . . . . $ 7.00

Carmel, California, picture in center, *By the Sea,* white ceramic, 3½" d. . . . . $ 5.00

Colorado Springs, Colorado, silver color coating on metal, *Seven Falls,* Occupied Japan, 4½" d $13.00

Copenhagen, Denmark, *Langeline Kobenhavn,* nymph on rock, symbol, 4" d $15.00

Duluth, Minnesota, brass triangle, *Aerial Bridge,* 4¼" sides. . . . . $ 5.00

Florida, compressed wood, Florida in relief on rise, 4" d. . . . . $ 4.00

Florida, pale blue ceramic, scene of birds in center, 6¼" d . . . . $ 5.00

Germany, Baumholder, silver plate, enamel seal of town at edge, 4" w . . . . $ 7.00

Germany, Rothenburg, triangle, gold edge, picture of city gate in center, 2½" sides . . . . $ 6.00

Las Vegas, Nevada, white ceramic, fry pan shape, decal in center of scenes of Las Vegas, 7" l . . . . $ 5.00

London, blue ceramic, cream bottom, white letters in center, 4¼" d. . . . . $ 6.00

Los Angeles, California, copper coating, *Farmers' Market,* letters cut out around edge of coaster & ashtray, 5½" w . . . . . $ 6.00

Mexico, De Sante Acapulco, red pottery, crude, high rise, 3" w . . . . $ 4.00

Milwaukee, Wis, small blue rect with iridescent rim, flowers in center, 3¾" l . . . . $ 5.00

Minnesota, state shape, white ceramic, 3¾" l . . . . $ 4.00

Missouri, silver color metal, map etched in center, one rest, 3½" d. . . . . $ 5.00

Monarch Pass, Colorado, amber plastic with pieces of mineral rock embedded around hexagon ashtray, 7½" d . . . . $ 9.00

New York City, hammered aluminum, buildings in relief in center, three rests, 5" w. . . . . $ 8.00

New York City, Times Square scene, silver color metal, 4¼" d . . . . $ 7.00

Newport, Oregon, Taquina Bay Bridge, crystal glass with picture in center with felt backing, 3⅝" sq . . . . $ 8.00

Old Czechoslovakia souvenir, bronze, from Ljubljana, a town in Czechoslovakia, 3½" d. $17.00

Plains, Georgia, peanut shape, tan ceramic, *Went Nuts in Plains, Georgia,* 5⅜" l . . . . $ 6.00

Roma, Hotel Mediterraneo, cream ceramic, green rests on rim, picture in center, 4½" d . . . . $ 7.00

San Francisco, ceramic, scenes of San Francisco in center, ornate rim, 6⅛" d. . . . . $ 8.00

San Francisco, foot shape, tan ceramic, *We got a kick out of San Francisco,* 5" l . . . . $ 5.00

San Francisco, copper coating, *Cable Car,* picture in relief in center under glass, cut out letters around the edge, 5" d. . . . . . . $ 8.00

Sault Ste. Marie, Michigan, white ceramic, picture in center of boat & locks, silver edge, 4¾" d . . . . $ 6.00

Washington, DC, cream ceramic, coaster & ashtray, picture of period dress couple in center, 4⅞" l . . . . $ 8.00

Washington, DC, copper coating, *The U.S. Capitol,* ornate rim, two rests, 5¼" w . . . . $ 5.00

Schroeder's
ANTIQUES
Price Guide

. . . is the #1 best-selling antiques & collectibles value guide on the market today, and here's why . . .

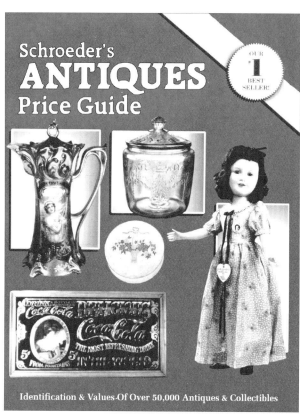